AN ELIZAB␣ PURIT␣

Arthur Golding the Translator of
Ovid's *Metamorphoses* and also of
John Calvin's *Sermons*

BY

LOUIS THORN GOLDING

ILLUSTRATED

RICHARD R. SMITH
New York   1937

SET UP BY BROWN BROTHERS LINOTYPERS
PRINTED IN THE UNITED STATES OF AMERICA
BY THE FERRIS PRINTING COMPANY

ARTHUR GOLDING'S MOTHER

Portrait of Ursula Marston Golding painted by an unknown artist in 1563. Now in the possession of the author.

FOREWORD

The importance of Arthur Golding's beautiful rendering of Ovid's *Metamorphoses* to Shakespeare has long been recognized, but the conspicuous place which that versatile translator occupied in the general cultural background of the Age of the Faerie Queene has not, I believe, been fully realized by scholars. This lack of appreciation has doubtless been due in the main to the fact that no adequate account of the man and of his work has been available. It seems, therefore, a happy circumstance that at last a life of Golding, with a detailed record of his various literary activities, has been attempted—as a "labor of love" by one of his descendants, who already, in other ways, has laid wreaths at the shrine of this great Elizabethan. Students of our early literature will, I am sure, welcome the present volume, and be duly grateful for the wealth of new information which the industry of its author has been able to supply.

JOSEPH QUINCY ADAMS.

The Folger Shakespeare Library,
Washington, D. C.
April, 1937.

PREFACE

Arthur Golding was the most voluminous translator of the Elizabethan Era. His Englishing of Ovid's *Metamorphoses,* Cæsar's *Commentaries* and other classics has gained for his name a secure place in the history of English literature. His translations of John Calvin's sermons and writings and those of other French reformers did their part in bringing to the English people the doctrines of the intellectual leaders of the Protestant Reformation; they bore their fruit in the revolution of English life and government that marked the seventeenth century.

Golding was born three years after Elizabeth and outlived her the same period. His active life, therefore, practically coincided with the reign of the great Queen, and his work is part of the record of that time.

A member of a wealthy county family connected by marriage with the highest nobility, associated with and patronized by the greatest Englishmen of his day, the translator of thirty-odd works (many of great bulk and importance), and the inheritor of large landed properties, he died in obscurity. So soon was he completely forgotten that standard biographical authorities have been unable to give the place or date of his birth, or of his death and burial, and have been able to record but few details of his life and family.

The purpose of the present book is to reconstruct from

meager facts gleaned in several years of research from the public and private records of England, as well as from the slight self-revelation offered in the dedications of his books, the life story of one of the substantial, if not brilliant, figures of The Golden Age of English Literature.

No new evaluation of the literary quality of his work has been attempted, but quotations from four centuries of criticism and analysis have been gathered in a separate chapter.

My acknowledgments are due to Dr. Joseph Quincy Adams, Director of the Folger Shakespeare Library, Washington, D. C., for his encouragement to persist in this work and his critical reading of the manuscript.

Through the kindness of Dr. M. W. Wallace, Principal of University College, Toronto, I have been permitted to make helpful use of data in the introduction to the reprint of Golding's translation of Theodore Beza's *Tragedy of Abraham's Sacrifice* edited by him for the Toronto University Studies (Toronto, 1906).

L. T. G.

Brookline, Massachusetts
April, 1937

CONTENTS

APPENDICES

CONTENTS

x

ILLUSTRATIONS

Chapter I

BIRTHPLACE AND FAMILY

ARTHUR GOLDING's childhood was passed in the parish of Belchamp St. Paul's in the charming countryside between the rivers Stour and Colne, in the northwestern corner of the county of Essex. This district lies fifty miles or more northeast of London, and twenty-five miles or so southeast of Cambridge, on the western edge of the long sweep of rolling land that stretches from the low marshy shores of the North Sea and gently rises towards the western boundaries of East Anglia. From earliest times a land of fields and woods, of hedgerows and pleasant running waters, the region stands today much the same as when nearly four hundred years ago Arthur Golding played around Belchamp Hall, the home of his father, which was set near the top of the low watershed separating the Stour and the Colne. Then as now this was a land of the farmer, lacking, however, the good roads, the solid bridges and the excellent postal service of today. The slender song of the skylark even then trilled down from "the blue vault of heaven," the stirring music of the chaffinch burst from the hedges, and in May there was the glory of the blossoming thorn that divides the well-kept fields; but there were probably more meadows for grazing the sheep whose fleeces supplied the wool-weaving industry of the neighborhood.

I

The beauty of the region has bred great artists. Gains-borough, born five miles from Belchamp St. Paul's at Sudbury, declared he derived his first love of art from the beauty about him. Constable, born at West Bergholt fif-teen miles away, made the middle reaches of the valley of the Stour famous as "The Constable Country," and the scenes of his pictures "The Valley Farm" and "Flatford Mill" still draw art-loving pilgrims. No one, who has not walked or driven along the banks of the Stour and watched the piled-up clouds sweep their shadows over the woods and field-checkered slopes of its lovely valley, can fully appreciate how completely the great landscape painter caught its charm.

In ancient days as now it was a land of the small holder. The great, with a notable exception, had gen-erally passed East Anglia by. The historic family of Vere, however, was located there from the days of the Conquest and stood preëminent in wealth and power. For 600 years the Earls of Oxford came from this family to play nota-ble parts in camp and in court, and to leave their names large on every page of English history. Macaulay re-ferred to them as the "longest and most illustrious line of nobles that England has seen" and, in *Lady Clara Vere de Vere*, Tennyson used the name to typify the utmost in birth and lineage. Their stronghold, Castle Hedingham, had from the twelfth century on stood only four miles south of Belchamp St. Paul's upon a hill overlooking the river Colne. Its great central tower, all that is now left standing, is regarded today as the finest Norman keep in England. To this castle, when Arthur was twelve years old, came his sister Margery after her marriage in Belchamp St. Paul's church to John de Vere, the sixteenth Earl of Oxford.

The East Anglian land, without the natural and easily defended barriers of mountain ranges or deep rivers, afforded no more obstacle to the marauding Danes than it had to the Romans of an earlier day of invasions. Both peoples have left traces. Names of Danish origin are found in the Domesday Book and are still noted today. Frequently, too, relics of the Universal Conquerors are found. Sites of Roman camps, for instance, are scattered over the territory and Colchester, the Roman Camalodunam, is but twenty miles from the district that commands our especial interest. It is from this town, so tradition has it, that Constantine started for his victory at the Milvian bridge and the mastery of the world.

Even as this countryside lay open to invasion, so it was easily accessible to the missionaries of the Cross. Christianity has always been strong in East Anglia; today, as for hundreds of years, every few miles is marked by a village church. The traveler is interested to observe that with almost every new horizon brought into view by a turn of the road, the low square tower of a typical English church of the fourteenth and fifteenth centuries appears. Indeed from the top of a moderately high tower in the village of Foxearth, about four miles from Belchamp St. Paul's, one may count fourteen churches.

The northwest corner of Essex still holds its ancient name of Hinckford Hundred and the parish of Belchamp St. Paul's carries back to almost as ancient an origin. The name Belchamp is generally assumed to have been derived from the French, with the meaning of "beautiful

3

fields." Some insist, however, and with good reason for their opinion, that the name is of Anglo-Saxon origin and hence much older than the Norman occupation. Dugdale indeed asserts that, when the lands in this neighborhood were granted to St. Paul's Cathedral by Athelstan, the grandson of Alfred the Great, before the year 941 the Latin deed rendered the name as "Bylcham." [1] For nearly a thousand years then this delightful rural neighborhood has borne a name, which is now shared by two other parishes, Belchamp Water and Belchamp Otten, all watered by Belchamp brook. One would prefer to believe that the French etymology is correct as it so aptly applies to the surroundings.

Throughout this district flourished in the fourteenth, fifteenth and sixteenth centuries the weaving industry of England. Here dwelt master weavers or clothiers who financed and controlled the cottage industry. Their varying degrees of prosperity are still marked by the size, beauty and elaboration of the churches in the villages where they lived, for upon them they lavished their wealth. Beginning three miles north of Belchamp St. Paul's with the ancient village of Clare, whose name furnished the title of the Dukes of Clarence, and stretching away to the east there is a string of villages, Glemsford, Long Melford, Lavenham, and Kersey, to mention only

[1] Dugdale, Sir William, Norroy King at Arms, *History of St. Paul's Cathedral*. London, 1818. Page 292.—Ekwall's *Dictionary of English Placenames* (Oxford 1936) says that the first syllable is probably derived from the old English word "baelc" meaning a roof made of beams and the second from the old English word "ham" meaning a manor or homestead, hence Belchamp means a house with a beamed roof—(It seems that the spelling may well have become Gallicised during the time of the ascendancy of the French language, to fit the French definition which the situation so obviously suits.—Author).

4

GLEMSFORD CHURCH AND THE GOLDING CHAPEL

The two windows at the right are in the chapel for the building of which John Golding left £40 in his will made in 1495. Over these windows is the inscription, "John Golding and Joan his wife founded this chapel, upon whose souls God have mercy."

the principal ones, in all of which cloth-weaving was the chief industry and in each of which the beauty of the church attests that industry's ancient prosperity and the piety of those who engaged in it.

Arthur's great uncle, John Golding, a clothier of Glemsford, in his will of 1495, provided for the handsome chapel which adds to the beauty of Glemsford church. (Appendix No. 1). At Lavenham, a still richer clothier, William Spring, furnished most of the money wherewith to build what is still recognized as one of the most beautiful country churches in England. This, like the one at Long Melford, its rival in beauty and the possessor of the famous Clopton stained glass, is very large —far larger than the shrunken population of the village now needs. All these churches in fact stand as monuments to a time when all the people attended public worship and when wealth was held best used that went to enlarge and beautify the house of God.

The church dedicated to St. Andrew, the parish church of Belchamp St. Paul's, was not thus favored, for no wealthy clothier resided in the parish. It was and is one of the smaller and more modest structures, solidly and fairly built, with a massive tower and flint-coated walls, and a list of vicars running back six hundred years. (Appendix No. 2). Close beside it in the fifteenth and sixteenth centuries was Belchamp Hall, which today, much altered, is known as Paul's Hall, a comfortable and substantial farmhouse.

One of the choice possessions of the parish is the carefully preserved Manor Roll, described thus by the Keeper of the Manuscripts in the British Museum:

5

Terrier in Latin of the Manor of Belchamp St. Paul's Co. Essex made 17 July, 1576, the Lordship of which was farmed by William Golding from the Dean and Chapter of St. Paul's Cathedral. At the end are some coloured plans. Paper A.D. 1576. Contemporary brown leather binding (repaired) stamped with the Tudor rose, pomegranate, royal arms, triple-towered gateway portcullis, fleur de lis, and binder's trademark. The same stamps are found on the binding of the British MS. 32103 (transcripts of evidence relating to Lancaster), and 37270 Book of the Manor of Bronham, etc., Co. Wilts. The general design of the cover of the former closely resembles that of the present MS.

One of the colored plans referred to is an interesting drawing of Belchamp Hall, then the residence of William Golding, which is elsewhere reproduced in this book. The present Vicar of Belchamp St. Paul's, the Reverend R. F. Flynn, in writing of the Manor Roll, says of this house:

Here the Golding family lived. There was John Golding, the head of the family, whose daughter Margery married the 16th Earl of Oxford in the parish Church in 1548. Then came Thomas and William, many times referred to in the Roll. Next, Arthur, who is not once mentioned. The Hall was many roomed, with a sweeping drive from the king's highway. Walled gardens, and stone archways gave an air of distinction to the home of the Goldings. The Manor Roll then takes particular notice of the surroundings. The dimensions of the fish house of 36 feet, "of the Dove House 'tiled,' " of the water mill "constructed by Mr. Golding," and the pightel.

The Manor Roll consists of a list of all the lands in the parish. Each field is described by name and each is pictured. Most of the land is noted as having been held in leasehold by Arthur's brother, William, who inherited it from his older brother, Sir Thomas Golding.

6

In Belchamp Hall Arthur Golding spent his early boyhood. Whether he was born here is not recorded, neither is the month nor day of his birth. The year, however, was 1536, as is shown by the inquisition upon the will of his brother Henry, who died in 1575. This document filed in 1576 states that "his brother Arthur forty years of age, succeeded him." [2]

The *Dictionary of National Biography* and other books of reference refer to Golding as having "probably" been born in London. There seems to be no foundation for this statement. His father, John Golding, it is true, was an auditor of the Exchequer, and therefore may be presumed to have been a resident of London at one time or another. Careful but vain search has been made in the Record Office and elsewhere for proof that John Golding dwelt in the city at the time of Arthur's birth. Clearly enough he spent considerable time there a number of years before, for he was admitted to the Middle Temple at a meeting of the Parliament in April 1520. The record on this reads:

John Goldyng, in the Exchequer was admitted and is pardoned exercising all vacations and offices in the Temple. And he has licence to be in commons and out of commons at his liking, except in Christmas week, if he be in town. And for having such an admission, he granted to the Fellowship 26s. 8d. [3]

In 1523 he was named with three other "auditors of The Court of Exchequer" in a subsidy laid upon "members of the Inns of Court and Court Officers." The subsidy

[2] Inquisition 19, Eliz. Feb. 7th. (Quoted in Morant, Rev. Philip, *History of Essex.* Vol. II. Page 180.)
[3] Hopwood, Charles Henry, *Middle Temple Records,* Minutes of Parliament, Vol. I. Page 61.

was laid upon those having over £40 and as John had £66 he was assessed 66 shillings.[*]

Later he appears to have removed from London. We hear of him in Essex a few years afterward, actively engaged in prosecuting those found in possession of forbidden bibles and testaments. He was there in 1527, for his first wife, who died in that year, was buried in Belchamp St. Paul's church on December 27th, and an altar tomb was erected for her in the chancel. He, too, was buried in it when he died twenty years after, but this tomb has long since disappeared. By inheritance from his parents, John Golding was a large landholder in the neighborhood, and it now appears clear that he lived at Belchamp Hall for a number of years before Arthur's birth in 1536. His children were all young at the time, the oldest but sixteen. There were two sets of them, four by his first wife and two or three by Arthur's mother, his second wife. John continued to live at Belchamp until his death in 1547, by which time he had eleven children in his family. It was hardly likely that with a flock of youngsters and with his many interests in Essex and Suffolk he temporarily removed his residence to London at about the time of Arthur's birth. It is, therefore, safe to assume that Arthur was born, as he died, at Belchamp St. Paul's.

The Goldings were a very ancient family. The name was known before the Conquest and bearers of it were numerous in the eastern counties in the days of Edward the Confessor. Correctly spelled, it first appears in *The Chronicles of Battel*, a history of the village which sprang

[*] Lay Subsidy, Divers Counties, Bundle 240, No. 273. P.R.O. (This abbreviation for Public Record Office, London, will be used hereafter in these footnotes).

up about Battle Abbey while it was being built. Internal evidence shows that the *Chronicles* were written about the year 1176. The Latin manuscript Domitian Aii of the Cottonian Collection of MSS. in the British Museum was translated in 1846 by Mark Antony Lower and published in London in 1851. The recital which begins with the securing of the land and the starting of work in 1075, records the history of the abbey and its village for nearly a hundred years. The monkish author, possibly Abbot Odo, says that when the building of the abbey was in process, "a goodly number of men were brought hither out of neighboring counties and even from foreign countries, and to each of them the brethren, who managed the building, allotted a dwelling place around the circuit of the abbey and they still remain as at first apportioned with their customary rent and service."

Then follows a list of 115 messuages and the name of the holder of each with the rent and required service. The rent varied from five pence to seven pence per annum payable at Michaelmas. The service was to find a man for one day to make hay in the meadow of Bodeham and also a man at the "reparation" of the mill. Also each had to make one seam (eight bushels) of malt. In the list the Golding entry appears thus:

84-85—to Golding, 5 pence and labor; of another adjoining it at 5 pence and for this he neither makes malt nor finds a man for the meadow or the mill.

The messuages were granted apparently to mechanics who were engaged in the building of the abbey and to those who supplied the needs of the workers. In nearly

9

half the entries the trade of the holder is given. There were shoemakers, weavers, cooks, herdsmen, a goldsmith, swineherds, a bell founder, several bakers, two carpenters, a clerk, a priest, two secretaries, a gardener, and a scourer. The names are mixed, a majority being clearly English, although, among the mechanics' names, there are a number that are Norman. There is no indication of the occupation of the other grantees. They may have been artisans of other trades not mentioned or they may have been merchants and so forth. It is hardly likely that there were among them day laborers, as such persons at that time were serfs. Nothing in the narrative indicates why the Golding named was granted two messuages at the lowest cash rental or why he was relieved of service on account of one of them. Whatever his business at Battel was, it needed more space than granted to the others and was advantageous to the brethren as the favorable terms he received indicate.

The derivation of the name is of course not perfectly certain. According to *Patronymica Britannica* (London, 1860, p. 132) Gold was both an Anglo-Saxon baptismal name and a term of affection. It appears to have given rise to such surnames as Golding, Goldwin and others having Gold as the first syllable. The Danish suffix "ing" with a signification of place points to a Danish background. This theory is to some extent sustained by the coupling of the name with "Stoke" as in Stoke-Golding a Lancashire village, whose name has survived from the days of the Danish occupation as have such better known names as Stoke-Poges, Basingstoke, and Stoke-on-Trent.

In the Domesday Book are found a number of names,

10

none spelled Golding but all close enough to make it likely that they at least belonged to persons of the same sept or clan. The Norman clerks who recorded the results of William's great survey naturally had trouble with the vernacular, a compound of Saxon and Danish. They spelled by ear with varying results. Thus the name appears as Goding, Godinc, and Goldinc. Godinc was preferred for, of eleven entries of land in Suffolk and Essex, six show this form, while four are spelled Goding and one Goldinc. It seems probable, however, that the last syllable should be the same in all and that in only one case did the clerk record the spelling of the first syllable correctly.

The name, in its correct form, begins to appear in the records about the middle of the thirteenth century. In 1257 one Gilbert Golding, court records show, was accused of withholding a deed to land in Cavendish but was acquitted and his accuser held "in mercy for false claim." [a] Later, variance of spelling constantly appears. The "y" is frequently substituted for "i"; a final "e" is sometimes used, and occasionally a "w" is interpolated in the first syllable so that "Gowlding" results. In more modern times a "u" appears in the first syllable making the name Goulding, which one branch of the family still retains.

Occasional references in public documents of the thirteenth and fourteenth centuries indicate that persons of this name had acquired wealth or held rank in the army or navy and possessed the confidence of the crown. According to the Suffolk Lay Subsidy Lists, when Parlia-

[a] Suffolk Assize Roll, No. 820, membrane 23 dorso. P.R.O.

ment in 1282, in the reign of Edward I, levied a subsidy of one-thirtieth for the support of the war to complete the subjugation of Llewelyn the Welsh chieftain, Hugo Golding of Ipswich was rated as worth £166, the highest in that town. He was assessed £5 8s. 8d., which, however, was credited against the £10 which he had lent to the king the previous year for the same purpose.[5]

From fourteenth century documents, written in Latin, we learn of the martial activities of Goldings whose names are spelled with a "y." Towards the middle of that century one Thomas Goldyng went to France with Edward III on the campaign which culminated in the spectacular victory of Crécy on August 26, 1346. He seems to have been a man of consequence, for his name is included in the list of persons who had "letters of protection," issued by Edward himself, at Sandwich on June 20th in the nineteenth year of his reign, to those "who set out for parts over sea with the king in his service."[6]

Near the end of the reign of Edward III we hear of one Johannes or John Goldyng, the captain of the man of war "La Mighel" of Hull, who was authorized by the King on the 28th of January 1374 to impress seventy mariners in the counties of Essex and Suffolk for service on the king's ships.[7] The Hundred Years' War was then going against Edward and men were badly needed for the fleet, whose early success at the battle off Sluys had been reversed in the actions of later years, particularly

[5] Lay Subsidy. Suffolk 242, 40-42 (Proceedings Suffolk Institute of Archaeology, Vol. 12, New Series, Pages 137 to 142.)

[6] Rymer, Thomas. *Foedera*. London, 1825. Vol. 3, Part 1. Pages 48 and 49.

[7] *Ibid*. London, 1830. Vol. 3, Part 2. Page 996.

12

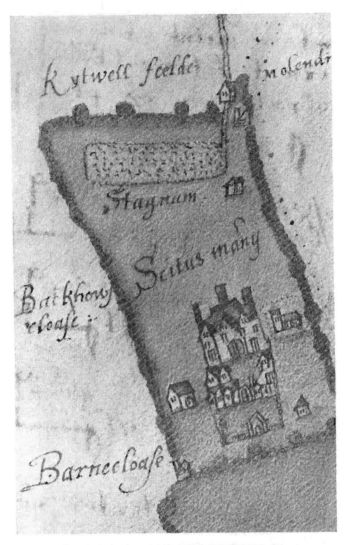

BELCHAMP HALL AND SURROUNDINGS IN 1576

From a colored plan in the Manor Roll or "Terrier in Latin of the Manor of Belchamp St. Paul's" preserved in the church archives. This building replaced the one occupied by John Golding at the time of Arthur's birth. It was erected by Sir Thomas Golding at a cost of £4,000 in 1566.

that fought off Rochelle not long before by John Hastings, Earl of Pembroke, the King's son-in-law; therefore the impressment of seamen was general in the eastern and southern coastal counties. A translation of the order for this early use of the notorious "press gang" is printed in full in Appendix, No. 3.

During this century and well into the next, numerous Goldings and Goldyngs were, as the records show, conveying land or paying taxes at various places in Suffolk and Thomas Golding who held land in the manor of Swifts in Preston left a will which was proved at Kettlebaston, Co. Suffolk, May 31, 1454. His widow's name was Ethelreda, a case of the late survival of Anglo-Saxon nomenclature. From about the middle of the fifteenth century on, the family began to rise in importance and wealth and Robert Goldyng of Glemsford, who died in 1470, acquired a coat of arms with these armorial bearings: Gules, a cheveron Or between three Bezants—the Crest, a Dragon's head Vert guttee d'or gorged with a collar with two rings also Or.[8] This was Arthur's great, great grandfather. Thus, solidly placed in the neighborhood, this branch of the Goldings presently entered upon a series of matrimonial alliances that greatly increased its wealth and, by the middle of the sixteenth century, had connected it with the lordly house of Vere.

The first whom Hymen helped to improve the family fortunes was Thomas Golding of Greys in Cavendish, Co. Suffolk, Arthur's grandfather. Whether the fact that he chose an heiress for his second wife indicates that in marriage he had an eye to the main chance, or that the lady

[8] Records of the College of Arms. London.

13

was the fortunate possessor, not only of broad acres but of charm and beauty, no one now can say. At all events she was Elizabeth Worthy, of unusually distinguished lineage. (Appendix No. 4) The daughter and heiress of John Worthy of Worthy's Place, the owner of Bloomsters Manor and other large and valuable properties in the neighborhood of Halstead. These Thomas passed on by will to their son John in addition to a share of his own already large holdings.

John, Thomas's eldest son by Elizabeth Worthy, emulating his father's example, began his matrimonial experiences by marrying an heiress. She was Elizabeth, the widow of Reginald Hammond, a co-heir of her father, Thomas Tonge, of West Malling, Co. Kent. After this lady died November 27, 1527, John married another heiress; this time, Ursula, daughter and co-heir of William Marston of Horton, Co. Surrey, a member of a noted and wealthy family (Appendix No. 5) who brought to him her half of her father's very large properties. By these marriages and the properties they brought to him, together with his own patrimony enlarged by his activities for the Exchequer and improved no doubt by the opportunities thus opened to him, John became a rich man. This is shown by the inquisition into his estate held by the Court of Wards in 1548, a year after his death. (Appendix No. 6).

By his first wife John had four children, Thomas, William, Margery and Elizabeth and by his second seven, Henry, Arthur, George, Edmund, Mary, Dorothy, and Frances.

Thomas, the eldest son, achieved considerable wealth

14

and position. He was knighted and, as Sir Thomas Golding, was Sheriff of Essex and Hertfordshire in 1563 and again of Essex alone in 1569. He maintained the matrimonial policy of the family by marrying Elizabeth, daughter and co-heiress of Thomas Roydon of Peckham, Co. Kent. She was the widow of William Twisden, Esq.

William, the second son, contented himself with the quiet activities of a country gentleman. He also married a co-heiress, Elizabeth, daughter of Edmond West of Cornard, Co. Suffolk. She was the widow of John Bukenham, Esq. After his brother Thomas died in 1571, he succeeded to the lordship of the Manor of Belchamp.

Elizabeth married Roger Wingfield of Co. Norfolk.

But it remained for Margery to confer social distinction upon the Golding family by marrying on the 5th of August, 1548, John de Vere, the sixteenth Earl of Oxford.

Of Ursula's children, Henry, the eldest, acquired considerable property and also many debts; he had been burgess of the borough of Malden, and, at the time of his death in 1575, was a member of Parliament for Colchester.

George inherited his father's business ability and acquired a handsome property but achieved no other distinction.

It was left for Arthur to give the family name the genuine and lasting fame of having furnished a scholar and poet to the Golden Age of English literature.

Edmund, having graduated from Peterhouse, Cambridge, entered the church and became Rector of Birdbrook, Co. Essex, a few miles from Belchamp St. Paul's.

Mary married Anthony Beeke of Reading.

15

Dorothy married Edmund Docwra of Thatcham, Co. Berks, and Frances married Mathew Bacon of Shelfayn, Co. Norfolk.

Of John Golding's six sons only Arthur left male heirs, so that the name, at least in this branch of the Golding family, has been carried down since that time by his descendants.

REAR WING OF PAUL'S HALL

Unchanged portion of Belchamp Hall, as rebuilt by Sir Thomas Golding in 1566.

Chapter II

FORMATIVE YEARS

THE only fact about Arthur Golding's formal education that is positively known is his matriculation at Jesus College, Cambridge, at the Easter term in 1552. He was entered as a "fellow commoner," a status which was customarily given to the sons of wealthy families and for which payment of thirty shillings was made. Fellow commoners were privileged persons. They had their meals with the fellows of the college and enjoyed release from most of the disciplinary rules of the institution. According to Mr. Arthur Gray, Master of Jesus College and the historian of Cambridge University, there are no records of the length of Golding's stay or of his activities while in residence.[1] Mr. Gray suggests that he left without taking a degree, because the changes in the college after the accession of Queen Mary were offensive to his strong Protestant leanings. This theory, which has much to commend it, gives us at least a clue to the length of his studies at Cambridge. Edward VI died July 6, 1553, but Mary, on account of the brief "reign" of the pitiful Lady Jane Grey, was far too much occupied with establishing and consolidating her hold upon the throne to do much towards stamping out the Lutheran heresy

[1] Address of Mr. Arthur Gray at the Dedication of the Golding Memorial Window.

until late in the year. The "Marian" persecution which fell so heavily upon England and especially the eastern counties, did not therefore get into full swing until early in 1554. In the meantime controversy had again flared up at Cambridge from the embers of the disputes of four or five years before, when Martin Bucer, the German reformer, had for two years been Regius Professor of Theology, as the appointee of Cranmer, at a salary of £100 a year, three times that of his predecessor.[2]

Bucer was a distinguished German divine and one of the leaders of the Reformation in western Germany who had been the chief pastor of the reformed faith at Strasburg. Compelled to flee from there in 1549 with Paul Fagius, his chief disciple, he had accepted the invitation of Cranmer to come to England. Here he was received with honor and appointed to Cambridge. Fagius also was given a post at Cambridge, but died before he went there to take up his duties. Bucer speedily achieved a position of great importance in the English religious world and came to be regarded as a sort of court of final resort in the complicated and confused theological discussions of the day. He was drawn into sharp controversies by some of the popish adherents in the university, the asperity of which was not softened by the knowledge of his (for the day) munificent salary. Envy and jealousy are not recently discovered failings, and, although he died in 1551 after a residence of less than two years, Bucer left bitter enemies. Finally, nearly three years after, when Mary had come to the throne, at the instigation of Cardinal Pole, a "purge" of Cambridge was ordered. The reformers

[2] Harvey, A. E. *Martin Bucer in England.* Marburg, 1906, page 29.

were driven out and the reformed doctrines condemned. The body of Bucer, although then dead four years, with that of Fagius who had been dead six, was dragged from its grave, "tried" for heresy, condemned, and burned at the stake February 6, 1555. Of course such a university was no place for a young man of Protestant leanings and Arthur left Jesus College without taking a degree. If, as is hardly likely, he remained until the "purge" was under way, he had but little more than two and a half years of academic training.

Since this is all that is known of his college days it may be well to examine, as far as possible, the schooling that preceded them and, still more important, the social and religious conditions surrounding and influencing him in his formative years. As Belchamp St. Paul's was far too small a village to sustain a school and Clare, three miles north, rather too far away for daily trips to school, John Golding undoubtedly had a resident teacher at Belchamp Hall for his brood of youngsters, as was the custom of the wealthier country gentry. Sometimes it happened that the vicar of the parish church was a man of parts who could and did undertake the training of the children of the manor house. The Reverend Stephen Lufkin came to be vicar at Belchamp St. Paul's in 1545.[8] He has left no record; but, as the only representative of the learned professions who is known to have been in close contact with Arthur's childhood home, it may be that when he came there he took over the teaching of nine-year-old Arthur and his brothers and sisters. Mr. Lufkin remained at Belchamp until 1558. Long before that, however,

[8] Belchamp St. Paul's Parish Records, see Appendix No. 2.

Arthur and the other children had departed from the Hall.

When John Golding died in 1547, he left his principal estate to his eldest son Thomas, according to the law of primogeniture. To Ursula his wife he gave a life interest in Bloomsters Manor near Halstead, about seven miles to the south. This manor, of about two hundred and thirty-five acres, had come to John's mother, Elizabeth Worthy, from her father, in whose family it had been for several generations and took its name from William Bloomster, who had owned it in the reign of Edward II. After Thomas Golding's death in 1504 Elizabeth Worthy married Anthony Poley and lived at Bloomsters for many years. John Golding, who was young at the time of his father's death, probably lived there in his youth. He inherited Bloomsters when his mother died in 1534 and is contemporaneously referred to as of Halstead and Belchamp St. Paul's. The manor house was built in the style commonly used by the country gentry of the period and still stands at the top of Windmill field about a mile from Halstead. To it Mrs. Ursula Golding removed after the marriage of her stepdaughter Margery in the summer of 1548. With her went her seven children, including Arthur who at the time was twelve years old.

Of the four years before his entry into Jesus College there is no record, but in all probability he went to school in Halstead, then a considerable village, where, as was customary, there was a grammar school for the sons of the gentry in which very fair grounding in the classics could be had. The move to Bloomsters, however, opened a new phase in the real education of Arthur Golding.

20

BELCHAMP HALL TODAY
(Now called Paul's Hall) Side View.

Bloomsters was but four miles from Castle Hedingham, the home of the Veres, whither his half-sister Margery had lately gone as the bride of the Earl of Oxford. Thus, during his adolescence and in his most impressionable years, opportunity was given him to contact the life and customs of a great nobleman's residence. His mother had been a second mother to her stepdaughter, the young Countess of Oxford, who was a very young child when Ursula Marston became John Golding's second wife. Not only had she reared and trained the little girl as her own but she had still been mistress of Belchamp Hall when Margery was married to the Earl, a year after the death of her father.

Ursula Marston Golding was a superior woman. As a stepmother she held the children's respect and affection; (no mean achievement in that—or this day). That she was recognized as a leader among the women of the county families of the neighborhood is indicated by her inclusion in the women beneficiaries of a curious will made by Edward Walgrave of Sudbury in 1544. The testator, after many bequests added: "I bequeath and give to every lady and gentleman whose names ensueth, whose prayers I do desire, to each of them for a pore token of remembrance, a duckett of 5 shillings apiece praying them of their charity to give 20 pence of the aforesaid to the most pore people of their parishes." [*] The list of twenty-six names included, among other men and women of whom this age knows nothing, Lady Clopton of Melford Park, whose family gave the famous stained glass in Long Melford Church, Mistress Spring, whose family had fur-

---

[*] *East Anglican*, New Series, 7, 1897-98, page 325.

nished most of the money to build the beautiful Lavenham
Church, and Mrs. Ursula Golding. Their husbands were
not mentioned.

Ursula Golding's portrait, painted in 1563, shows a
firm, though not a stern character. Fixed purpose and
strong will are indicated by the direct but not unkindly
glance, square jaw and rather thin-lipped mouth. Not a
forbidding face, yet that of one not easily swayed.
Traces of youthful comeliness remain, and over all lies
the air of one well assured of herself and her place in the
world. After studying the picture, one readily believes
that heredity had no small part in developing the deep
religious convictions and the determined puritanism that
became Arthur's most notable characteristics.

Castle Hedingham was the home of a very rich, sport-
loving man, of no great energy or force of character, John
de Vere, the sixteenth Earl of Oxford, as inclined to gen-
erosity and hospitality as to ostentation and display. Writing of him in 1598, Stow says:

The late Earl of Oxford, father of him who now liveth, hath
been noted within these forty years, to have ridden into this City
and to his house by London Stone with eighty gentlemen in a
livery of Reading tawny and chains of gold about their necks
before him and one hundred tall yeomen in the like livery to follow him without chains but all having his cognizance of the blue
boar embroidered on their left shoulders.[5]

John de Vere had little taste for the politics of the day,
but yet had skill and luck and pliability enough to save
head and property in a time when many a noble lost both.

[5] Stow, John. *A Survey of London.* (Written in 1598.) London,
1890, page 115.

22

He was amenable to woman's wiles and to official pressure. After his first wife's death (she had been Lady Dorothy Neville, the daughter of the Earl of Westmoreland) a certain "Mrs. Dorothy, waiting woman" to his only child Catherine, then a girl of nine or ten, caught his eye. Banns for their marriage were twice published. Yet this marriage never took place, for the Lord Protector Somerset prevented it.

Catherine got her father into further trouble about the same time by her mere existence. Somerset, casting a greedy eye on the vast Vere estates, wheedled or frightened the Earl into an agreement for the future marriage of the little girl to the Protector's son Henry, then a child of seven. He induced Oxford to consent, on February 1, 1548, to a "fine," in the interest of these children, which would have deprived collateral Vere heirs of the bulk of the estate. But this marriage never took place and, after the fall of Somerset, Parliament annulled the "fine" and made provision for a proper recognition of the children of Oxford's brothers.

Castle Hedingham, under such a master, was hospitable to the new doctrines and practices set forth by Archbishop Cranmer, eagerly embraced by the young King and sternly enforced by the strong hand of Somerset. Edward VI, the scholarly and precocious youth who was upon the throne, was more interested in theology than in government. Under the influence of Cranmer, he devoted the full energy of his feeble frame to religious studies and observances. It became the style to be religious, that is, to be, or pretend to be, deeply interested in matters of doctrine. Such was the situation when Arthur went with

23

his mother to Bloomsters, close neighbor to, and under the strong influence of the Castle. Here he spent the next four years, years which left their mark upon his entire life.

At an early period the church had established a strong hold on the minds of the inhabitants of Essex. The county, before Henry VIII closed them, had had two mitred abbeys and six others, twenty-two priories and three nunneries, nine hospitals, three colleges, and two preceptories.[6] Four of these were within easy reach of Belchamp St. Paul's and other places near which there had been Goldings for several hundred years. They were the Frère Primonts at Sudbury, the Augustinian Friars at Clare, the Dominicans at Babwell and the Franciscans at Cambridge. All of these, the recipients of the devout testamentary bounty of the pious, had grown rich. Arthur Golding's ancestors, too, had been among those to remember them in their wills. His grandfather Thomas of Cavendish had in 1504 left forty shillings to each of those orders for the saying of masses for his soul. His great uncle John of Glemsford had left them each ten shillings to sing Gregory's Trentall for the same purpose. Thus the closing of these monasteries and of other institutions deeply affected the minds of the people who, as usual, could not sense that the old order was breaking down and the new was coming in.

Yet for years the people of the eastern counties had shown an increasing disposition towards independence of thought. They were readily accessible to the doctrines of

[6] Morant, Reverend Philip. *History of Essex*. London, 1769. Introduction.

the German reformers and had constant news of the progress of the rebellion against the Papacy. Their position
near the North Sea, in easy and frequent communication
with the Low Countries, where the new doctrines flourished, had early made them fertile ground for the sow-
ing of the seeds of Protestantism. As the government,
however, was not yet as Protestant as the people, Arthur's
father had been energetic in enforcing the order of Tun-
stall, Bishop of London, and later of Archbishop Ware-
ham, to prevent the circulation of English translations of
the scriptures. When William Tyndale printed his translation of the New Testament in Germany in 1525, copies
soon were smuggled through the eastern ports. Strong
efforts were made to prevent entrance of the book and
for some years afterward many arrests were made, particularly in the parishes of Birdbrook and Bumpstead near
Belchamp St. Paul's. Secret meetings were held for scripture readings and there was a general revolt against the
doctrine of the real presence in the sacrament and against
the worship of the saints, etc. As official rigor softened
with the development of the dispute between Henry and
Clement over the divorce of Queen Catherine, Protestant
voices became louder. Nevertheless ecclesiastical control
and repression were still strong. But reform was in the
air and could not be entirely stifled. In 1530 one William
Worfley "priest and hermit" was abjured for preaching
at Halstead "that no one riding on pilgrimage on a soft
saddle and an easy horse under him should have any merit
thereby but the horse and the saddle." [7]

[7] This and foregoing references to persecution in Essex are from T. W.
Davids' *Evangelical Nonconformity in the County of Essex*. London, 1863.

25

This was a long step forward from the time when Arthur's grandfather Thomas had provided, in the will above referred to, for a vicarious pilgrimage to clear his sins. He had left twenty pounds "and more if necessary" for the services of an "honest priest" to make the journey to Rome and Jerusalem to pray en route for his soul and those of his friends. Thomas also created a testamentary trust through the operation of which, twenty-four persons, who should each year pray for his soul, would have their taxes paid, to the extent of six shillings. (Appendix No. 7). Perhaps this sort of thing was not customary, but, if Thomas's methods were unusual, his purpose was not. The protest of the "priest and hermit," although too early for his own comfort, undoubtedly expressed the growing dissatisfaction with the idea that man's eternal salvation could be procured by such methods. These events were before Arthur's birth, but they form part of the foundation for the religious background of his early years which was so profoundly to influence the formation of his character.

During the four years between Arthur's removal to Bloomsters and his going to Cambridge, whether at home, at school in Halstead, or at Castle Hedingham, the boy must constantly have heard of the changes in the church services and methods as well as of the book of common prayer the Archbishop had prepared at the order of the King. At Jesus College he heard more; those who held to the Papal tradition were silenced if not convinced. Thus his boyhood rounded into youth under the constant influence of the new ideas. In his second year at college the world fell to pieces. Edward VI died, confusion followed, and finally the Roman Catholic Mary Tudor

26

came to the throne and reaction got under way. Essex felt it sharply. When the reëstablishment of the rule of celibacy among the clergy was ordered, eighty-nine in the county were deprived of their livings because they would not give up the wives they had married or the families they had reared. But even worse followed when the wave of persecution by axe and stake swept over the country and claimed seventy-two victims in Essex. The scourge reached every corner of the county and near Bloomsters a particularly spectacular horror took place.

In 1554, Thomas Hawkes, described as "gentleman and priest," was burned at the stake in Coggeshall, only about five miles from Bloomsters. This terrible event must have left a deep impression as great crowds attended. It is even possible if Arthur had by that time returned from college, as is probable, that he was among those who witnessed the scene. Fox's *Book of Martyrs* tells this thrilling story:

before Hawkes was burned some of his friends asked him to give them a sign "whether the pain of such burning were so great that a man might not therein keep his mind quiet and patient." Hawkes promised that if the pain were tolerable he would lift his hands above his head before death. Then when his skin had been drawn together, and his fingers consumed with fire, so that all men thought certainly he had been gone, suddenly and contrary to all expectations the blessed servant of God being mindful of his promise aforemade, reached up his hands burning in a light flame which was marvelous to behold, over his head to the living God and with great rejoicing, as it seemed, clapped them three times together.

As Fox was on the Continent at the time and got his information from reports this account is interesting not be-

cause it may be believed literally but because it indicates
the tremendous impression made upon the spectators and
the consequent spread of the legend of the event. Those
who asked the question were clearly in a state of religious
exaltation, and were indeed weighing in their own minds
the possibility of defying the flames.

This was not the only horror in the neighborhood but
this alone would have been sufficient to make a vital and
lasting impression upon an eighteen-year-old lad and to
explain the bitter hatred of popery that marked Golding's
later years. Whether or not Arthur returned to Bloomsters before or after Hawkes suffered, he found life there
changed. Though, by reason of Oxford's prompt support
of Mary, that household and all other connections of the
Vere family were safe, they were so only as long as they
were quiet and, at least outwardly, embraced the ancient
faith. For the remaining three or four years of Mary's
reign Arthur probably remained at home helping his
mother and elder brother Henry in the administration of
the manor. Doubtless he continued his studies and may
even have worked at translation. As religious subjects
were too dangerous in that day of persecution, Arthur
turned to the classics and delved deep into their history
and literature.

Thus this period was a time of preparation for the
group of classical translations which, a few years later,
placed him in the front rank of English scholars. Evidence of this is found in the letter dedicatory of his translation of Justine's *Trogus Pompeius*, addressed in 1564
to his brilliant young nephew Edward de Vere, the seventeenth Earl of Oxford. He says, "I long since vowed to

28

BLOOMSTERS MANOR TODAY

This had been the home of his grandmother and afterward of his mother, and was Arthur Golding's home in his later boyhood and early manhood.

dedicate this work to your father." As this was only two years after John de Vere's death, it is clear that the words "long since" refer to a time much earlier when he already was at work on the book.

Of the details of his life during these years nothing is of record. Nor indeed is anything definitely known until we hear of him in London in 1562. It is safe to assume, however, that he lived a quiet and retired life. The position of his brother-in-law John de Vere was none too secure, for towards the end of Mary's reign, he was under suspicion by the Catholic party. The statements in the *Dictionary of National Biography* and elsewhere that Golding was in the service of the Protector Somerset and in that of Sir Henry Sidney appear to be without foundation. (Appendix No. 8).

It has been assumed that he acted as tutor to his nephew Edward. No definite record has been found indicating such a connection which, however, would appear reasonable in view of the factor of relationship as well as the fitness of the one and the youth of the other. Two other persons, however, are mentioned as having been Edward de Vere's tutors. The first was Sir Thomas Smith, who later succeeded Sir William Cecil as principal secretary of state in 1572 when the latter, lately created Lord Burghley, was made Lord Treasurer. Smith's service is believed to have begun during the period under discussion; but how long it lasted is not known.[8] Later and during a part of his stay at Cecil House, which occurred before he went to Cambridge, the young Earl was under the tutelage of

[8] Ward, B. M. *The Seventeenth Earl of Oxford.* London, 1928, page 11.

Lawrence Nowell who in June, 1563, wrote to Cecil: "I clearly see that my work for the Earl of Oxford cannot be much longer required," and asking therefore for other employment.[9] This Nowell was Dean of Litchfield, a brother to Alexander Nowell, the learned Dean of St. Paul's. His most noteworthy service to letters was the preservation of the famous Beowulf Manuscript, which, later secured and saved from oblivion by Sir Robert Cotton, is now one of the chief treasures of the British Museum. Nowell's name, with the date 1563, is at the top of the first page of the manuscript.[10]

It would therefore appear that such share as Golding may have had in the education of his nephew was limited to the period after his return from Cambridge, when he was a very young man and the boy but five or six years old. It is evident, however, that Arthur was in close contact with the lad and was interested in and observant of the progress and the development of his nephew's brilliant mind. This is made clear in the dedication to him of his translation of *Trogus Pompeius:*

I have had experience thereof myself how earnest a desire your honor hath naturally grafted in you to read, peruse and communicate with others as well the histories of ancient times and things done long ago, also of the present state of things in our days.

Possibly this statement is the basis for the assumed tutorship, but such words may well have been the result of the natural contact and association between a scholarly uncle and a clever nephew, rather than have arisen from

[9] Lansdowne MSS. No. 6, Art. 54, British Museum.
[10] Sir Israel Gollancz in introduction to *The Caedmon Manuscript*. Oxford, 1927.

the formal relation of pupil and scholar. Certainly Golding, in his dedication (1571) of *Calvin's Commentaries on the Psalms*, to the young Earl of Oxford, then of age and about to be married, speaks as an uncle "by the duty wherein nature hath bound me to you." The tone of the address is strongly admonitory, almost in the manner of an anxious and worried father. There is nothing of the teacher in it.

When Elizabeth came to the throne in 1558 the scene changed for Golding as well as for the country. The fear of persecution was withdrawn from the Protestants and England breathed a sigh of relief. The new Queen was far more politically than religiously minded and, although some twenty-nine clergymen in Essex were finally deprived for failure to obey the acts of supremacy and uniformity, there was nothing like the persecution of the previous reign. Castle Hedingham and all its occupants and retainers felt the change especially; Bloomsters and its family as well. With the political astuteness which had served him so well in Mary's reign, John de Vere was quick to turn to the new Queen and was one of the peers who accompanied Elizabeth from Hatfield, her semi-prison, on the journey to London to take the throne.

Elizabeth, as the granddaughter of Henry VII, had inherited a love and a respect for wealth and for those who possessed it. Hence she was friendly to John de Vere, who soon had a chance to display his taste for ostentatious hospitality in the entertaining of one of the first of the bearers of royal offers for Elizabeth's hand. In 1559 Oxford was appointed to entertain the Duke of Friesland, son of the King of Sweden, who came to England to offer

Elizabeth marriage with his brother, Prince Eric. Oxford did the honors royally and, in the words of an old chronicler, "shewed the Prince great sport." [11] The same year his wife Margery, Countess of Oxford, was appointed lady-in-waiting to the Queen, [12] and, two years afterward, August 14-18, 1561, Queen Elizabeth was his guest on one of the "progresses" which she so delighted to make. [13]

In 1560 a commission was appointed to "restore true religion" to the University of Cambridge and on the 30th of July of that year the University, in the most solemn manner, made full atonement by reversing the decree of heresy and the sentence of burning, and restored Bucer and Fagius to full communion with the reformed church. Bucer's old friends and disciples in Strasburg celebrated this event by issuing a pamphlet in Latin which gave the "true history" of Bucer's life and death, and of his burning and his "restoration." This Golding translated and published in 1562, the first of his known publications. As we have seen he had a particular interest in this event on account of his stay in Cambridge, for he had either been there when the ridiculous performance took place or had observed it from his home at Bloomsters. This was his only translation of a religious character, until he brought out Calvin's *Treatise on Offences* five years after.

During the four years from the accession of Elizabeth to John de Vere's death, Castle Hedingham was the scene

[11] Markham, Clements R. *The Fighting Veres.* Boston, 1888, page 22.
[12] Nichol, John. *The Progresses, and Public Processions of Queen Elizabeth.* London, 1823. Vol. I, page 37.
[13] Cottonian MSS. Vespasianus C. XIV. Page 481. British Museum. (Printed in Nichol, John. *The Progresses, and Public Processions of Queen Elizabeth.* London, 1823. Vol. I, pages 92-104). See Appendix No. 16.

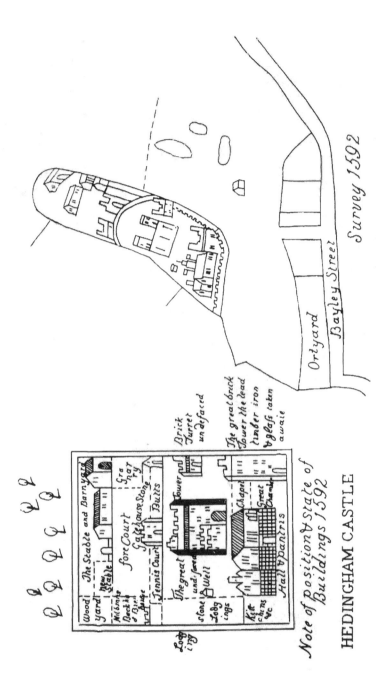

PLAN OF HEDINGHAM CASTLE IN 1592

Survey of condition made by order of Lord Burghley who was then moving to protect the interests of his grandchildren, their father, the Earl of Oxford, having despoiled the property.

of much gaiety. Golding, who was in his early twenties, found nothing in his associations there to turn him to the study of religious literature. On the other hand there was much to deepen and strengthen his interest in the classics. It has been a surprise to many that so stern a puritan as Golding later showed himself to be, should have translated the *Metamorphoses* of Ovid. It is easy, however, to see that the new spirit of life in the country and in the castle, coupled with the opportunity to observe, and probably to associate with the great, possibly with royalty itself, would stir interest and imagination and make him drink in eagerly the Roman poet's tales.

Then, too, he doubtless went up to London or traveled elsewhere as was the custom of young men similarly situated. For he was after all the son of a wealthy county family; his sister was a countess, his brother a knight, and he himself was on friendly terms with his brother-in-law, one of the wealthiest of the great nobles of England. London was the natural goal for such a young man. There he found associations which again strengthened his interest in the classics. At that time the Inns of Court were the centers of most of the intellectual activity of the city, and it was natural that Golding should have visited among them. His father had been a member of the Middle Temple forty years before, and various others of his name and probably related to him had held membership in one or the other of the Inns. He is said to have been a visitor to Gray's Inn in 1561,[14] but the fact is not set down in the Inn's records. It seems very likely, however, because Sir

[14] Conley, C. H. *First English Translators of the Classics.* New Haven, 1927, pages 41-132.

William Cecil was a member of that Inn and a friend of John de Vere, who in his will left him a "great horse." Here then, Arthur probably began the acquaintance with Cecil because of which the latter appointed Golding "receiver" for Edward de Vere in his minority.

Chapter III

IN THE GREAT WORLD

WHEN the Earl of Oxford died, his son Edward, Margery's child and Golding's nephew, was twelve years old. As heir to the vast possessions of the noble house of Vere and to the high rank and great title of Earl of Oxford, the boy was a subject of royal solicitude. According to the custom of the time the heirs of great nobles, in their minorities, were made wards of the crown and Queen Elizabeth therefore directed that Edward be placed in charge of Sir William Cecil, who the year before had been appointed Master of the Wards.

John de Vere died on August 3, 1562, and a contemporary writer has left this interesting picture of his funeral four weeks afterward:

On the 31st day of August was buried in Essex the good Earl [of Oxford] with three Heralds of Arms, Master Garter, Master Lancaster, Master Richmond, with a standard and a great banner of arms, and eight banner rolls, crest, target, sword and coat armour, and a hearse with velvet and a pall of velvet, and a design of scutcheons, and with many mourners in black; and a great moan was made for him.

From the same source we learn that

On the 3rd day of September came riding out of Essex from the funeral of the Earl of Oxford his father, the young Earl of Oxford, with seven score horse all in black; through London and

Chepe and Ludgate, and so to Temple Bar between 5 and 6 of the afternoon.[1]

In this company in all probability went Arthur Golding, the newly appointed "receiver" for the young Earl, on his way with him to take up residence in Cecil House, Sir William Cecil's residence on the Strand, then but lately finished, where the Principal Secretary of State lived with a household of eighty persons at a cost of from £40 to £50 per week. The house was large and handsome, ornamented with four turrets, and inside was "curiously beautified with rare devices." It stood on the north side of the present street near Somerset House, in the midst of a large garden. The name, three hundred years afterward, was revived in the neighborhood by the famous Hotel Cecil which was for nearly fifty years the most renowned hostelry in London.

It is not entirely clear what the functions of the office of "receiver" were, but Golding appears to have had some business or financial guidance of the interests of the young Earl and of his younger sister Mary. In the State papers are found records which indicate this phase of his activities. These are receipts in Latin in which he signed his name Arthurum Goldyng and acknowledged the receipt of money from the bailiffs of estates inherited by the young people. (Appendix No. 9).

At any rate it is clear that Golding, appointed by Cecil who was well known for his astuteness and his skill in judging men, must already have developed substantial qualities of mind and heart. The fact that he had a part in

[1] *The Diary of Henry Machyn,* London (printed for the Camden Society, 1848), pages 290-291.

the management of the vast Vere estates is sufficient evidence of the confidence reposed in him when it is realized that those estates were among the greatest in the realm. Some fifty years earlier an offer of twelve thousand pounds as yearly rental for only a portion had been made to the fourteenth Earl of Oxford.[2] There is reason to believe, however, that in Golding's time the estates were heavily encumbered with debt, due to the lavish extravagance of the sixteenth Earl. Margery, the widowed Countess of Oxford, in a letter (1563) seeking to be relieved of responsibility in connection with her husband's will, complains of the burden of "those things which, in my Lord's lifetime, were kept most secret from me. And since that time the doubtful declaration of my Lord's debts have so uncertainly fallen out that" she wishes to leave the whole matter to her son that the "gain, if any there be" might come wholly to him.[3]

Golding's work for his nephew and niece was not limited merely to finances. Soon he was called upon to defend their dearest interests. Within a year of his appointment an attack upon their legitimacy and their mother's and his sister's honor was made by their half-sister, Lady Catherine Windsor, the only child of John de Vere's first wife. This move, which not only threatened their right to the Vere estates, but their titles and their names as well, was of vital import. That it should have been left for defense to Golding, then twenty-seven years of age, is further evidence of Cecil's confidence in his ability.

[2] Morant, Reverend Philip, *History of Essex*, London, 1769, Vol. 1, page 294.
[3] Lansdowne MSS. No. 6, Art 20, British Museum.

37

The complete details of the vicious attack upon the validity of his sister Margery's marriage to John de Vere and the legitimacy of his nephew and niece, which Golding was now called upon to resist, are not to be found after the lapse of nearly four hundred years, but enough has been brought to light to piece out the main facts of the story. It discloses a daughter ready to accuse her dead father of bigamy, and to stamp her half-brother and sister as bastards.

Golding's action in the matter, at least that part of it that has come down to us in the records, is shown in a petition in Latin now on file in the Public Record Office (State Papers Domestic, Eliz. Vol. 29, No. 8) which is endorsed in Cecil's hand "Arthur Golding's petition for my lord of Oxford."

The document which is not in Golding's holograph having probably been prepared by a clerk, may be translated freely as follows:

Arthur Goldyng, gentleman, uncle of my lord Edward, Earl of Oxford, and of the Lady Mary his sister—

Being informed on the report of several persons that Catherine, wife of Lord Edward Windsor, Baron de Stanwell, has entered a vigorous demand and still urges that the most Reverend Matthew, Archbishop of Canterbury, shall decree that the afore mentioned lord Earl of Oxford and Lady Mary his sister be summoned to produce witnesses (if they shall think it concerns their interest) to be received, sworn and examined about certain articles touching and concerning the said Earl and his sister under protestations of "not consenting unless &c." Arthur Golding alleges and to the effect of all right alleges the petition of the said lady Catherine to contain grave prejudice of the lady the Queen and to touch the legitamacy of the blood and right of hereditary possessions of the said Earl and his sister and alleges

38

the aforesaid Earl to have been and to be a minor of fourteen years and known and of record to be under the ward, tutelage and care of the said lady the Queen with all and singular his lands, tenements and hereditaments which of right are and ought to be in the possession and rule of the said lady the Queen during his minority. And for the same reason by the common law as by the statutes of the realm, and also by the privileges of the Court of Wards and Liveries no plea or controversy may be moved or any other be recited, set in motion or proposed before any ecclesiastical or secular judge, which touches directly or indirectly the person, state, things, goods, lands, possessions, tenements or hereditaments of the same in any way or in any manner during his minority in the Court of Wards and Liveries of the said lady the Queen save before the master and council for the same Court to this deputed by the strength of the law of this realm. And further he alleges that the said lady Mary the sister of the said Earl was and is a minor of fourteen years and her right and interest to depend directly on the right and title of the aforenamed Earl. Therefore he asks that the most Reverend to decree by reason of the premises that it be superseded, until special licence in this part be obtained, according to the laws and customs in like causes in the said Court of Wards and Liveries lawfully used.

28 June 1563.

Very extensive and careful searches at Lambeth Palace and at Canterbury have failed to bring to light the "articles" of Lady Windsor's charges, nor can any record be found of any suit having been brought by her in the Court of Wards and Liveries as Golding declared she must do. Whether or not any formal written charges were filed by her in the Archbishop's Court is not clear. The fact that they are not now to be found is, however, no proof that they were not filed, as they may well have been lost or taken from the files at the instance of Golding and de-

39

stroyed in order finally to silence the scandal. It is also possible that Lady Windsor had only made a verbal application to the Archbishop who hesitated to act. Golding says that he acts "on the report of several persons.", Quite possibly the Archbishop did not wish to act and was glad to be inhibited. Perhaps he gave a hint to Golding through one or more of the "several persons." At any rate it was a nasty family mess. Great names and vast properties were involved and Matthew Parker the Archbishop was a bookish man who usually avoided all controversy. Normally, matters relating to marriage were under the jurisdiction of his court, but this case may have appeared to him one that might well be left alone. At any rate, it is clear that Golding's warning petition was accepted by him as properly stating the law as to minors under the control of the Queen, for, in a later case, involving his episcopal rights in the rents of certain lands of John de Vere, he brought suit against the young Earl Edward in the Court of Wards and Liveries.

In order to get at the story which lay behind this bitter family quarrel, it is necessary to go back sixteen years, before the young Earl and his sister were born and Lady Windsor was but a child. In 1547, with the accession of the boy Edward VI to the throne, his uncle, Edward Seymour, the Duke of Somerset, seized power as Lord Protector, and entered upon his tyrannical and avaricious course. John de Vere was one of those who suffered at his hands. Oxford lay under some real or pretended accusation—the details of which have not come down to us. Morant in a footnote says that the Protector "convented" Oxford before him on a criminal charge but there are no further details. (See Appendix No. 10). Matters at any rate stood thus in June, 1547, when Sir Thomas Darcy the husband of the Earl's eldest sister Elizabeth Vere wrote the following letter to William Cecil then at the outset of his remarkable career.

Sir Thomas Darcy to Wm. Cecil, June 27, 1547.

After right hearty commendations these shall be to advertise you that according to my late conversation had with you in my lord's graces gallery at Westminster, I have by all means that I can inquired of the matter between my Lord of Oxenford and the gentlewoman with whom he is in love namely Mrs. Dorothy late woman to my lady Katherine his daughter. And upon conversation had with them both, I have found and do perceive them to be in the same case that they were in when my said Lord of Oxenford was before his lord's grace and no other, saving that the banns of matrimony between them were twice proclaimed in one day. Other treaties or solemn conversation hath not been before witness but only been in secret between them twin. Sir if it shall stand with my lord graces pleasure to have this matter further stayed, as my lord of Oxenford's honor wealth and preservation considered, I think it very expedient and may right well be, then I beseech you I may be thereof advertised. And yet, you will move his grace to direct his letters to Mr Edward Green of Sampford in whose house the said Dorothy doth now continue, commanding him by the same neither to suffer my said Lord of Oxenford to have access to her nor she unto him. And that no privy messengers may go between them, which as I suppose will be the surest way to stay them. And upon further advertisement to be had from his grace, if it shall so stand with his pleasure, I will enter in conversation with my lord Wentworth for a marriage between my said Lord of Oxenford and one of his daughters and as they, upon sight, what other treaty may agree, so to proceed in the same. Sir upon your motion to be made unto my lord's grace concerning the premises I pray you I may be advertised by this bearer of his pleasure in the same, which

41

knowing I shall right gladly endeavor myself to accomplish by the aid of the Blessed Trinity who have you in his continual preservasion.

From Heddingham Castle the xxvij day of June (1547)

By your loving friend

THOMAS DARCY

Endorsed

From Sir Thomas Darcy Knight

State Papers (Domestic) Edward VI Vol 1. No. 45.

It is clear from this letter that Oxford had been under suspicion; at least he had been under examination before Somerset, and this love affair had been known. Also it is plain that Darcy had been sent to Castle Hedingham to report on the progress of the affair. Apparently it was coming close to the final conclusion of marriage, so Darcy made his recommendations for the thwarting of the lovers. But Darcy saw in the precarious position of the Earl an opportunity to benefit the family of a near relative. Lord Wentworth, one of whose daughters he suggested as a wife for the Earl, was Darcy's own cousin. If Oxford was so keen to marry it was better that he should bestow his hand and his property upon one of Darcy's relatives. But Somerset knew a better way. He was a cousin of both Wentworth and Darcy and if he had no daughter then unmarried to put forward for the post of Countess of Oxford, he had a son Henry, then but seven years old, whom he would marry to Oxford's daughter Catherine, then not over ten years old. Under the cover of the honor of this alliance with the cousin of King Edward and the threat of the actual or invented criminal charge, the Protector induced Oxford to betroth Catherine to Henry and to agree to a "fine" which practically stripped his collateral heirs of the great Vere possessions. It took a few months' separation from "Mrs. Dorothy" and probably considerable pressure from Somerset but on February 1, 1548, John de Vere signed the "fine." On the same day Oxford made a new will which was witnessed by Thomas Golding, Arthur's eldest half-brother.[4] The exact relations of Thomas with John de Vere and his connection with the Protector can only be inferred from the benefits conferred upon him and his family by Somerset and from the unusual nature of a letter (almost certainly to him) by the latter two years later in which the Protector calls him his servant. In the meantime, in November, 1547, Parliament had granted the chantry lands to the Crown. Their liquidation was in every neighborhood a juicy plum and in Essex this fell to Thomas Golding who, in the words of Holman's *History of Halstead*, "knew how to improve his interest to get a large share of them." [5]

With the granting of the "fine" Somerset lost interest in John de Vere's love affairs, for he made no opposition when on August 5, 1548, thirteen months after Darcy's letter and but five months after the granting of the "fine," Oxford was married in Belchamp St. Paul's church to Margery, Thomas Golding's full sister and Arthur's half-sister. That John de Vere was under some sort of observation or control by Thomas Golding is evident from Somerset's leter to "——" Golding just mentioned. (See Appendix No. 8). Thomas Golding was riding on the crest of the wave and well knew how to steer a prosperous

[4] Records of the College of Arms, London.
[5] Holman, Reverend William; *History of Halstead* (Holman MSS., Colchester Museum), pp. 62-65.

course in these troublesome days, for just at this time
1549-50 he was knighted and in 1550 he was made collector of the subsidy in Essex, another lucrative appointment. Sir Thomas was skillful enough to avoid being involved in Somerset's fall two years later and seems not
to have incurred the enmity of John de Vere when the
latter was freed of fear of Somerset by the Protector's
fall. Even when Parliament voided the "fine" in the interest of the marriage of Catherine with Henry Seymour
(which never took place) and John de Vere was in favor
with Northumberland in the last days of Edward's reign,
there is no record that he had any enmity towards Sir
Thomas Golding who continued to prosper. What became of that lovelorn maiden "Mrs. Dorothy" we do not
know, but her story is apparently behind Lady Windsor's
charges which Arthur Golding opposed. Almost a hundred years afterward the story appeared again when in
1660 Lady Windsor's great grandson laid claim to the
Lord Great Chamberlainship on the ground that Lady
Catherine was the child of the sixteenth Earl of Oxford's
"only lawful wife." [6]

These events, happening when Arthur was still a boy
were probably not known to him at the time, but were
doubtless told him later by Sir Thomas. With Darcy's
letter in Cecil's files, they furnished the key to the situation. Finally with the unquestionable evidence of his sister Margery's marriage, he was in a good position to meet
Lady Windsor had she brought suit in the Court of
Wards and Liveries. In view of the easily proven fact of

[6] Lord Winsor's Petition, *Journals of the House of Lords*, Vol. XI,
p. 227.

44

HEDINGHAM CASTLE TODAY

From a photograph by permission of Miss Musette Majendie, the present owner of the estate.

John de Vere's marriage to Margery Golding and the existence of the record in Belchamp parish register, it is not clear why Lady Windsor should have made her charges unless she relied upon childhood memories. The Mrs. Dorothy, described in Darcy's letter as a "gentlewoman," was in all probability the companion or governess of the little girl who at the time was certainly not more than ten years of age. (Lady Dorothy Neville, her mother, was married to John de Vere in 1536.) Dorothy's relations with the motherless child were doubtless intimate and she probably told her she was about to marry her father, perhaps told her she had done so, which would not have been so great a stretching of the truth considering the publishing of the banns twice in one day. John de Vere must have been entirely under Mrs. Dorothy's influence when Darcy acted just in time. At any rate, Lady Windsor transmitted to her family her belief that Oxford's marriage had been unlawful, a belief they still held a hundred years after. Perhaps the fact of the twice published banns might have appeared as a cloud upon the marriage, since publication of banns three times was a necessary preliminary to lawful marriage. It was a technical point, but the technicalities of legal procedure were no less stubbornly urged in Elizabeth's time than they are now. The Archbishop had jurisdiction over marriage; if his ecclesiastical conscience could be aroused, perhaps something could be done. So Lady Windsor and her lawyers may have argued, though nothing came of their endeavors although for generations the Windsor family believed they had a case.

The frustrated romance of Mrs. Dorothy and her

easily discouraged lover, John de Vere, has for more than three hundred years made its appearance in the many contests for the post of Lord Great Chamberlain, which have made this one of the most famous cases in Heraldic jurisprudence. This office, asserted to be hereditary in the Vere family, after the death of the eighteenth Earl of Oxford without male heirs, passed to Lord Willoughby the son of Margery Golding's daughter Mary by her marriage with Lord Willoughby de Eresby. In 1660 it was held by his descendant, the Earl of Lindsay, whose title to it was attacked by Thomas, Lord Windsor, descendant of Catherine Vere, so the contest was between the descendants of two half-sisters. At this time John de Vere, on this account, was described as "not as wise as his fathers" which, when one considers the vigor of Aubrey de Vere, companion of William the Conqueror at Hastings, or John de Vere who commanded at Bosworth for Henry of Richmond, may be considered as letting the sixteenth Earl off easily. This statement and Mrs. Dorothy's sad story persisted in later contests for the office and have been heard, possibly finally, as recently as 1902, when, in a sort of general struggle for the office, it seems to have been held that the office ceased to be hereditary in the Vere family after the death of the fifteenth Earl, so there was no need to have so often dragged out this sixteenth century romance. In all this, however, it escaped attention that John de Vere's daughter used this story as a basis for charging her half-sister and brother with illegitimacy and, in effect, her father with bigamy, or that Arthur Golding defended them.

46

Chapter IV

HIS MOST FAMOUS WORKS

HOWEVER actively Golding may have been engaged in the affairs of his nephew and niece, he found leisure for classical studies and for translation, of which the latter was from this time onward to be the chief occupation of his life. Notwithstanding he was busy with the interests of the young Veres and the attack upon their legitimacy, in 1563 he published his translation from the Latin of Leonard Aretine's (D Bruni) *History of the Wars between the Imperialls and the Gothes for the possession of Italy.* This was the first of five classic translations that were to come from his pen in four years and to place him in the front rank of English translators. This work he appropriately dedicated to his host and immediate chief in the affairs of the young Veres, Sir William Cecil.

In the spring of the next year, 1564, he published his translation of Justine's *Abridgement of Trogus Pompeius* which he dedicated to the young Earl of Oxford, then but fourteen years of age and about to receive a degree from Cambridge University. This history, long a favorite of Renaissance students, he holds up to his nephew, and says he knows no one "to whose estate it seemed more requisite and necessary." He urges him to let the example of Epaminondas and other classic heroes "encourage you to

47

proceed in learning and virtue and yourself thereby become equal to any of your predecessors in advancing the honor of your noble house." The whole tenor of the dedication is affectionate and admiring and shows more sentiment than the stern Puritan exhibited elsewhere.

The next year, 1565, Golding published the first portion of the work for which he is most famous, his translation of the first four books of Ovid's *Metamorphoses*. This was not without an inward struggle between the scholar and the puritan in him. Conscience stood at his elbow while he wrote. He was of that considerable body of Protestants whose advocacy and practice of purity of life gave them that name. Apparently he was not concerned with dogma, nor was he a foe to prelatealism. Thus he differed from those later Separatists who through persecution and civil war carried the name of Puritan to a secure and significant place in the history and language of England.

To such a man, the morals or the lack of morals, in the *Metamorphoses* must have come as a shock. To the scholar on the other hand, Ovid's lively tales must have been fascinating. In the introductory matter of the first four books it is easy to see Golding's difficulty. He had chosen as patron Robert Dudley, Earl of Leicester, then scarcely entered on his surprising career. For some years before, and for many years afterward, Leicester was known as a generous patron to translators of the classics, and it is apparent that Golding did not fear the effect of Ovid's tales upon the Earl. Rather he considered him wise and discerning enough to reject the evil and admire the good. In the prose letter of dedication the translator said:

If this woorke was fully performed with lyke eloquence and connyng of endyting by me in Englishe, as it was written by Thauthor thereof in his moother toonge, it might perchaunce delight your honor too bestowe some vacant tyme in the reading of it, for the nomber of excellent devises and fyne inventions contrived in the same, purporting outwardly moste pleasant tales and delectable histories, and fraughted inwardlye with most piththie instructions and wholesome examples, and conteynyng bothe wayes most exquisite connynge and deepe knowledge.

.　　　.　　　.　　　.　　　.

The which if it maye please you too take in good part, I accompt my former travell herin sufficiently recompensed, and think myself greatly enforced too persever in the full accomplishement of all the whole woorke.

However to ease his conscience Golding placed this warning on the title page:

> With skill heede and judgment thys work must bee red
> For else to the reader it stands in small stead.

Others besides Leicester, however, would see the work. Of their discretion he could not be so sure; therefore he felt it necessary to protect them against this first draught of the strong waters of mythological lore. And so he prepared an address "To The Reader" using the metrical form of the poem itself. This Preface sets forth the theory already advanced by medievalists concerning the allegorical nature of the tales and their purpose to serve as warnings to the reader. He began:

I would not wish the simple sort offended for too bee,
When in this booke the heathen names of feyned Godds they see.
The trewe and everliving God the Paynims did not knowe:

.　　　.　　　.　　　.　　　.

49

Some woorshipt al the hoste of heaven: some deadmens ghostes &
    bones:
Sum wicked feends: sum woormes & fowles, herbes, fishes, trees
    & stones.
The fyre, the ayre, the sea, the land, and every ronning brooke,
Eche queachie grove, eche cragged cliffe the name of Godhead
    tooke.
The nyght and day, the fleeting howres, the seasons of the yeere,
And every straugne and monstruous thing, for Godds mistaken
    were.

After he had sketched the faults of the denizens of
Olympus, and pointed out the madness of considering
them Gods, he takes this thrust at contemporaneous
morality:

So would too God there were not now of christen men profest,
That worshipt in theyr deedes theis Godds whose names they doo
    detest.
Whoose lawes wee keepe his thralles wee bee, and he our God
    indeede.

To make sure that the reader will understand that the
characters in the tales are not themselves, but merely sym-
bols for certain types of human beings, with all their
faults and failings, he sets out the cast of the allegory and
lists the performers thus:

By Jove and Juno understand all states of princely port:
By Ops and Saturne aucient folke that are of elder sort:
By Phoebus yoong and lusty brutes of hand and courage stout:
By Mars the valeant men of warre that love too feight it out.
By Pallas and the famous troupe of all the Muses nyne,
Such folke as in the sciences and vertuous artes doo shyne.
By Mercurie the suttle sort that use too filch and lye.
With theeves, and Merchants whoo too gayne theyr travell doo
    applye.

50

By Bacchus all the meaner trades and handycraftes are ment:
By Venus such as of the fleshe too filthie lust are bent,
By Neptune such as keepe the sea: by Phebe maydens chast,
And Pilgrims such as wandringly theyr tyme in travell waste.
By Pluto such as delve in mynes, and Ghostes of persones dead:
By Vulcane smythes and such as woorke in yron, tynne or lead.
By Hecat witches, Conjurers, and Necromancers reede,
With all such vayne and devlish artes as superstition breede.
By Satyres, Sylvanes, Nymphes and Faunes with other such
    besyde,
The playne and simple country folke that every where abyde.

That this personalizing of the vices of Jove's court may
not seem mere illustrative rhetoric he brings home the
lesson individually thus:

Now when thou readst of God or man, in stone, in beast, or tree
It is a myrrour for thy self thyne owne estate too see.
For under feynèd names of Goddes it was the Poets guyse
The vice and faultes of all estates too taunt in covert wyse.

He is not surprised that the heathen gods take the form
of animals and remarks:

And when the people give themselves too filthie life and sinne,
What other kinde of shape thereby than filthie can they winne?
So was Licaon made a Woolfe: and Jove became a Bull:
The tone for using crueltie, the toother for his trull.
So was Elpenor and his mates transformed intoo swyne,
For following of theyr filthie lust in women and in wyne.

Man's dual nature, the struggle of the flesh with a
soul endowed with reason by God, is pointed out. If we
are ruled by reason, Golding says we may count ourselves
men, but, if we yield to fleshly lusts, then we are but
beasts. He continues:

51

This surely did the Poets meene when in such sundry wyse,
The pleasant tales of turned shapes they studyed too devyse.
There purpose was to profite men, and also too delyght
And so too handle every thing as best might like the sight.

The reader is reminded that the Poets' lessons and
benefits are so hidden that they may be seen by but few.
Again he gives warning:

And therefore whooso dooth attempt the Poet woorkes too reede,
Must bring with him a stayd head and judgment too proceede.
For as there bee most wholsome hestes and precepts too bee found,
So are theyr rockes and shallowe shelves too ronne the ship a
    ground.

Some persons he says "seeing vyce shown lyvely in his
hew" are led off into like errors while others condemn the
book too severely and wish it burnt. Of these he says:

These persons overshoote themselves, and other folkes deceyve:
Not able of the authors mynd the meening too conceyve.
The Authors purpose is too paint and set before our eyes
The lyvely Image of the thoughts that in our stomackes ryse.
Eche vice and vertue seemes too speake and argue too our face,
With such perswasions as they have theyr dooinges too embrace.

He lays it upon the conscience of the reader not to condemn the author if some wicked ones are urged towards
vice. Let the reader search his own heart he says, and
continues:

Then take theis woorkes as fragrant flowers most full of pleasant
    juce
The which the Bee conveying home may put too wholsome use:
And which the spyder sucking on too poyson may convert,
Through venym spred in all her limbes and native in hir hart.
For too the pure and Godly mynd, are all things pure and cleene,
And untoo such as are corrupt the best corrupted beene.

52

He disdains in advance the criticism of those whose feelings are so tender that they must reject all not Divine. Equally he repulses those who twist and warp matters plainly written with good intent. He rests his case with the "gentle reader" whose favor he expects on account of the wealth of "godes and jewells" in the *Metamorphoses*.

Mo darke and secret misteries, mo counselles wyse and sage,
Mo good ensamples, mo reprooves of vyce in youth and age,
Mo fyne inventions too delight, mo matters clerkly knit,
No nor more straunge varietie too shew a lerned wit.
The high, the lowe: the riche, the poore: the mayster, and the
 slave:
The mayd, the wife: the man, the chyld: the simple and the
 brave:
The yoong, the old: the good, the bad: the warriour strong and
 stout:
The wyse, the foole: the countrie cloyne: the lerned and the lout:
And every other living wight shall in this mirror see
His whole estate, thoughtes, woordes and deedes expresly shewd
 too bee.

Still fearful of criticism as one beguiling the innocent to vice, he washes his hands of blame in a final warning:

Now to thintent that none have cause heereafter too complaine
Of mee as setter out of things that are but lyght and vaine:
If any stomacke be so weake as that it cannot brooke,
The lively setting forth of things described in this booke,
I give him counsell too absteine untill he bee more strong,
And for to use Ulysses feat ageinst the Meremayds song.
Or if he needes will heere and see and wilfully agree
(Through cause misconstrued) untoo vice allured for too bee:
Then let him also marke the peine that dooth therof ensue,
And hold himself content with that that too his fault is due.

53

The entire address which runs to two hundred and twenty lines is printed in full in Appendix No. 11 and will repay a reading. It is the most vigorous and characteristic expression of the translator in the poetic form.

Notwithstanding Golding's efforts to render Ovid's tales beneficial, or at least innocuous to his readers, he apparently became convinced that he had overrated the protective quality of their "reason," to which he had so strongly appealed in the Preface. The reaction of the public to the First Four Books was probably quite different from what he had expected. Then too the excursions of his fellow translators into the fields of definitely immoral classic literature were disturbing. In the next year, 1566, Adlington brought out his translation of *The Golden Ass* of Apuleius which doubtless startled Golding. He was himself, however, under the influence of a moral and intellectual antidote. At that time he was engaged in translating Calvin's treatise on *Offences*, wherein the sins of the flesh and the spirit were discussed and their evil effects pointed out. This vigorous denunciation of human frailties occupied him even while he was working on the remaining eleven books of the *Metamorphoses* published in 1567. The *Offences* appeared shortly after the completed Ovid. The latter was again dedicated to the Earl of Leicester. This time, however, Golding replaced the brief prose letter of dedication with a long and elaborate explanation in metrical form, of his theory of Ovid's philosophy. Then, to make certain that no one should misunderstand the tales as anything but allegorical demonstrations of human vices and virtues and their consequences, he proceeded to point out plainly the hidden

54

meaning of each of the fifteen books. (Printed in full in Appendix No. 12).

Moreover he reprinted the Preface with minor verbal changes adding, however, a few lines that referred seekers of fuller explanation to the dedicatory letter. Thus, doubly explained, the complete translation of the *Metamorphoses* was given to a public which welcomed it so eagerly that it passed through eight editions. For nearly sixty years it remained without challenge or competition.

Yet Golding was apparently dissatisfied with his failure to impress Elizabethans with the fundamental ethical purpose that he saw in the *Metamorphoses,* for he never again translated a classic that in any degree bordered on the immoral or improper. In fact, he did not translate any other classic for ten years, and at that time he did the unexceptionable work of Seneca dealing with·"benefits" or "the doing of good turns."

At the same time he had Ovid in hand, indeed between the first and second editions of the Roman poet, he produced another work, second only in importance, the translation of *Cæsar's Commentaries.* This was done under interesting conditions, and at the suggestion of Cecil under whose peculiar patronage Golding stood.

John Brende a very able scholar whose translation of Quintius Curtius's account of the campaigns of Alexander the Great, published in 1553, had been most successful, had been engaged in the translation of *Cæsar's Commentaries* when he died, having finished the first five and one-half books. Golding in the customary dedicatory letter to Cecil tells how he hesitated to undertake the work of completion because of his ignorance of the warlike matters and other subjects treated. But, since Brende's manuscript had been sent to him by Cecil, and "remembering that earnest endeavor conquereth all things," he undertook the task. When it was finished he found himself in a delicate position. His friends urged him to lay aside Brende's work and translate the whole from the beginning. He shrank from doing so but finally yielded. But he was doubtful how this action would be received and says in the letter:

Wherein how my doings may be liked of others I know not. This I most humbly desier your honor, that you will take my paines & trauell in that behalfe in good worth. For I haue not done it, because I thought my selfe of more skill and experience than maister Brend (which I confesse my yeeres giue me not) neither because I would in defacing his glory, (which were a point of lewdnesse) goe about (as the Latin prouerb saith) to pricke out the Crowes eyes. But I haue done it, partly moued by the persuasions aforesayd, and partly because I was desirous to haue the body of the whole story compacted vnyforme and one stile throughout. For so I thought it should be both more alowable among such as are of knowledge, and also more acceptable to the Reader, when neither part of the work might be an eye sore to the other. Furthermore forasmuch as it is knowne vnto many, that the sayd Copie was committed vnto mee, I haue forborne to build vpon that foundation, least I might haue ministred occasion to such as loue cauelling, to say I had eyther hatched other byrds Egges, or else presumed to finish the picture of Venus that Appelles left vnperfect.

He finished the Cæsar in the autumn of 1565 and dated his dedicatory letter October 12th of that year, less than ten months after he finished the first four books of the *Metamorphoses*, December 23, 1564. Like the Ovid this was warmly received, particularly by the students of history and military affairs and later by the gentlemen volunteers who learned the art of war while fighting in the Netherlands against Spain. A second edition was issued when interest was keen in military matters in 1590, for England had eight thousand men under Sir Francis Vere sustaining the cause of the Dutch and had just had four thousand in France to help Henry of Navarre.

One of those soldiers who learned their trade in the Netherlands, that nursery of the English military tradition, was the renowned "Captain of Plymouth." Longfellow in *The Courtship of Miles Standish* makes the book under discussion one of the two which composed that redoubtable warrior's military library:

Fixed to the opposite wall was a shelf of books, and among them
Prominent three, distinguished alike for bulk and for binding;
Bariffe's Artillery Guide, and the Commentaries of Caesar
Out of the Latin translated by Arthur Goldinge of London,
And, as if guarded by these, between them was standing the Bible.

Golding may have been justified in his modest doubt of his own military knowledge, but later he was not without connections and close acquaintance among the leading English soldiers of the day. Lord Willoughby de Eresby who had been commander-in-chief of the English in the Netherlands was the husband of his niece, Mary Vere, daughter of his sister Margery. Sir Francis Vere, who succeeded Lord Willoughby in the chief command in the Low Countries when the latter was sent to France, was the cousin of his brother-in-law, the Earl of Oxford, and brother to Horace, Lord Vere, who with him became famous in history as "The Fighting Veres."

57

Chapter V

BUSY AND SUCCESSFUL

THE five years 1562-1567 were crowded with activities. In addition to the duties of "receiver" for the young Veres, Golding had the burden of defending the charges brought against them by Lady Windsor. Notwithstanding all this he produced five translations from the Latin, two of them major works recognized at the time and since as of the first importance.

He was moving about a good deal during this period. We see him in the first two years at Cecil House, but apparently he left there for good in the early part of 1565. The fact that Edward Vere had gone to Cambridge and had taken a degree there in the summer of 1564 may have changed or discontinued Golding's duties as "receiver." At any rate we still find him at Cecil House during the Christmas season of 1564, for on December 23rd he dated his letter of dedication of the First Four Books of the *Metamorphoses* from there. Some time after that, however, he went down into the country again and we find him at Belchamp St. Paul's in the autumn, for his dedication of *Cæsar's Commentaries* is dated as of that place, October 12, 1565. It was natural that he should be at Belchamp, his brother's house, for Bloomsters Manor, the home of his later boyhood and early manhood, was no longer open to him. His mother had died quite recently, though we do not know the exact date. She had sat for her portrait in 1563, but, by 1565, Bloomsters (in which she had a life estate) has passed to her husband's heir, Sir Thomas Golding. By him it had been sold to one Roger Martin of Long Melford, who caused a survey of the manor to be made, August 7, 1656. We next find Golding at Barwicke, a manor belonging to the Vere estates in White Colne, Co. Essex. From here he dated the completed translation of the *Metamorphoses*, April 20, 1567.

These frequent moves might indicate that he was still single, as no record has been found of where or when he was married. His wife, however, was Ursula Roydon, the daughter of John Roydon of Chilham, Co. Kent. Little is known of her or her family, but it appears likely that she was related to Sir Thomas Golding's wife, as both were Roydons from Kent, Lady Golding's father having been Thomas Roydon of East Peckham in that County. At any rate indications are that Arthur's marriage had not yet taken place, not only on account of his frequent moves and his residence in other men's houses, but also because he had no children, at least no boys, when his brother Sir Thomas made his will in 1569; nor do we learn of the birth of his eldest son Henry until the child is mentioned in Henry Golding's will early in 1575. We find no record of Arthur's renting a house until 1575 nor of his leasing or owning one until two years later. This, however, is not surprising, since Golding, as a younger son, had to make his own way, especially after the death of his mother. Possibly this event, bringing a new need to earn money, may have had some influence in the decision he seems to have made, after he finished the *Metamor-*

phoses, to devote his time to religious translations. Possibly also the influence of Calvin's *Treatise on Offences,* which he had translated and which was published in 1567, as well as his doubtful experience in trying to convert Ovid into a moral tract, may have had weight. At any rate, there was at this time a growing interest in the works of the French reformers. Printers were willing to pay for translations of religious books for which there was a steady demand that increased until volumes of Calvin's sermons were "best sellers."

The religious quarrels in France were eagerly followed in England as they grew in ferocity, until the crowning horror of St. Bartholomew's Day in 1572 shocked the English public. Before that, however, the religious issue, complicated by high politics, had been brought home to the people by the flight of Mary Queen of Scots into England, and by the fears her pretensions to the throne aroused, backed as they were by Spain. It became evident that there was to be a fight to the death between the Pope and the Protestants. Naturally, therefore, the writings and sermons of Calvin, the intellectual leader of the more aggressive branch of the new religion, were in demand, as were those of lesser leaders of French religious thought. So for the next fifteen years Golding devoted practically all of his time to their translation.

In these busy years, beginning with his going to London in 1562, he seems to have become well known to that group of young poets, gathered about the Inns of Court, whom Jasper Heywood described in the preface to his translation of Seneca's *Thyestes* (1560). Among others Heywood mentioned North, Sackville (Lord Buckhurst),

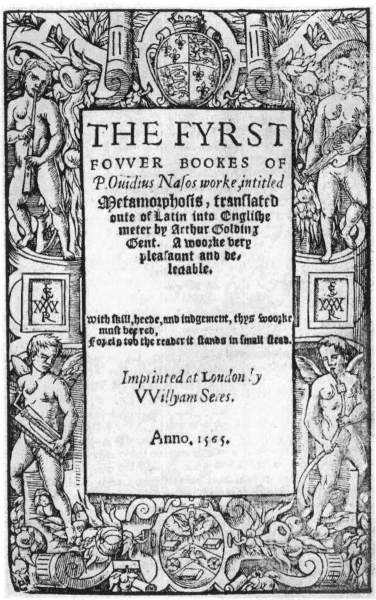

THE FYRST

FOVVER BOOKES OF
P. Ouidius Nasos worke, intitled
Metamorphosis, translated
oute of Latin into Englishe
meter by Arthur Golding
Gent. A woorke very
pleasaunt and de,
lectable.

With skill, heede, and iudgement, thys woorke
must bee red,
For els too the reader it stands in small stead.

Imprinted at London by
VVillyam Seres.

Anno, 1565.

TITLE PAGE OF THE FIRST FOUR BOOKS OF THE
METAMORPHOSES

Baldwin, Googe and Blundeville, of the latter of whom he wrote:

And there the gentle Blundeville is by name and eke by Kynde,
Of whom we learn by Plutarch's lore, what frute by Foes to
    fynde.

After the publication of *The First Four Books of the Metamorphoses*, it was Blundeville who wrote that Golding "by the thondryng of his verse hath sat in chayre of state."

Thomas Peend, a member of the Middle Temple, a translator from the Spanish, and with Blundeville and others a writer of verses introductory to Studley's *Agamemnon*, published in 1565 *The Pleasant Fable of Hermaphroditus and Salmacis* from the fourth book of the *Metamorphoses*. In his dedication to Nicholas Sentleger, Peend wrote

When I had employed some time in translating Ouids Metamorphosis, and had achyued my purpose in parte therof, intendyng to haue trauayled further: I vnderstoode that another had preuented me. And so, I was resolued to stay my laboure, & to reserue that to the use and behofe of my pryuat frend: whych I intended to haue made comen to euery man. . . . And thus neither my first labours shall altogether syncke: nor I shall seeme to abuse the wryter or reader of those foure bookes of Metamorphosis whych he so learnedly translated all redye." [1]

Peend possibly shrank from competition with one already successful and accredited or he may have been discouraged by the "friends" who Golding says "advised him" to put aside Brende's work and translate *Cæsar's*

[1] Brydges, Sir Egerton and Joseph Haslewood, *The British Bibliographer*, Vol. II, page 344, London, 1812.

Commentaries from the beginning. Or he himself may have been a member of the group. At all events the incident was complimentary to Golding and showed him accepted by a contemporary as a leader among literary men.

For the next two years we have no record of his work, for he published nothing which has come down to us. There is a hint, however, in one of his later works which indicates that he continued his labors upon religious subjects. In the letter dated December 31st, 1573, dedicating his translation from the French of Calvin's sermons on the Book of Job, he addresses the Earl of Leicester and speaks of his

accustomed favor, whereof, I have had so often trial heretofore in accepting divers works of mine though containing good commendable and Godly matters, yet not of like substance, importance and travel unto this.

The only works which we know he had previously dedicated to Leicester were the two editions of the *Metamorphoses.* These he certainly would not have described as containing "godly matters," so it seems clear that the "divers works" he refers to were, as he indicates, unimportant and have not survived. Some of these were probably issued in these years, for he appears to have finished at least a book a year and sometimes two.

After hearing of him at Barwicke in 1567 we have no record of his whereabouts until 1569. During these two years and the next he appears to have devoted himself to the liturgy of the church, probably at the instance of Sir Walter Mildmay. In 1569 he published a translation of a "postil or exposition of the Gospels as they are to be read at the church services" and dedicated it to Mildmay from London. This had been written in Latin by Nicholas Heminge and the translation was so successful that Golding was urged to provide a similar guide to the epistles. He, therefore, chose for the purpose a Latin work by David Chytræus. This he translated and dedicated to Mildmay, March 31, 1570, from Belchamp St. Paul's under the title "a postil or orderly disposing of the epistles for the church services for the entire year."

Just when he moved to London from Barwicke is not clear, but he was there in 1569 and probably before, and that city was doubtless his residence at this period despite his occasional visits to Belchamp St. Paul's. It is clear that he was there after 1570, for he published Calvin's *Commentaries on the Psalms*, 1571; Beza's *Catechism*, 1572, and Bullenger's answer to Pope Pius V's Bull excommunicating Elizabeth, 1572; all from London.

He was working at this time on a group of important religious works, Marlorate's *Exposition of the Revelations of St. John*, and Calvin's sermons on the books of Job and Galatians, all of which were published in 1574. These were all large volumes containing, altogether, over eighteen hundred pages. From the St. John we get definite information as to his residence for he dated that book "from my lodgings in London, the last day of August 1574." In his dedication of the Epistle to the Galatians, he is more specific dating it "from my lodging in the forestreet without Cripplegate, Nov. 14th, 1574." As a young man and a younger son, he lived modestly at this period, not even within the city walls, but he already dis-

63

played the surprising industry that fifteen years later called forth Webbe's eulogium, "him which hath taken infinite paynes without ceasing, traulleth as yet indefatigably, and is addicted without society, by his continual laboure."

Naturally he was often at Belchamp St. Paul's, the home of his boyhood, occupied after the death of his father by his brother, Sir Thomas Golding, an important man in the neighborhood. Sir Thomas died in 1571 and Golding's presence at Belchamp St. Paul's at about that time might have been caused by the imminence of that event. This event did not change his relation to the house, for he was on good terms with his sister-in-law, Lady Elizabeth Golding. Furthermore we find that he was again there four years later when he "finished" his translation of Beza's *Tragedy of Abraham's Sacrifice*. Notwithstanding these sojourns in the country, there can be little doubt that from 1565 on, for fifteen years at least, his real residence was in London. During this long period he turned out an immense quantity of work. We have record of eighteen books published during this time, all definitely religious in character, except the completed *Metamorphoses* and the Seneca on benefits. Some of these were of great bulk, including three large volumes of the sermons of Calvin upon the Book of Job and St. Paul's Epistles to the Galatians and Ephesians.

In his dedication to Leicester, of his translation of the sermons on Job in 1573, he modestly says that

This worke is the first of any great weight that ever I translated out of the French tongue to be published. I crave it as a special favor to myself and as a benefit to the church of God that where

64

any faults shall be found I may be made privy to them and I will be as forward as the forwardest to amend them.

He might well say that this was a work of great weight since it contained one hundred and fifty-nine sermons and occupied seven hundred and fifty-one royal folio pages containing over twelve hundred thousand words. Other important works of this period were his translation of Calvin's *Commentaries on the Psalms* in 1571 and his translation of Theodore Beza's *Abraham's Sacrifice* which he "finished" at Belchamp St. Paul's in 1575 and which was issued in an illustrated edition by Thomas Vautroullier in 1577. The Letter dedicatory of the *Commentaries* to his nephew the Earl of Oxford in 1571 is a vigorous appeal to the young man and is expressive of Golding's sense of responsibility for the youth and his fear that he would desert the Protestant religion. He adjured him by "the duty wherein nature hath bound me to you and the care I have of the church and my native country, to consider how God has placed you upon a high stage in the eyes of all men. If your virtue be not counterfeit, if your religion be sound and pure, if your doings be according to true Godliness, you shall be a stay to your country and an increase of honor to your house. But if you should become either a counterfeit Protestant or a professed Papist or a cool and careless neuter (which God forbid) the harm could not be expressed which you should do to your native country." He says he does not "mistrust" Oxford but speaks "because of the perils of the present world where all means possible are practiced to overthrow Christ's kingdom." He warns him "that the devil hath more shapes than Proteus; first and foremost, the obstinate-

65

hearted Papists, the sworn enemies of God, the pestilent poisons of mankind and the very welsprings of all errors, hypocrisy and ungraciousness."

Even though he was addressing his nephew this was still very vigorous language to use towards one of the greatest and wealthiest nobles of England. Oxford was a favorite of Queen Elizabeth who used to send for "her Turk," as she nicknamed him, to dance with her. He was then twenty-one years of age, had just won the highest prize in the great tournament and was about to be married to the daughter of Lord Burghley. Golding says he does not "mistrust" but one may read in this lecture his knowledge of the wild youth of Edward de Vere and some premonition of the fact that the Earl would actually do this very thing—become a Papist—though only for a brief time.

Golding was on the crest of the wave of literary success in these years. His family was prosperous and increasingly prominent, one brother a knight and sheriff of his county, another, a large landholder and a member of Parliament. His nephew Oxford, with whom he apparently had always kept on good terms, had not yet entered on the career of reckless folly which marred his life and destroyed his fortune but was apparently on the road to a very high place in the affairs of the nation. These years in fact may be set down as the highwater mark of Golding's life. He was achieving very considerable social and professional success; and was busy and happy in his chosen field of work. The financial troubles which were to cloud the latter part of his life had not yet appeared, for a careful search in the Record Office disclosed nothing in the

66

way of financial transactions to disturb him until after the death of his brother Henry in 1575. At this time he appears to have been purely a literary man, having no part in politics or official life, undisturbed by the responsibilities of wealth, moving in a circle of power, brilliance and intelligence. In 1573 he was made a member of the Inner Temple "without payment." (Appendix No. 13). This high honor, corresponding in a measure to the present LLD. degree, was occasionally conferred upon eminent Englishmen and among whom at about this time who received it was Sir Francis Drake.

During this period Golding also enlarged his acquaintance among learned and important men. The bookish Dr. Matthew Parker, who practically had been compelled by Queen Elizabeth to take the archbishopric of Canterbury, made vacant by the death of Cardinal Pole, had in 1572, with the assistance of the eminent antiquarians William Camden, Sir Robert Cotton and others, organized the Society of Antiquaries, whose membership comprised the best known and most eminent students of ancient history and literature. Of this body Golding was a member. (Appendix No. 14).

In 1573 when a London tailor was murdered by his wife's paramour, the city was greatly excited by the crime and by the subsequent trial and execution of the wife and the other criminals. On this occasion, Golding wrote the first of his known original prose productions: *A Briefe Discourse of the Murther of G. Sanders.* It was re-issued by H. Bynneman in 1577 in a thin 16 mo. volume, now in the British Museum.

This is a close and intimate account of the crime, giving

67

its detection and punishment in such great detail, in a day when there were no newspapers and trials were not always public, that one would like to suggest that Golding had some special knowledge of the matter. The story tells of an unfrocked minister who, deceived by the woman's protestations of innocence, had fallen in love with her and was plotting her release, when he unwittingly betrayed his plans to "an honest gentleman." By this slip the plot was frustrated, and the love-smitten ex-preacher set in the pillory. So complete is the account that it appears quite possible that Golding himself was "the honest gentleman" and thus, being brought into close contact with the case, got all the details. The crime was one of the most celebrated of its day and created a tremendous sensation. The Privy Council itself directed the search for the murderers, and the Court of Kings Bench sat in Westminster Hall for the trial. The occurrence was dramatized in 1599, though not by Golding, under the title *The Warning of Fair Women.*

Although his austere puritanism and his modest means probably prevented close social relations, he was now in association, on the side of their higher interests, with many of the great Englishmen of the time. Their number included Lord Burghley, the master statesman of Elizabeth's reign; the Earl of Leicester, who was supposed to aspire to the Crown Matrimonial—not without encouragement from Elizabeth; the Earl of Huntington; his own nephew the Earl of Oxford; Sir Thomas Bromley, later Lord Chancellor; the Earl of Essex; Sir Walter Mildmay, founder of Emmanuel College, Cambridge; Sir William Drewrie; Sir Christopher Hatton, Captain

68

FIRST HOUSE GOLDING RENTED

"The Griffins," one of the oldest houses in the village of Clare, where Golding lived in 1575-76.

Staircase in "The Griffins." Balusters identical with those in communion rail in Clare Church.

of the Queen's bodyguard and later Lord Chancellor; Dr. Matthew Parker, Archbishop of Canterbury; and many others less distinguished in the great world, but active in the affairs and pursuits of the Society of Antiquaries.

In 1575 Golding went down to Essex and dated from Belchamp St. Paul's his illustrated translation of Theodore Beza's *Tragedy of Abraham's Sacrifice*. Quite possibly he returned to Essex to be near his brother Henry. The latter, whose health was declining, had made his will in March and died in December, leaving Arthur large but encumbered properties, which involved him in many lawsuits as we will see later. In 1575 Golding rented a house "The Griffins," which is still standing in the village of Clare, three miles from Belchamp St. Paul's and about seventeen miles from Little Birch, Henry's home. This is the first we hear of his taking a house. After the death of Henry he probably felt it necessary to remain in the general neighborhood for we do not hear of his being back in London until March 1577.

As noted before, the date of his marriage is unknown. It is certain, however, that in 1569 he had had no children, at least no boys, for in that year his brother, Sir Thomas, made a will which clarifies that fact. This brother was childless himself and "myndinge the advancement of his house, name and kindred and to preserve the lease to them" he devised to trustees the Manor of Belchamp St. Paul's, of which he had bought a ninety-nine year lease in 1566 from the Dean and Chapter of St. Paul's. This he did so that after his death and that of his wife Elizabeth, it should pass for life to his brother Wil-

69

liam and to his first male heir if any, and in like manner to his brothers Henry and Arthur and George and then to his cousin George Golding. It is evident from this that at the time of the will none of the brothers had male heirs. But in the will of March 20, 1575, Henry Golding mentions Arthur's son, Henry. Just when this child was born is not of record, but later events indicate that the boy was very young at that time, certainly less than six years of age. Golding had three other sons, George, Thomas and Percival, who were born later, as well as four daughters. Of the birthdates of three of the girls, Jane, Alice and Elizabeth, we have no record and any or all of these may have been living at the time. The fourth, and youngest, was Dorothy, who outlived her mother and became her sole executor. Yet the fact remains that no matter how many children he had in 1575, he felt the need of a separate establishment and satisfied this want by renting "The Griffins."

The move to the country did not interrupt his literary labors for he finished his translation of Calvin's Ephesians at Clare on January 7, 1576 and the *Warfare of Christians* at the same place nine days later.

Chapter VI

CHIMERICAL GOOD FORTUNE

A TURNING point in the life of Arthur Golding was reached in 1575 with the death of his brother Henry. The latter apparently left Arthur a rich man. Soon, however, it developed that Henry's great properties were practically mortgaged to the Queen, and that Henry's wife, Alice, had been left a life interest in the principal estate, that of Little Birch. These causes involved Arthur in a series of lawsuits that occupied his time and drained his resources for twenty years. He was forced to battle for his good name, for the possession of his inheritance and even for the cattle on his estate.

The hold of the Queen upon Henry's property grew out of a friendly action—the giving of security to help his friend Thomas Gardiner who had gotten in debt to the Exchequer either through embezzlement or confusion of his accounts in his office of chirographer of the common-pleas and master of the fine-office. Gardiner was a pedantic person with an urge to rhetorical expression and a taste for classical reference who seems to have had a distinguished career at King's College. At one time he was in Cecil's service, and was returned to Parliament in 1557. After Elizabeth's accession he was appointed to this post.[1]

[1] Cooper's *Athenae Cantabrigienses*, London, 1858, Vol. I, page 515.

He was a voluminous letter writer. For almost forty years he wrote frequently to Burghley and quite a number of his letters, always in either Latin or Greek, have been preserved. Most of them refer to his difficulties with the Exchequer and are filled with appeals for help. He appears to have been more than once in prison. We get a somewhat hazy picture of the troubles he brought upon Henry and Arthur and an interesting account of his efforts to protect both in three of these letters. The first, in Latin, dated in August 1572 may be freely translated thus:

Most honoured: Scarcely had your letter been read to me by my clerk, when Henry Golding the uncle of the most noble hero of Oxford came to me in the city from his house, full of anger and indignation, making many bitter complaints against me, because some Royal Magistrate of Essex, had interferred with him and his tenants on my account on the grounds of a royal writ. I bore it ill that trouble had been caused to my friend.

The matter stands thus: Richard Smith, as your honour knows, is in the Exchequer and would that I could say I am free of his levity, or crime, or danger. He has my bond in which Golding my surety is involved with me. The money being paid we both are free according to law. It happened through my accustomed negligence that the bond remained in Smith's hands. Fanshawe, having seen the bond, not only Minos and Radamanthus, but even Jove himself being unwilling, sent royal messengers with a royal writ to Golding's estates, tormented his tenants and cruelly tortured Golding himself.

This cause was brought back to judgment, by my consent and Smith's and with the agreement of the honourable Mildmay. The Sum of my request and petition is this that you will give your letter to this messenger, to Fanshawe, that he is not to molest Golding and is to reserve the whole cause for you. I would seek this rhetorically from your honour with many words, did I not

72

know well your prudence and equity. Give me then this small boon, and God keep and guard you.

Your most humble Suppliant,

THOMAS GARDINER.[2]

We do not have to accept too literally Gardiner's assertion that he had paid the money, for, with his "accustomed negligence," he may have been mistaken in this. Nor need we literally believe the statement that Henry Golding was "tortured." But it is easy to see that Smith and Fanshawe were seeking to do in a mild way for Elizabeth, what Empson and Dudley did for her grandfather by more strenuous persecution.

Gardiner's protest to Burghley was of doubtful benefit to either Henry Golding or himself. The latter saw his lands indented to the Queen and Gardiner appears not to have cleared himself and probably went back to prison. The phraseology of the letter indicates that he was free at the time but he had been in prison the previous year for on May 4, 1571, he had written the Lord Treasurer asking pardon for "his error" and begging to be released from confinement.[3]

Henry Golding, a member of Parliament for Colchester and a former Burgess of Malden, had owned the Manor of Easthorpe and the Manor of Little Birch, both in Suffolk, as well as much other property not immediately connected with these estates. Easthorpe consisted of four messuages, three hundred acres of land, twenty acres of meadow, one hundred acres of pasture, six acres of

---

[2] Lansdowne MSS. No. 39, Art. 83, British Museum.
[3] Lemon, Robert, *Calendar of State Papers, Domestic Series of the Reigns of Edward VI, Mary, and Elizabeth, 1547-1580*, London, 1856. Vol. I, page 412.

wood, and rentals to the value of one hundred shillings in Easthorpe, Messinge, Great Birch, Little Birch, Copford, Stamway, Layre de la Hay, and Fordham as well as the advowson of the church of Easthorpe. The Manor of Little Birch was even larger and even more important. It had originally been in the possession of the Tendering family, whose name had been given to the Hundred immediately north; from them it had passed to George Foster, the first husband of Henry's wife. From the details given in a subsequent lawsuit it appears that the Little Birch property consisted of three hundred and sixty acres of pasture, one water mill, six hundred acres of land, sixty acres of meadow, eighty acres of wood, and four hundred acres of heath and furze, in Little Birch, Great Birch, Copford, Stamway, and Layre de la Hay. In addition to these there was much other property and the advowson of the church of Little Birch.

George Foster left two daughters, Joan and Mary, and to them he had bequeathed one-half of his estate to be divided between them and a life estate in the other half to his widow with the reversion to them. After Henry Golding married the widow he purchased the portions left the daughters as well as their reversionary rights in the portion left to their mother. In his will ' he left his wife, or rather confirmed unto her, the life estate left her by her former husband Foster with a reversion "to my brother Arthur Golding during his life and after his decease to my nephew Henry Golding his son in tail male." Henry, however, apparently did not have entire confi-

' Henry Golding's Will proved Feb. 11, 1576. P. C. C. Doughty 8, P.R.O.

74

dence in Arthur, for as a warning to him, he included the
following curious provision:

Provided alwaies and my verie meaninge is That if my brother
Arthure shall by himselfe or any other by his procurement and
assent molest vex, or trouble my welbeloved wife in the quiett
possession and holdinge of such lands as I have assigned to her
then I will my saide wife and her assignes shall have in consideration of the vexings and molestacion to be donne by my saide
brother or anie other by his assent and procurement all mannor,
landes, tenementes, and hereditementes to her bequeathed by the
space of five yeares after her decease.

Golding's agreeable social and literary associations in
the great world were interrupted by this chimerical good
fortune. The trouble it brought upon him finally took
him away from London. He did not appear eager to live
in the country, for two years after his brother's death he
was granted permission to alienate the Manor of Easthorpe to Richard Atkins; something interfered, however,
as the transfer was not made for some years. After his
stay at Clare he had returned to London, and, possibly
because of the presumed improvement in his financial
condition, leased or bought a house, for in 1577 he dedicated to Sir Christopher Hatton his translation of Seneca's
work on benefiting from his house in the parish of All-
Hallows-on-the-Wall. How long he lived in this house
is not certain. There is evidence to show that he was there
in 1584, as the records of the parish state that at that time
"Jeane Clarke, servant of Mr. Golding of this parish, was
buried." Also it appears that on the twelfth of May 1589,
Mr. John Morgan of Chilworth, Co. Surrey, and Mar-
gerye Golding, daughter of Mr. William Golding of

75

Belchamp St. Paul's, Co. Essex, Arthur's brother, were married by licence from the Archbishop of Canterbury, no doubt from the house of her uncle.[5] However, whether or not he retained the All-Hallows house, he moved down into Essex for a certain period of time, for on March 7, 1580, he leased from his brother George the Manor of Netherhall in Gestlingthorpe.

George had purchased Netherhall, March 1, 1579, from their nephew, the Earl of Oxford, who at that time was busily wrecking the great estate left him by his father. One of the Earl's spendthrift excesses was the lavishing of gifts upon the Queen. About this time he gave her a notable one. On New Year's Day, 1580, he presented Elizabeth with "a fair jewel of golde, being a shippe garnished fully with diamonds and a meane perle pendant." [6] If the price of Netherhall went for the purchase of Elizabeth's New Year's gift it was merely following the tradition of the past, for the ancient manor had first been part of the dowry of Good Queen Eleanor, and had later been part of the dowry of Anne of Bohemia, Richard II's first queen. Henry VII had granted Netherhall to John de Vere, the thirteenth Earl of Oxford, who commanded the victorious Tudor forces at Bosworth, and from him it descended to Edward de Vere. The manor house still stands on the side of the road from Gestlingthorpe to Belchamp St. Paul's. It has been so completely altered and modernized, however, that there is probably very little of the original structure left. There were good reasons for Golding's move to the country at this time.

[5] No trace of this house remains as the whole parish including its church was swept by the Great Fire of London in 1666.

[6] Cooper's *Athenae Cantabrigienses*, London, 1861, Vol. II, page 390.

He still owned Easthorpe, which he had not yet been able to convey to Atkins, and in 1579 his legal troubles over Little Birch had begun. Netherhall was conveniently placed for him to watch his interests in both properties, being located abut a dozen miles from either; besides it was near Belchamp St. Pauls.

The story of his troubles over Little Birch begins with the story, ever old, ever new, of flaming youth and the desire for self-expression. George Foster had had two daughters, Joan and Mary, and the latter was a wild and wilful young woman. Nearly twenty years before she had been married to Robert Walgrave, Esquire, but the marriage did not hold. That is it did not hold her. With considerable informality she divested herself of the tie to Walgrave, and found "consolation" with one William Sanckye. These acts, of course occurred some time before, during the lifetime of Henry Golding, her stepfather. He felt some responsibility for the conduct of this imitator of Bluff King Hal who, though she could not create an archbishop to give her a divorce, could and did devise a substitute that did as well. For her, Henry had made certain provisions in his will. By 1579 William Sanckye was dead, and Arthur Golding was deaf to Mary's demands for what she supposed Henry had left her in his will. She brought suit against him therefore in the Court of Chancery describing herself as Mary Sanckye, "widow" of William Sanckye.[7] In her suit she declared that George Foster, her father, had owned lands and houses in Essex and Suffolk of the yearly value of £300 and that after his death a great part of the property descended to her

---

[7] Chancery Proceedings, C 2 Elizabeth W. 26/37, P.R.O.

and her sister and the reversion of the rest after the death of Alice their mother.

Afterward, she went on to say, her mother married Henry Golding, who in right of his wife became seized of some of the said property and, while she was under age, Henry Golding "ded use diverse wayes and meanes to gett and obteyne of the sayd Mary the moiety of the property as well as the reversion of the remainder residue and she was brought to be contented to bargayne and sell her half and her portion of the reversion for far less value than they were worth." She also asserted that her **portion** was worth £700 of which about twelve years before she lent £400 to Nicholas Mynne, Esq., a near kinsman of Henry Golding, and he and his brothers John and William Mynne had bound themselves to William Ayloffe, Esq., her uncle and to Henry Golding (because she was then under age) to repay the money, which should have been done eight years before. For this, Mynne had charged the Manor of Kettleston in Suffolk (of the yearly value of £40) for one thousand years, with a yearly rent of £12 as interest and as security for the payment of the £400. Because about two and a half years before, Henry Golding had died and Arthur had succeeded him, the interest which Henry had bought from her became his. She complained that Nicholas Mynne for three years had not paid the yearly £12 promised nor repaid the £400, and that Arthur Golding would not help her as he favored his kinsman Nicholas Mynne and his brothers. Mary seems to have had some grounds for discontent but it is hardly clear why she should sue Golding except upon the theory that as the ultimate beneficiary of Henry's will

78

he was responsible for having its provisions carried out notwithstanding the fact that George Golding had been appointed executor and was then living.

Henry Golding had had a stepfather's troubles but had tried to grapple with them as best he could as appears from these clauses in his will:

Item, whereas there is owinge unto Marry Waldgrave by Nycholas Mynne foure hundred powndes, and by my selfe one hundred threscore powndes I will that my Executors do paye the same unto my welbeloved wife and my Cosin William Alaff to the use of the same Marye Waldegrave. Also that till she be paide the same she be allowed Tenne powndes of everie hundred towardes her livinge.

Item, whereas Robert Waldegrave standeth bounde unto me in one paire of Indentures touching the same Mary Waldgrave and hath knowledged a statute of the somme of seaven hundred powndes for the performaunce of the said Indenture and statute to my said wife and Cosin Aloffe prayinge them wiselie to foresee for the safetie of the said Marie Walgrave.

Through this antiquated legal phraseology and variegated spelling we can read the story of Henry's embarrassment. Here was a wild young stepdaughter whose marriage was not turning out well and who wanted to be quit of her husband who was willing, probably too willing. Here was the widow Alice Foster, his wife, siding with daughter Mary, and here was Henry realizing his responsibilities and determined to limit them by insisting upon husband Walgrave giving his bond to protect Henry, apparently from the task and burden of Mary's maintenance. So it was fixed up and Henry wrote it into his will and shouldered the responsibility upon Mary's cousin and her mother. Perhaps the adjustment would have been successful if Mary had not sought "consolation" with William Sanckye. But this action, while condoned by her mother, found no favor with Arthur, the puritan. So, when he refused to press Nicholas Mynne, the charge of undue influence was brought against the dead Henry. This charge, later to become a basis for the suit against Arthur, seems to have been forgotten or forgiven at the time of the settlement, possibly in return for Henry's careful provision for Mary in his will and his prayer to Cousin Aloffe and her mother to "wiselie foresee for the safetie of the said Marie Walgrave."

Mary did not get very far with her case. Depositions were taken at Coggeshall, which is a few miles from Little Birch, and the following extracts are from the report as filed in the Record Office:

Michael Darbey of Colchester tailor aged 50. "He sayeth that he harde never Henry Goldinge his Master nor I do not thincke that his said Master wolde unjustly seke the land of the plaintiff."

"He sayeth the said Complainant Mary Walgrave did sogyn at his Master Mr. Goldinges house from the separating from her husband Robert Walgrave; how longe he knoweth not."

Alice Golding widow aged 50 said "that Marye Walgrave complainant was with the said Henry Goldinge with a Judge to thentente to acknowledge a fyne of her right in the said landes that the said Complainant wepinge before the Judge whereupon the Judge refusinge to take knowledge of the said Fyne, and that shortly after she came before an other Judge and acknowledged her fyne."

"That she knew the Complainant was very well contented at the request of Arther Goldinge defendant and also of her owne good will that a good end to be made betwene the said Arther Goldinge Nicholas Mynne and the complainant her daughter for

80

the said fouer honndred pound & the arrerages of the rent of forty pound which good ende yt could not be at noe tyme obteyned to her knowledge." [8]

Apparently this testimony defeated Mary Sanckye's efforts and ruined this case for she proceeded to try again, but before doing so she again "consoled" herself, this time with Robert Cryspe. Robert, with proper gallantry undertook Mary's case, and, in his own name and that of Mary his "wife" as plaintiffs, brought suit in the Court of Star Chamber against Arthur Golding and made the same allegations adding, however, Mary's complaint that Arthur was trying to defraud her of her property and money.[9] To this Golding made the following devastating answer:

The bill of complaint is infamous and slaunderous, And is exhibited into this most honorable Court for malice and vexacion and onely to put this defendant to great and unnecessary charges and expences, and to bring him into discredit and note of obloquie by the infamie and slaunder thereof.

That Robert Crispe one of the complainants "is not husband of the said Marie but that she is the espowsed and lawful wief of one Robert Walgrave Esquier yet living at Thornedon" in Essex, therefor he could have no legal right in this suit.[10]

In the meantime Alice, who seems to have been a very soft-headed person quite under the control of her daughter and who by her husband's will had a life interest in the estate of Little Birch, had been cajoled by the much "consoled" Mary into giving a lease of the premises to Robert Cryspe.

[8] Chancery Depositions (Eliz.-Chas. I) W. 15/16, P.R.O.
[9] Star Chamber Proceedings. Eliz. C. 7/3, P.R.O.
[10] *Ibid.*

With the situation standing thus it is easily seen that Golding's affairs were in bad shape and that it was wise for him to come down from London and settle nearer to the disputed properties. Besides he was about to undertake a monumental work. He had previously described the translation of Calvin's *Sermons on Job* as a "weighty" task but he would have needed a more strenuous adjective to describe the work of translating that divine's *Sermons on the Book of Deuteronomy*. Calvin preached two hundred sermons on this book. He began on March 20, 1555 and finished on July 15, 1556. As translated by Golding these sermons occupy twelve hundred and fifty folio pages and contain upwards of one and one-half million words. In his brief introduction Golding displays his admiration and enthusiasm for the work and concludes with this rhetorical outburst:

> For if we have an eye to the author of the groundworke; it is God and not man. If to the Lawemaker; it is the Lawe of the Judge and the whole world, the lampe of life, the wellspring of wisdome, the touchstone of truth, the rule of right, the ground of goodnesse, the bond of blessednesse, the loadestarre to life, the opener of our understanding, and the governour of our wits; the faithful following whereof is the way to welfare, the procurer of peace, the path of true pleasure, the entrie of immortalitie, and is the harbourer of happiness.

The sermons were bound up with an elaborate concordance containing over five thousand headings and more than twice that number of references by Abraham Fleming, the well-known religious writer and translator of the day who had been associated with Golding and the publishers in other matters. The volume was printed by

George Bishop at London in 1583 and contains one of the earliest examples of the publisher's blurb. This was not on a fancy colored cover as our modern publishers place it but decently installed on a page by itself and signed by "Thine vnfayned, T. W. the Lord his unwoorthie Servaunt." T. W. stands for Thomas Woodcock. He says that his remarks which are addressed to the Christian Reader, are

in all holie love and affection, to make this carelesse generation more studious to labour to abound both in sound knowledge and the trueth, and in all holie obedience to the same. In which respect, not onelie are these few lines written at this person, but this noble worke of Master Calvin's Sermons upon Deuteronomie published, and that in our owne native language; wherein what paine and acts hath beene bestowed with them might comefoorth as is beneficiall to the Christian Reader as might be, though I myselfe may speak much in trueth as an argument of some weight, to induce the goodly brethren to the buying and reading thereof; yet letting that point pass as a matter in which to be stood upon, I minde onely to press those things, and that also in very fewe words, which shalbe most material. And that is; that as al states and conditions of men may out of the same fetch many profitable points for their instruction both in faith and obedience towards God and man; so particularly if a man would overthrow Atheists, or confute Papists, and other Heretikes, or wound the wicked, or encourage the fainthearted or comfort the afflicted conscience cast downe with the fight of Sinne, or performe any other service towards God, myselfe, or other men, he shall have matter, and that in great store plentifully ministred unto him for the performance of these and of other dueties whatsoever. Wherefore I would advise thee (good Reader) to get it speedilie, to reade it diligentlie, to remember it faithfullie, and to express it fruitfullie in thy conversation, to the glory of God, the profite of his people, and the salvation of thine owne soul through Christ.

This Thomas Woodcock at one time handled most of Golding's translations of Calvin's sermons and writings. July 15, 1578, he paid the Stationers' Company twenty shillings for a license to publish translations of the following sermons of Calvin: Deuteronomy, Job, Galatians, Ephesians and his Commentaries on the Psalms. At the same time he was licensed to print a number of other religious books, twenty-nine in all. Luke Harrison, the well-known printer, had had an interest in these books which after his death was sold to Woodcock.[11] All of Calvin's books, with the exception of *Deuteronomy*, had already passed through one edition. A note in the *Register of the Stationers' Company* from which this record is taken says: "Woodcock has not paid his part of the license for Deuteronomy which is to be paid when imprinted." This may account for the almost pathetic tone of the "blurb" and the energy and ingenuity of the sales talk.

There was another reason why Golding was willing to leave London. He had become pretty much disgusted with the metropolis. He felt that the world was evil, the people of London especially. His puritan blood rose at the sight of what was going on there and, when the earthquake of April 6, 1580, startled the world, it was to him the plain voice of the Almighty warning mankind and especially the English. In expressing this view he wrote the second of his two known original prose works *A Discourse Upon the Earthquake*. This is the tragically earnest appeal of one deeply opposed to evil, who feels upon

---

[11] *A Transcript of the Registers of the Company of Stationers of London*, Ed. Edward Arber, 1875, Vol. 2, page 332. July 15, 1578.

himself the heavy responsibility of warning mankind to repent and reform.[12]

During his residence at Netherhall, Golding, in the summer of 1583, seems to have made a serious effort to clear his property of the inherited debt to the Queen which was the result of Henry Golding's over-confidence in Thomas Gardiner. This he did by a friendly suit against the latter in the Exchequer Court in which he was loyally supported by Gardiner himself even to the extent of a rather bald attempt to bribe the Lord Treasurer. The story is told in another of that individual's flamboyant Latin letters to Burghley. This long letter which is here freely translated and quoted in part is dated June 25 and is couched in quite different terms from the crisp protest of eleven years before. Misfortune and imprisonment had taught Gardiner to be obsequious and he now addresses Burghley as "Most noble hero" and signs himself "Your abject suppliant." He reiterates that he is not bound by his bond either to the Queen or to Richard Smith and asks why he is dragged into court, but does not object because

I ought to guard and protect Arthur Golding, my very dear and intimate friend, from every danger which might in any way come to him from Smith. . . .

Wherefore in the name of all your justice I beg of you that you grant me the benefit of natural right and the public laws, which will be to my great good fortune or, what I still more desire that, granting those petitions, which recently my friend Golding has explained in a schedule, in both our names, directed

[12] This is the earthquake referred to by Shakespeare in *Romeo and Juliet*, Act 1, Scene 3, where the nurse, seeking to fix Juliet's age, says: " 'Tis since the earthquake now eleven years."

85

to your honour, you would be pleased to have us both conjointly defended and increased by your kindness. . . .

For as through many years we have been united, by great use and fellowship of letters, which is the sweetest bond of friendship, so too this suit touches my conscience of justice more separately so that I desire that some satisfaction in this kind and in many ways be made to my friend Golding. And since nothing much remains to me, but some small corroded trifle, I know not what; take, I beg, anything as you may judge fair, from that store, nor fear for your honour (however much Thomas Fanshawe, that terror and thunderbolt of the court, may resist) but that it is lawful to taste the wholesome and delicate food from this store. Therefore, in the name of all your honour, help Golding and me conjointly. Of your divine clemency, save our ship from those rocks upon which it is being dashed. . . .

He insists that when State papers and royal exchequer accounts are examined by fair judges that it will be shown that he has "emerged from that filthy sink of vile debt." He urges Burghley, who knows "how hazardous and uncertain this matter is for me and into how many directions it spreads and turns," to permit "my ministers and clerks" to take part in the investigation that it may be shown "on whose authority this debt began to be contracted."

After this hint that he has been made the scapegoat of others, he bursts into a fervent declaration of his entire confidence in Burghley's disposition to do him justice and concludes:

Now I have kept faith with my friend Golding, as I should, and I humbly beg that I may understand that this letter has been of avail with your honour and has been of much weight to relieve our cause. God load your honour with felicity.[13]

[13] Lansdowne MSS. No. 39, Art. 25, British Museum.

86

Whether it was the invitation to Burghley to help himself to the "corroded trifle" or the suggestion of a sixteenth century "frame up" or the arguments and explanations of Golding that proved effective, is not clear but evidently the result was prompt and favorable, for only ten days later, on July 5th, Gardiner wrote Burghley a letter, in Latin like the others, which is a paean of joy and gratitude. The Lord Treasurer seems to have been unexpectedly friendly, so much so as to leave Gardiner almost speechless, for he says:

> I cannot yet in truth discover with what words I am to thank your honour or just what kind of speech I am to use. And yet I confess that I am not so lacking in words nor altogether destitute of the faculty of speech, though nevertheless no word occurs to me, which either is equal to your divine merits towards me or seems to attain to the least part of your merits. I see myself entirely hemmed in on all sides, who am compelled to explain the power and strength of no common kindness in common words. To conclude in plebeian and vulgar words then, since I have all my fortunes constituted by your divine goodness, if you bring the kindness you have begun to an end, and since in returning thanks nothing in my opinion can be too much, so I resolve and determine, all these same things shall ever be in your power and are more subject to your commands than to mine. . . .

Words again failing he falls back upon classical allusion:

> No sort of kindness perishes which is conferred upon anyone by a prudent man, not even when it meets with ingratitude. Marcus Antonius, that same who was duumvir with Augustus, when he was so pressed by the arms of Augustus that he almost despaired of escape, said with almost his last words that after his death he only would endure, in as much as, while he lived, he had done good to his fellows, by which it may be understood that a certain immortality follows our kindnesses like a shadow.

He concludes by remarking:

Since your honour bade me be brief, the rest, my friend Golding will tell, speaking face to face.[14]

Such fervent thanks and the reference to his fortunes being "constituted" and his determination to put "all these same things" in Burghley's power quite plainly indicate that the Lord Treasurer had put aside Gardiner's offer of the remnants of his estate. Possibly Thomas Fanshawe, who was the Queen's Remembrancer of the Court of Exchequer, was too much a "thunderbolt" even for the Lord Treasurer. At any rate, Gardiner got his request for an examination with "my ministers and clerks present" without the sacrifice and seemed to feel that his case was as good as won.

The final results, however, could not have been as satisfactory as he hoped, for Golding's lands were not freed of the Queen's claims which continued to plague him for many years afterward, and he, himself, seems to have remained either in prison or under suspicion and close observation, as indicated by the letters he continued to write to Burghley for the next six years.

The extent of the obligation Henry Golding assumed for Gardiner's debts is not clear but that individual was heavily involved as appears from a letter written to Sir Robert Cecil, principal secretary, January 16, 1596-7. One George Peckham appeals for help because "for twelve years his lands and living had been extended on account of a bond he made to the Queen for 6,500 li; parcel of the debt of 26,000 li, owed to her Majesty by

[14] Lansdowne MSS. No. 39, Art. 26, British Museum.

88

Thomas Gardiner, sometime one of the tellers of the Exchequer." Peckham says he is in great extremity and has had "to sell the bed he lies on and has kept this Christmas more like Lent." [15]

[15] *Calendar of the Salisbury Manuscripts at Hatfield House*, Vol. XII, page 23, London, 1899.

Chapter VII

MORE LEGAL BATTLES

THE STAR CHAMBER proceedings brought by the current "husband" of Mary Walgrave were no more successful than the Chancery proceedings had been. In the meanwhile, however, Cryspe and Mary were in control of the Little Birch estate, for Alice, Henry's widow, had withdrawn to Bradwell near Coggeshall. This situation was all to Golding's disadvantage, for the property suffered at the hands of its occupants. At that time the felling of timber was the usual way of despoiling leased property. Mary understood this well, for she had already sold wood from her portion of the estate, when she was first in possession of it after her father's death and before the sale to Henry Golding. Arthur would have liked to have proceeded against Mary and Cryspe but was afraid to do so on account of the stern warning in his brother's will. He therefore decided to appeal to his old friend Lord Burghley and did so, as appears from the following in Hunter's *Chorus Vatum*:

There is a bill in the Exchequer 14 Feb. 1585, to Lord Burghley from his daily orator Arthur Golding—Whereas his late brother Henry Golding, Esq., deceased left him in present possession only the manor of East Thorpe which was encumbered and gave the manor of Little Biral (Birch) with other lands to Alice his wife, with a clause prohibiting said Arthur from molesting her;—whereas one Robert Crispe a very troublesome and unquiet person marrying one Mary Waldegrave daughter of said Alice and wife of one Robert Waldegrave, Esq., yet alive and undivorced, under colour of that unlawful marriage obtained of the said Alice a lease of the said Henry Golding's chief mansion house & has committed waste and spoil—He prays that he may proceed against Crispe without incurring the penalty of his brother's will.[1]

This appeal brought no early results, for it was not until the sixth of July, 1587, that the Exchequer Court took final action which was expressed in the following decree:

> Upon hearinge of the matter betwene Arthur Golding and Robert Crispe for and concernynge the possession of certeyn landes and tenementes in the occupacion of the sayd Crispe and extended for the Queens Majestie for the debt of Henry Goldinge deceased. It is ordered in the presence of the said Arthur Goldinge that all matters in controversie depending betwene the sayd parties be compromytted to three persons indiffrently to be chosen by theym to be by those three harde and determynded And if the sayd Crispe shall refuse the same and not otherwise to compounde the controversie about the sayd possession before Michaelmas next comynge that then the possession of the sayd landes and tenementes shalbe delyvered to Sir Thomas Lucas knight to the Queens majesties use according to the extent by process of this Court.[2]

This was not a very beneficial remedy for Golding's troubles. It looked as if he were bound to lose either way. If the arbitrators decided for Cryspe, he lost, and if they decided against Cryspe and Cryspe refused to abide by the decision, the property was to go to the Queen; Golding therefore was between the devil and the deep sea.

[1] Hunter, Joseph (1783-1861) *Chorus Vatum Anglicanorum*, Vol. II, pp. 435-440. Additional MS. 24,488. British Museum.

[2] *Exchequer Orders and Decrees*, Vol. 13, f. 90d. P.R.O.

Apparently there was one chance, and that was that Cryspe would refuse and the Queen's agent would take over the property and then Golding could recover it by paying the debt. Golding must have been disgusted when he saw the decree, but this judgment was thoroughly characteristic of the attitude of the Queen towards her debtors. She was a good collector and a thrifty woman and if you owed her, you paid, but if she owed you, it was different.

Worse than that, the decree of the court had not relieved Golding from the penal clause in Henry's will and the arbitrators apparently took that into consideration. Alice, Henry's widow, had died the previous year so, according to the will, Arthur was shut out of the estate for four years more because of "vexings and molestacion," presumably in bringing the suit in the Exchequer Court. This was a triumph for Cryspe but he did not live to enjoy the whole period, as he died and Golding finally gained possession in 1589. This was a particularly difficult time for Golding, as the debt was still due the Queen. Furthermore certain annual charges upon the property, made by Henry Golding, were still in operation and had not been paid after Alice Golding's death. And in the long legal battle Golding had received no income from it.

After he became Henry's heir Golding was always in need of money. Like many other literary persons he showed but little aptitude for business, notwithstanding his experience as "receiver" for his nephew. In fact, the only transaction that is of record, in which he made any profit, was probably due to the advice of his brother George. In 1576 George and Arthur bought twelve acres of land in Wyke, Co. Essex, for forty-two pounds. Two years after they sold this land for about eighty-nine pounds.[3] Now, however, Golding was steadily borrowing money, endeavoring at the same time to sell the properties he had inherited. His borrowings were particularly heavy during the time he was making the effort to oust Cryspe. On November 23, 1586, he borrowed £1,000 [4] from Richard Atkins of London, and the previous year, on February 13, 1585, he had borrowed £700 from Richard Andrew of Oxford. The latter borrowing finally got him into serious trouble as we will see later.

In 1585 he began to sell the fine properties left him by his brother George, who had died the previous year. The first to go was the Manor of Waltons in Suffolk and with it went a ninth of Little Birch. Waltons was located about ten miles south of Colchester and four or five miles from Little Birch. It was really a very important estate as the description in the records indicates. The buyers were Richard Moseley and Thomas Phillippes, Gentlemen, and they got

ten messuages, ten tofts, two mills, six dovecotes, twenty gardens, fifty acres of land, one hundred and fifty acres of meadow, five hundred acres of pasture, two hundred acres of wood, two hundred acres of heath & furze, six acres of marsh, £5 rent and common of pasture for all beasts in Purleigh, Mundon, Woodham Mortimer, Lawlinge, Woodham Ferris, Danburie on the Hill, Cole Norton, Stowe Maris and Northfambridge as well as the third part divided into three parts of the manor of Little Birch, and the third part divided into three parts of one water mill, four hundred acres of land, forty acres of meadow, two

[3] Feet of Fines, Essex, Easter, 20 Elizabeth. P.R.O.
[4] Close Rolls, 28 Elizabeth, part 25. P.R.O.

hundred acres of pasture, sixty acres of wood, three hundred acres of heath and furze and 20s rent in Little Birch, Great Birch, Copford, Stanway and Layer de lahay as well as the third part divided into three parts of the advowson of the church of Little Birch.[5]

It seems hardly possible that all this was conveyed free of debt as the given price was only £400.

Netherhall in Gestlingthorpe, Co. Essex, where he seems to have lived from 1580, probably up to the time of the sale, he disposed of in 1586. This manor had lands in Water Belchamp, Weatherfield, Castle Hedingham, and Little Yeldham, and was sold to John and William Cooe, but the record in the Patent Rolls does not disclose the amount paid.[6]

We have seen that Golding within a year or a little over a year borrowed £1,700 and sold very large and valuable properties. Whether he paid some of the proceeds to the Queen and thus lessened the charge upon Little Birch is not clear, but in 1591 it was apparent, from a decision in another lawsuit, that the property had been very largely cleared. Atkins, from whom he had borrowed the £700, had in 1583 paid him for the Manor of East Thorpe, which Arthur had been given permission to sell to him in 1577. What occasioned the delay is not shown in any of the records, but, when the sale was finally made, Atkins paid £480.[7]

In 1587 Arthur's brother William died at Belchamp St. Paul's. William, some sixteen years before, had inherited that manor from his elder brother, Sir Thomas,

[5] Feet of Fines, Essex, Hilary 27 Eliz. P.R.O.
[6] Patent Rolls, 28 Eliz. part 4 M 25. P.R.O.
[7] Feet of Fines, Essex, 25 Eliz. P.R.O.

in accordance with the latter's Trustee will. William left a nuncupative will dated the 8th of February, 1587, which reads as follows:

The sayd William Golding calling for Elizabeth his wief sayd unto her, Besse, I have nothing to give thee in consideracion of the long tyme that thou has been with me, But I woulde you should have all that I have and I pray you paye my debtes and have consideracion of my daughters. And then the sayd Elizabeth aunswered, Sir I will paye your debtes yf I sell all that I have to my smocke, and after the sayd William Golding about three of the clocke in the nighte following dyed at his house in Belchamp Saynte Paule aforesayd.
Witnesses. William Maslevile, James Armond.[8]

William's widow was not reduced to the necessity of parting with her smock in order to pay her husband's debt or to care for his memory. She provided an altar tomb for him and later one for herself in the chancel of the church at Belchamp St. Paul's, which, however, have long since disappeared. The only trace remaining is an assemblage of the brasses which adorned them in a tablet in the floor of the church, a relic of some "restoration." One of these brasses represents a man in armor, presumably William. Why he was represented in armor is not clear, as there is no record of his having engaged in any military activities. The following is the inscription, cut in brass:

Here lieth the bodie of Elizabeth one of ye daughters & coheires of Edmund West late of Cornard Esquire, first married to John Buckenham Esquire by whom she had Edmund yet living & Dorothie deceased, and after married to William Goldinge

[8] P.C.C. Rutland 16. P.R.O

95

Esquire by whom she had Edward & Elizabeth deceased and Margery and Mary yet living. Obiit xx May 1591.

William's death made no difference to Arthur because his sister-in-law continued to occupy Belchamp Manor until her death in 1591. His other sister-in-law, Sir Thomas's wife, had been left a life estate in it so Arthur did not come into possession of the manor until her death in 1593. He did not immediately go there to live, because for some time thereafter he is still referred to as Arthur Golding, Esquire, of Little Birch.

Notwithstanding the heavy borrowings and large sales of valuable property in the previous few years, Arthur in 1590 borrowed £10 from his sister-in-law, Sir Thomas Golding's widow. In the Folger Shakespeare Library in Washington there is what is believed to be the only existing signature of Arthur Golding. It is signed to a document which reads as follows:

Memorandum that I Arthur Golding of Little Birch in the countie of Essex. Esquire have borrowed of my very good sister in law the Lady Golding this sixth of May 1590 the sum of xli of lawful English money, and w'ch I received from her by the hands of her servant Gyles Gold. In witness whereof I have written this bill in mine own hand & subscribed thereto my name
By me Arthur Golding.

Even though Golding after the death of the "very unquiet person," Robert Cryspe, in about 1589, gained possession of the manor of Little Birch, it was by no means a quiet possession. When George Foster's daughter, Joan and her husband, Henry Peryent, in 1565 sold to Henry Golding the portion left her by her father, they reserved, as was frequently the custom at that time, an annual pay-

96

ment or rental from the lands conveyed, to the extent of £16 per annum. This had doubtless been paid during Henry's lifetime and also after his death. According to Arthur's statement, Alice, then in possession of the property, had purchased from Robert Spring, who was the son of Joan by her second husband, the right to receive this £16. After Alice's death Robert Cryspe retained possession of the property under the penal clause in Henry's will, but he did not pay this £16 per year, so that after his death Thomas Peryent, Joan's son by her first marriage, and one John Songer, acting as bailiffs for Robert Spring, distrained Golding's cattle, consisting of nine cows and two steers. This was in June, 1590, and must have been a hard blow, for Arthur was almost pennyless, having been compelled to borrow £10 only the month before. Golding, however, put up a bold front and summoned them to answer or, as we would now say, to show cause for this action. Their defense was to set up the facts above related and to complain that for the whole year of 1588 Golding had not paid the £16.⁹

In this connection an inquisition was held at Chelmsford, on the 17th of April, 1591, "where it was considered that the said Arthur Golding should pay £10 1s. damages." Thereupon Arthur again had recourse to the Exchequer Court and at the Easter Term, 1591, sued Peryent, Songer and Spring. This step was probably taken because the Exchequer had jurisdiction over the interest the Queen held in the property. Golding hoped that on this account the Exchequer would interfere, with the claim that these payments endangered those to be made to the

⁹ Coram Rege Roll 1315 M 316. P.R.O.

Queen. In his bill of complaint Golding recited the descent of the property, its transfer with the annual rent charge of £16 (with a penalty of £4 for arrearage) and continued "the said Henry Golding the plaintiff's brother being seized of the said moiety was indebted to the Queen in certeyn greate summes of mounye." Therefore all his lands were seized and extended to the Queen's use and at the time of this suit all the debts had not been paid. He alleged furthermore that, during the two years after the death of Alice, while Cryspe still held the premises, neither Spring nor Peryent received or made any claims to the said rent. "But when Robert Cryspe died Thomas Peryent conjecturing that your Suppliant was lyke ynowgh to recover the possession of the premises & of the residew of his living which had bin most injuriously deteyned from hym a long tyme took a distress for the half years rent."

Golding being "desyrous of quiet for that he was even in maner overwhelmed with the multitude & greatnesse of the Incumberances that lay uppon him at present" offered £8 which Peryent refused saying that in accepting he would lose the arrearages. Golding, or his counsel, apparently stressed the point that Peryent had made no demand upon Robert Cryspe for the rent during 1588 and therefore by such failure had forfeited his right to receive it, because he asked Robert Spring for his part of the deed by which he conveyed the rent to Alice, hoping apparently to find something therein to sustain this point. Spring replied that he remembered the deed but had lost it.[10]

[10] Exchequer Bills and Answer, Eliz. Essex 105. P.R.O.

At the Michaelmas Term in the same year, on October 12th, Golding's counsel procured a subpoena calling Peryent, Spring and Songer into court to make "a better and more direct answer upon oath to the particular points of the said bill of the complainant." [11] Fifteen days afterward the Court handed down its decision as follows:

Whereas Arthur Goldinge gentleman heretofore exhibited his bill of Complainte in the Exchequer Chamber against Thomas Perient Robert Springe and John Songer concerninge one rent chardge of xvjli yerelie to be paied owt of the Manor of Little Birche in the Countie of Essex & owt of other landes and tenementes of the saide Arthures whereunto the saide defendants appeared & demurred in lawe to the saide bill alledginge that the said Arthure Goldinge hath noe cause of privilidge to holde suite uppon the saide Englishe bill here in this Courte againste the said defendentes and therefore praied judgement Nowe for that uppon the full openinge & debatinge of the said matter this daie in Courte by the Councell on bothe sides it appeareth that her Majesties debte is paied or otherwise assured to be satisfied by lawe for the saide debtes heretofore extended and that the saide landes are more in yerelie vallewe then they are extented for to her Majestie and alsoe that the saide rent was graunted before anie debte to her Majestye and that the saide suite commensed here by the saide plaintiff is but for delaye and onelie to gaine hinderaunce of the proceedinges for the said defendandtes in other Courtes It is therefore this day ordered that the said suite & cause shalbe dismissed this Courte and the saide plaintiff maie seeke his remedie elles where at the common lawe. [12]

No record is found that Arthur continued the litigation in another court. Perhaps he gave up and acknowledged

[11] *Exchequer Decrees and Orders*, Vol. 16, f.229. Michaelmas, 33 Eliz. (Oct. 12.) P.R.O.

[12] *Exchequer Decrees and Orders*, Vol. 16, f. 243 Michaelmas, 33 Eliz. (Oct. 27.) P.R.O.

that he was beaten—as he generally was when he went to law. From this judgment it would seem that Arthur had either made a payment on account or had perfected other arrangements so that the Exchequer felt that the Queen's interests were secured, and hence declined to interfere. This would account for the heavy borrowings of the previous years and show what Arthur did with the money. Whatever this arrangement was, it was not carried out because the Exchequer had to take steps to collect. At the Easter Term of the Exchequer Court, the sixth of May, 1592, the following order was entered:

Whereas the sheryffe of the County of Chester by vertue of proces out of this Court hath distrayned the Cattell of Jasper Lowyn Robt. Bireman Richard Brock Richard Bridgeman and other tenantes of the Mannor Litle Byrche much Byrche and Easthope in the County of Essex to the value of C^{li} and upwardes for the halfe yeres Rentes of the said Mannors due at our Lady day last accordinge to severall extentes of the said Mannors heretofore made for the severall debtes due to her Majestie which sayd rentes the said tenantes doe affirme by their Counsell that they have already payd to the sayd Mr. Goldinge upon ignoraunce not knowinge that the same was or ys due to her Majestie by the sayd extentes how be yet they doe offere to pay the same agayne to her Majesty yf yt shall please the Court to gyve them tyme tyll the next terme which beinge thought Reasonable It ys this day ordered by the Court that the said tenantes puttinge in bond to answere the said Rentes due at our Lady day as aforesayd accordinge to the sayd extent sometyme and the next trinity terme. That then the sherife of the sayd County shall presently release and discharge the sayd distresses taken by him as aforesayd And he shalbe therof acquited in this Court.[13]

[13] *Exchequer Decrees and Orders,* Vol. 19, f. 57. Easter 34 Eliz. P.R.O.

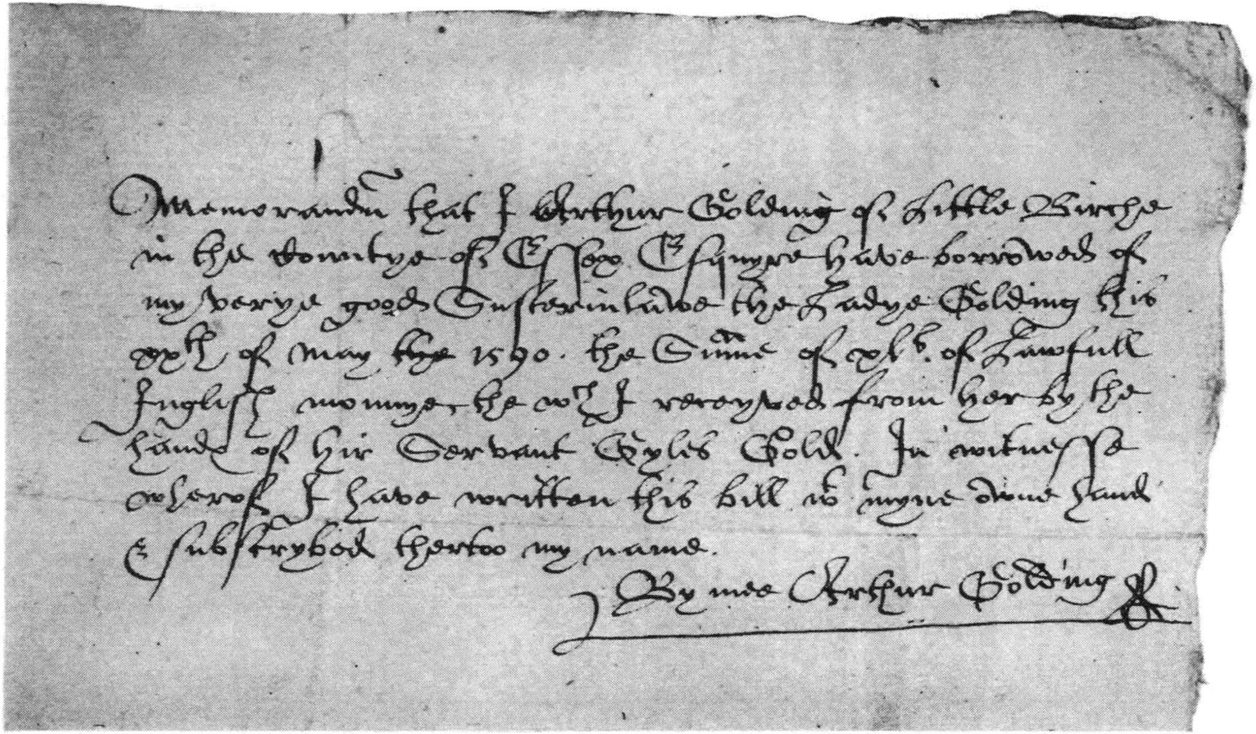

Just why the Sheriff of Chester should have acted does not appear, nor is there any record of what Golding's unfortunate tenants, thus required to pay their rent twice, did in order to get their money back. Presumably they had the right to sue him to recover, but the method employed by the Exchequer again indicates the vigor with which Queen Elizabeth collected what was due her.

About this time, his sister-in-law Elizabeth Golding, William's widow, having died, Arthur felt it necessary to look out for his interests in the Manor of Belchamp St. Paul's, so in May, 1591, he filed a petition in the Court of Chancery [14] which may be thus abstracted:

Artur Goldinge of Little Birche, Essex, gentleman and George Goldinge of Pistingford, Suff. gent. versus Robert Crane, Esq., William Tyffin of the Middle Temple Esq., and Richard Deering of Wye, Kent, Esq. That Sir Thomas Goldinge Knt. late of Belchamp St. Paul's deceased brother of the said Arthur and cousin of the said George was possessed of the manor or lordship of Beauchamp St. Paul otherwise Poles Belchamp and of the rectory and advowseon thereof by a lease made to him by Alexander Nowell Dean, and the Chapter of St. Paul's for 99 years from 2 Feb. 1565. Sir Thomas Goldinge lived there until his death in 1571.

As the said Sir Thomas had no issue he "myndinge the advancement of his house name & kindred & to preserve the said lease to them" about 1569 by indenture between him and Robert Crane, William Tyffin of the Middle Temple and Richard Goldinge of Sudbury, Suff. since deceased, and Richard Deeringe demised the property to

---

[14] Chancery Proceedings, Series II, 225/14, May 1591. P.R.O.

them so that after his death and that of Elizabeth, his wife, (who was living at the time of this suit) to the use of William Golding and his first heir male with remainder in like manner to his brothers Henry and Arthur, with remainder to his brother George and then to George Golding his cousin and four issues male with remainder to the brothers of his said cousin George Golding.

Sir Thomas's brothers William, Henry, and George Golding had all died without issue male therefore the interest in the property should come after the death of the Lady Elizabeth, his widow, to Arthur Golding and his first heir male and then to his cousin George Golding and his four issues male &c. The petition then continued "Albeyt your said orators doe nothinge doubte of the fidelitye of the parties aforesaid they all beinge gentlemen of good worshipp and Creditt and are assured therof," nevertheless Robert Crane and Richard Deering had never sealed the counter part of the indenture so that the plaintiffs were in doubt whether they could be trustees if the said William Tyffin should happen to die &c.

The result of this application must have been satisfactory. Furthermore Golding's fears as to the longevity of William Tyffin were unfounded for the latter survived Crane and Deering for more than twenty years. After the death of Sir Thomas there had been various suits in Chancery between William Golding and Elizabeth the widow of Sir Thomas, which presumably resulted in William's favor, for he seems to have obtained possession of Belchamp during the life of Sir Thomas's widow, notwithstanding the fact that she had been left a life estate in the property.

102

Chapter VIII

DEBTORS' PRISON

GOLDING's defeat in his legal battles with Peryent and the action of the Exchequer in sending the Sheriff of Chester to levy upon the cattle of his tenants in order to enforce the payment of the Queen's claims, had repercussions in another direction. It brought down his creditors upon him. After the manner of their kind his creditors pressed their claims for payment as his fortunes declined.

During his efforts to raise money while battling Cryspe for the possession of Little Birch, Golding borrowed wherever he could. One of these loans was from Richard Andrew of Oxford on the 13th of February, 1585. Although this loan was to have been paid within a few months, Golding succeeded in putting off settlement during the tedious course of the legal contests and even after Cryspe's death had put him in charge of the property. When, however, even that possession did not put an end to the successful suits brought against him, Andrew took drastic action by causing him to be put in the Fleet Prison for debt. The details of the preliminaries to this imprisonment have not come down to us. In fact, the only way we know that he was there is from an entry in the Close Rolls 35 Elizabeth, Part 18. This entry is dated May 31, 1593, and states that:

Richard Andrew of the City of Oxford, Gentleman, declared that Arthur Goldinge of London Esq. by the name of Arthur Goldinge of Little Birch, Essex, Esq. by his recognizance of 13 Feb. 1585 acknowledged himself bound in the sum of £700 to be paid at Whitsun following—"And where alsoe the saide Arthur by the Queenes writt therevppon awarded out of her Highe Courte of chaunceries and returned in the saide Courte is nowe in execution in the pryson of the Fleete vppon the saide Recognizaunce"—Andrew now wished to release quitclaim &c any actions, demands &c against the said Arthur.

Just how long he was in prison is not clear, for no record is to be found of the date of his commitment. Certain dates, however, enable us to approximate the length of his incarceration. We know that the Exchequer Court handed down its decision in his suit against Peryent on October 27, 1591. According to custom he was probably present in court at that time although the judgment does not so state. If he was, this would put the time of his confinement between these date, October 27, 1591 and May 31, 1593, a period of nineteen months. Except for the return of the Sheriff of Chester in the matter of the distraint of his tenants' cattle, May 6, 1592, we have no record of him between these dates, and there is nothing in this occurrence to indicate that he was then free. In fact, it may be that the Sheriff levied on the tenants' cattle because Golding was in the Fleet and thus beyond his reach.

Whatever the length of his confinement it must have come as a crushing blow after his hard luck with lawsuits. He was practically alone; all his brothers were dead and his eldest son Henry was not above twenty-two years of age at the oldest and possibly not over eighteen. His only living sister-in-law was Mary, widow of his brother George. As George was a rich man, she was probably in a position to help him and perhaps did so, for she felt kindly towards her husband's family. This attitude was indicated by a bequest to her nephew Henry in her will made some years afterward. Of Golding's own sisters only one married a man who appears in the record as being able to have been of any financial assistance. This was Edmond Docwra of Chamberhouse near Thatcham, Co. Berks, who married Dorothy. He himself, however, had been in financial trouble shortly before this, and had been forced to sell the estate in 1585. Nevertheless the families were friendly. Dorothy had named her eldest son after Arthur and he had named a daughter after her. Whether Arthur had help from this source at this time is not clear, but five years later Dorothy's second son, his nephew Sir Henry Docwra, afterward the first Lord of Docwra of Culmore, joined in a recognizance for £200 signed by him and his son Henry.[1]

A hint of the possible source of assistance in this predicament is found in the dedication of one of his translations two years later. In 1595 he published his translation from the French of Hurault's *Politicke, Moral and Martial Discourses*. This he dedicated to William Brooke, Lord Cobham, Warden of the Cinque Ports. In the customary letter of dedication, dated January 27, 1595, he makes reference to his troubles and expresses his appreciation of Cobham's help in this fervent paragraph:

"Forasmuch as being unknowne to your good Lordship, otherwise than by report, yet notwithstanding I have

[1] Lord Chamberlain's Recognizances, L.C. 4/193, P.R.O.

tasted of your goodness and favour, to my great comfort in my troubles, of the which when God will I hope I shall be well discharged, I acknowledge myself more bound unto your honor, than any service or abilitie of mine can extend unto, and therefore to testify my thankful and dutifull mind towards you, I have presumed to dedicate this my labour to your lordship."

It is evident from this language that such assistance as Lord Cobham rendered was in no sense personal, but was influenced rather by Golding's position as a leading scholar of his time. It is not now clear whether he secured his release through Cobham's help or through that of his dwindling family; all we know for certain is that in the spring of 1593 he was able to renew his efforts to realize upon his inheritance. The difficulties in which these bequests had involved him interrupted his literary work almost completely for, after he had finished the translation of Calvin's *Deuteronomy* in 1583, we have no record of any further publications except De Mornay's *Truth of Christianity* in 1587 and Hurault's *Discourses* in 1595. In the first case he did the work at the request of Sir Philip Sidney who had started the translation, and whose request was really a compliment to Golding's scholarship and integrity. Just at this time, besides, there was a slight pause in his legal battles, for he was then waiting for the lapse of the penal clause of his brother's will which kept him out of the possession of Little Birch until after the death of Cryspe in 1589. The Hurault translation may well have been prepared earlier, though not published till 1595 as a means of thanking Lord Cobham. From various references in the dedications of his books it appears that he was in the habit of preparing translations, particularly of the classics and of scientific and philosophical subjects, and then laying them aside for future publication. Some of these manuscripts were, indeed, found in his effects after his death.

When released from the Fleet Golding did not go back to his long-neglected literary work, but took up the pressing task of improving his financial position. The first step was to borrow more money. This was nothing new for him, but he turned to a rather surprising source. Apparently he swallowed his pride and forgave or forgot Thomas Peryent's legal triumphs over him, for he accepted a loan from him of £300.[2] On October 20, 1593, Arthur gave his recognizance, in which Henry joined, acknowledging that he owed Peryent that amount "to be paid at the feast of St. Andrew next." When this time came around, only forty days afterward, Golding was not yet in a position to pay, and the next year he was compelled to make a settlement to his disadvantage. At Michaelmas, 1594, he sold to Peryent eight acres of wood, and the moiety of two messuages, three gardens, one hundred and twenty acres of land, twenty acres of meadow, two hundred acres of pasture and sixty acres of wood in Great Birch, Little Birch, Copford, Stanway, Easthorpe, Layre de la Hay and Layer Bretton.[3]

Some or all of this property must have belonged to the Manor of Little Birch, because for the first time in this deed appeared the name of his son Henry to whom the Little Birch property had been entailed. Henry joined his

[2] Lord Chamberlain's Recognizances, Vol. 192, f. 347d., P.R.O.
[3] Feet of Fines, Michaelmas, 36/37 Eliz., P.R.O.

father in transferring the property and also warranted the transfer against his, Henry's, heirs. Henry probably had but lately come of age. He was born before March 1575 and after 1569. As the consideration named in this deed was only £200 it appears clear that the cancellation of the £300 recognizance was included. Henry had joined in that document and therefore Peryent was free to levy on any property of Golding even though entailed to Henry. With the entire Manor of Little Birch thus at the mercy of Peryent it is difficult to believe that the latter did not drive a hard bargain. Undoubtedly the conveyed lands were worth more than £500, especially in view of the statement of Mary Walgrave, in her suit against Arthur fourteen years before, that the property of her father, George Foster, in Essex and Suffolk was worth £300 per year. At the same time she had also said that Henry Golding had paid £2,200 for her portion of her father's estate, both in possession and in reversion. This purchase included some land in Suffolk, which she had inherited directly from her father and which Henry later sold. While these figures do not clearly fix the value of the Little Birch property those that were later used in transactions seemingly in connection with its ultimate sale to Sir John Petre indicate that £500 for a large portion of it was by no means its full value. After this "squeeze," Golding was still in difficulties, as is indicated by his pious remark the next year in his dedication to Lord Cobham, referring to his "troubles, of which when God will, I hope I shall be well discharged."

The next year, 1596, saw the beginning of the end of his ownership of the Little Birch property for which he

LITTLE BIRCH HALL ABOUT 1727

From a watercolor drawing in the possession of Charles J. Round, Esq., of Birch Hall. The ruined tower in the background is that of Little Birch Church. Arthur Golding nominated to the living in 1591. The building was destroyed by Parliamentary soldiers during the siege of Colchester (a few miles distant) in 1648.

had fought so many legal battles. In the spring of that
year he and Henry turned over to Robert Golding and
William Tyffin, according to the record:

the manor of Little Birch, one dovecote, two gardens, two hundred acres of land, twenty acres of meadow, one hundred and
fifty acres of pasture, thirty acres of wood and 10s rent in Little
Birch, Great Birch and Copford and the advowson of the church
of Little Birch warranted against all men. For which the plaintiffs (Robert Golding and Tyffin) gave £200.⁴

Tyffin was the lawyer who was trustee for his brother
Sir Thomas for the lease of Belchamp St. Paul's, and
Robert Golding was probably Arthur's second cousin, then
a leading member of the Inner Temple. As the amount
paid was but a fraction of the value of the property, it is
probable that this conveyance to two lawyers, closely connected to him, was not really a sale but a device to help
him escape his creditors. When he was fighting Cryspe
ten years before he had borrowed heavily from others as
well as from Andrew. In the Close Rolls, 28 Elizabeth
Part 25, November 28, 1586, we find the following
entry:

Arthur Golding of London acknowledged that he owed £1000
to Richard Atkins of London gentleman, which if not paid
should be levied on his lands.

If Atkins had been no more successful as a collector
than Andrew (before he had put him in the Fleet) and
the records do not show that he had been, Golding still
owed him. Action under the recognizance would cloud his
title to Little Birch so conveyance to his trustee and his

⁴ Feet of Fines, Easter, 38 Eliz., P.R.O.

cousin was a protection. Negotiations with Sir John Petre, later Lord Petre, were already in progress, he had received permission to alienate property to him in 1594, and this conveyance was doubtless the first step.[5] Petre acquired the property about this time according to Morant but the only direct record appears two years afterward, 1598, as follows:

Patent Roll, 40 Elizabeth, Part 4M 39—License for Arthur Golding Esq, and Ursula his wife and Henry Golding, gentleman and Joan his wife to alienate fifty acres of land called Parmeters and Chamberleys lying in Stanway, Great Birche and Little Birch in the County of Essex, held of the Queen in chief to John Petre, Knight and Thomas Petre Esq. his son and heir for ever—1 April.

These two fields may have been part of the Manor of Easthorpe or of Little Birch, for both manors had fields in the neighboring parishes and at this time it is not possible to separate them by description. It is probable, however, that they belonged to or were contiguous to Little Birch. About three months after their transfer we find the following puzzling record in the Close Rolls, 40 Elizabeth part 34:

Arthur Goldinge of Powles Belchampe, Essex and Henry Goldinge gentleman his son and heir acknowledged that they owed £4,000. to John Petre of West Horndon Essex Knt. and Thomas his son and heir. to be recoverable on their lands &c . . . 8 July 1598.

The exact character of this transaction is difficult to determine with certainty at this late day. On the face of the

[5] Morant, Reverend Philip, *History of Essex*, London, 1769, Vol. 2, page 184.

document it appears to be a mere acknowledgment of
debt, but the sum is so large that that is hardly likely.
It probably was a sort of penal bond given to insure the
performance of some contract by Arthur and Henry. As
the whole of the Little Birch property ultimately passed
into the hands of Sir John Petre it was possibly given to
insure the transfer of the remainder of the estate, which
two years before had been conveyed to William Tyffin
and Robert Golding. At any rate, this is the last record
of any transaction by Golding that has even a remote
connection with this fine estate, which he had struggled
so long to secure and which he enjoyed for but a few years.

From Petre, Little Birch passed through several hands
until it came into the possession of James Round of London who bought it in 1727 and "rebuilt" the manor house
as related by Morant. The reverend historian of Essex,
writing in 1769, says:

> Little Birch Hall was a very ancient edifice built chiefly by
> the Tendering and Golding families and ornamented in various
> places with nine escutcheons of their arms. But in 1727 and
> 1728 it was rebuilt in a handsome manner by James Round, and
> hath since been improved by the present owner.[6]

The Round family has held it for more than two hundred
years. In the nineteenth century the manor house was
replaced by the handsome mansion now known as Birch
Hall and occupied by Charles J. Round, Esq., the present
representative of the family. The illustration of Little
Birch, printed elsewhere, is from a water color drawing in
the possession of Mr. Round, who has kindly consented
to its publication here. It shows the building at a very

[6] *Ibid.*

early day. In the first edition of Morant's *History of Essex* (1769) there is an engraving on copper of Little Birch which shows the same building with the "improvements" referred to by the author. These consist of a stone wall before the house and the elimination of the stable or other offices which appear in the water color sketch, which is thus indicated to be that of the manor house after being "rebuilt" in 1727.

Whether this is the building occupied by Arthur Golding, with such changes as early eighteenth century taste dictated, depends upon the definition of the word "rebuilt." There is some evidence in the picture itself to support the theory that "rebuilt" in this instance meant important changes rather than complete reconstruction. Two-story bay windows were a common feature of Tudor buildings and the solid pediment and parapet shown could easily have replaced the crenellated parapet which, in the sixteenth century, still lingered from the days of castle turrets defended by archers.

Chapter IX

DECLINING YEARS

THE loss of Little Birch must have been a very heavy blow. It was by far the finest of his properties. Situated in a fair and fertile country but four miles from the ancient City of Colchester it was and is a dignified and worthy seat for a country gentleman. As soon as he had obtained possession Golding moved his residence there and signed himself as of Little Birch as long as he had the right to do so. He exercised the prerogatives of the manor and on May 19, 1591, nominated to the living of the church.[1] He clung to it even after he had, through the death of his brother Sir Thomas' widow, become the Lord of the Manor of Belchamp St. Paul's. It is significant of his waning fortunes that the evidence of his preference for Little Birch is found in the notes and other acknowledgments of debt that he continued to sign as lord of that manor. No longer can we trace his movements by the dedications of his books. So far as any record has come down to us his pen was idle. The long struggle to secure his inheritance appears to have occupied his time to the exclusion of interest in world affairs. At least we no longer find evidence of this interest through his translations and writings as formerly in regard to the excommunication of Queen Elizabeth, the massacre of St.

[1] Morant, Reverend Philip, *History of Essex*, London, 1769, Vol. 2, page 184.

Bartholomew's Day and the murder of Coligny, the visit of the Duc d'Anjou and the earthquake. Great events that changed the course of history filled the closing years of the sixteenth century, but he left no record of nor comment on them. The Spanish threat had passed away with the destruction of the Armada; the cause of religious liberty had won a great victory in the Edict of Nantes; but neither drew any comment from his pen. Doubtless, with his implicit faith in the direct interference of the Almighty in mundane affairs, he ascribed the overthrow of Philip's plans for the subjugation of England, to Divine power and regarded it as another evidence of His inexhaustible patience with a people who had not heeded the warning given by the earthquake. Had he been alive when it was put up he could have prepared the noble inscription for the monument that stands on Plymouth Hoe which records the defeat of the Armada and gives credit not to the gallant British seamen who took part, but in these words:

He blew with His winds and they were dispersed.

Whether Golding was ready to praise Henry of Navarre who delivered the Huguenots from persecution and granted them freedom of worship is not so clear, for he must have been shocked at Henry's remark that "Paris is worth a mass," and his acting upon that view. However oblivious Golding may have been to foreign events or foreign threats to England he was still ready to voice loyal admiration of the Queen and his simple philosophy of government in praise of monarchy. This he did in the dedication of his translation from the French of Jacques

Hurault's *Politicke, Moral and Martial Discourses* to
Lord Cobham in 1595 whose help had been so important.
This nobleman was a courtier of the first rank. He was
Warden of the Cinque Ports, Constable of the Tower,
Chamberlain of the Queen's household, member of the
Privy Council, Lord Lieutenant of Kent and Knight of
the Garter. Such a roll of honors indicates how high he
was in the favor of Elizabeth, and Golding displayed
almost a courtier's sense of the appropriate when he
addressed his fervent praise of the Queen and her government to a man so placed and favored. Nor did he lose
sight of the recipient's own vanity in the choice of a book
for dedication.

Jacques Hurault was a French soldier and statesman
and a man of force and discernment as his *Discourses* show.
In early life he had been in the army of the Duc
d'Anjou, afterward Henry III, at the victories of Jarnac
and Moncontour. He was Henry's adviser in later years,
being a member of the privy council at the time of his
dedication of his book to the King, October 28, 1588.
The Hurault family had been prominent in France for
many generations and had furnished councillors to Louis
XI and Louis XII. One branch were Lords of Cheverny
and their château is today second only in interest and
beauty, among the show places of the Loire, to that of
Chambord. As the early comrade and late adviser of the
last of the Valois, Jacques Hurault was competent to
write upon statecraft and war and Cobham could only feel
complimented to have the work of such a man dedicated
to him.

In the opening of the dedicatory epistle, after the direct

acknowledgment of gratitude quoted in a previous chapter, Golding goes on: "it is a thing ingrafted by nature, specially in those that are of best and noblest disposition to take delight in hearing and reading of such things as are most proper and incident to their own callings as whereof they have best skill and wherein they most excell."

With this subtly flattering introduction, he states his belief in the monarchical form and its basis in Divine action and purpose:

Of all the formes of government that have beene in the world, the Monarchie or Kingdome hath ever (as well by common and continuall experience, as also by the grounded judgement of the best practised politicians, and by the grave censure of the wisest men, yea and even by the ordinance & approbation of God) bin alwaies deemed and found to be most antient and sufficient, most beneficial and behoofful, most magnificent and honourable, most stable and durable, and consequently most happie and commendable; as which (besides many other most excellent prerogatives which I omit here) doth most resemble the highest soveraigntie of God, the onely one universall Monarch of the whole world, and is most agreeable to the first originall patterne of sovereigntie on earth, I meane Adam, whom God created but one, to have the dominion and lordship of all creatures under the cope of heaven.

The which being justly forgone by that first mans disobedience, God thought good in his wisdom to repair and set up againe much more large and magnificent than afore, in the person of one other man, namely of our Lord Jesus Christ, whom he hath made heir of all things, giving unto him all power both in heaven and earth, to reigne in glory everlastingly world without end. Who when he was to come into the world, in the last temporall Monarchie of the world, did thus much further beautifie and commend the state of Monarchie by his coming, in that he

116

vouchsafed not to come, afore such time as the state of Rome was brought into a Monarchie, and settled in the government of one sole soveraigne.

Such and so excellent is the matter whereof this booke doth treat. The which was written in French by one Jaques Hurault, lord of Vieul and Marrais, an honourable personage, and (as may wel appeare by his handling of the matters here treated of) of great learning, judgement, experience, and policie. Who for his prudence, gravitie, and loyaltie, was admitted to be of the privie counsell to his soveraigne lord and master the French king. Wherby he had fit occasion and meanes, to see into the states and forms of government, as well of forrein countries, as of his owne, and therefore might be the better able to discerne the truth of things, and to deliver his censure the more soundlie, concerning the managing of publike affaires and matters of state.

But now to come home out of Fraunce into England, and to applie the case more particularlie to our selves: I am fullie resolved, that if wee list to looke upon things with right judging eyes, and to consider them with well advised minds, we shall plainlie see there was never anie nation under the sunne, more bound to yeeld immortall thanks unto God for their state, Prince and soveraigne, than we be for ours; or to magnifie him more for the innumerable benefits receyved by that means, than we be. For first our state is that state which is most justly deemed the best and most excellent, namely a monarchie or kingdome, wherein one sole sovereigne assisted with a most grave Senat of prudent and sage counsailors, reigneth by wisedome, and not by will, by law and not by lust, by love and not by lordlinesse.

And unlesse we will denie the thing which the world seeth and gladly honoureth, and which we our selves have continually found and felt in experience now by the space of xxxvi years and upward, to our inestimable good and comfort: we must needs confesse that God hath given us a prince, in whose sacred person (to speake the truth in as few words as so great a matter may permit) there wanteth not anie heroicall vertue or gift of grace, that may beseeme or adorne the majestie of a kingdome, the

117

which thing is so much the more glorious and beautifull in her highnesse being both a woman and a virgin.

By whose means God hath also restored unto us the bright shining beames of his most holie Gospell, late afore eclipsed with the foggie clouds of superstitious ignorance and humane traditions, and the true ancient and catholike religion, borne down and in maner overwhelmed with the terrible stormes of cruell persecutions: a benefit wherunto none other can be comparable in this world. Of the which religion her Majestie hath continually shewed her self, not a bare professor, but a most earnest and zealous follower, and a most lightsome example to her subjects: directing all her studies, counsels and proceedings, to the setting forth of God's glorie, as well by advauncing and maintaining the same religion uncorrupted; as also by her most provident & motherly governing of hir people with all justice & clemencie, to their greatest tranquilitie benefit and welfare.

Whereupon hath also ensued Gods most mightie and miraculous protection of her majestie's most royall person, her realms dominions and subjects, from exceeding great perils, both forreine, civil and domesticall, such and so fitly contrived by the sleights of Satan & satanicall practisers, as but by the wonderfull and extraordinarie working of the divine providence, could not have beene found out, and much lesse prevented, avoided or escaped: an assured token of Gods speciall love and favor towards both soveraigne and subjects. To be short, so many and so great are the benefits which we received and still receive, by and from our most gracious soveraigne lady Queen Elizabeth, that I know not how to conclude her majesties most just deserved commendation, more fitly than with the verses of a certaine auncient Poet, written long since in commendation of that renowned prince of Britaine the noble King Arthur, the which verses I have put into English, with small alteration of some words, but no alteration at all in matter and sense, after this manner:

Hir deeds with mazeful wonderment shine everywher so bright,
That both to heare and speak of them, men take as great delight,
As for to tast of honycombe or honie. Looke upon

118

The doings of the noblest wights that heretofore be gone.
The Pellan Monarch fame commends: the Romans highly praise
The triumphs of their emperors. Great glory diverse wayes
Is yeeled unto Hercules for killing with his hand
The monsters that anoyd the world, or did against him stand.
But neither may the Hazel match the Pine, nor stars the sun.
The ancient stories both of Greeks and Latins overrun:
And of our Queene Elizabeth ye shall not find the peere,
No age to come will any yeeld that shall to her come neere.
Alone all princes she surmounts in former ages past,
And better none the world shall yeeld, so long as time doth last.

What remaineth then, but that all we her native subjects, knitting our selves togither in one dutifull mind, do willingly and chearfully yeeld our obedience to her gratious majestie with all submission faithfulnes and loyaltie, not grudging or repining when any things mislike us, but alwayes interpreting all things to the best; not curiously inquisitive of the causes of hir will, but forward and deligent in executing her commandements, even as in the sight of God, not for feare of punishment, but of verie love and conscience. Which things if we doe unfeinedlie, then no doubt but God continuing his gracious goodnesse still towards us, will give us daily more cause of praise and thanksgiving, multiplying his majesties yeares in health and peace, and increasing the honour and prosperitie of her reigne, so as our prosperitie also may with joy see and serve her manie yeares hence still reigning most blessedly: which are the things that all faithfull subjects doe and ought to rejoice in and desire, more than their owne life and welfare, and for the which we ought with all earnestnes to make continuall prayer and supplication unto God.

This is the only political expression of Golding that has come down to us. Coming towards the close of his life it may be taken as summing up his puritan philosophy in government as well as in personal action. Throughout his life he adhered to the simple belief in the sheltering guidance of God's will for the individual and here he enunciates it for the nation. It is crystallized in one word "obedience." Obedience of the sovereign to God, obedience of the subject to the sovereign, and over all the sheltering arm of Almighty protection from the assaults of Satan within or his agents without. A worthy expression of the old Puritan scholar's life rule in the terms of government. It would be unfair to such a sincere and consistent soul even to hint that he held to the cynics, definition of gratitude as "a lively sense of benefits yet to come," but it is difficult not to believe that Golding had hope that this eloquent tribute to England and Elizabeth put before such a courtier might reach the eye of the Queen herself to his own benefit. If so, he was doing no more than the practice of the time commended and doing it better than it was usually done. Here was no stultification of opinion, no prostitution of talent to an unworthy cause. The praise he eloquently voiced was in the minds and on the tongues of all Englishmen and has been confirmed by the judgment of posterity.

Whether or not the thought of benefit entered Golding's mind, he might well have been the recipient of royal favor. He had spent his life in literary toil that had received the high praise of his contemporaries in the same field. His labors in early life had opened one of the principal doors through which knowledge of classic lore came to inquiring English minds. Through his many later translations of Calvin's writings he had been one of the chief channels by which the stern doctrines of the Geneva reformer were disseminated as the seed which was to flower into an individualistic philosophy of religion and bear fruit in the irresistible charges of Cromwell's Ironsides.

The humble faith in the Divine approval and support of the monarchical principle so earnestly expressed by him lay deep in the hearts of simple English folk. It was cherished until illogically expanded and distorted by Stuart folly into the divine right of Kings. So altered, it was in half a century to bring Charles I to the scaffold through the stern purposes of men whose rigid doctrines had been nourished by the teachings of Calvin which Golding had done so much to spread. In this dedication he was expressing that deep current of mingled religious faith and civic duty, individually interpreted, that since that time has borne the English people forward to the great achievements of the British Empire. Elizabeth might well have honored and aided such a man in his old age and necessity. A pension or a sinecure—titles were for the soldiers or the wealthy. But Elizabeth did nothing, perhaps she never knew. And besides, if she did, honors cost money and Elizabeth was a thorough Tudor who took but did not give.

Probably during these later years Golding's health was poor. In 1589 Thomas Nash referred to him as "the aged Arthur Golding." He was probably tired and prematurely aged and may have been then worn down by disease so that although but fifty-three he seemed aged to Nash—himself then in the early twenties—an age when to the young and vigorous, elderly men seem older than they are.

A few years later there is some evidence of disability. In the diary of the notorious astrologer and philosopher

Dr. Dee, under date of September 30, 1597, there appears this entry:

John Crockar my good servant hath leave to go and see his parents. He went with Barthilmew Hikman and Robert Charles towards Branbroke, with Arthur Golding to cure of his fistula. John Crockar intendeth to returne about Easter or at Whitsuntide next. God be his spede.[2]

Dr. Dee, who had been a striking figure in London for many years and also a member of Archbishop Parker's antiquarian society, was well acquainted with Golding, although there is nothing to indicate any closer relation than this—physician and patient. Hikman was his chief assistant or manager at the sanitarium or nursing home which he conducted at Mortlake.

[2] *Private Diary of Dr. John Dee,* London (Printed for the Camden Society), 1842, page 60.

Chapter X

LAST SCENES

AFTER Golding's loss of Little Birch he went to live at Belchamp St. Paul's. There he still needed money, for the records show continued borrowings up to three years before his death. As the recognizances given for these loans were also signed by his sons, several times by Henry and once by Percival, it may be that he was using his credit for them rather than for himself. At any rate he seems to have lived the quiet life of a country gentleman in embarrassed circumstances for several years.

We can imagine and sympathize with Golding's anger when, towards the end of his days, May 17, 1604, there appeared an edition of his translation of De Mornay's *Trewenesse of the Christian Religion,* the title page of which, after stating that the work had been in part translated from the French by Sidney and finished by Golding, went on:

Since which time it hath been reviewed and is the third time published and purged from sundry faults escaped heretofore through ignorance, carelessnesse or other incorruptions by Thomas Wilcocks.

In the introduction Wilcocks praised the character and work of De Mornay and spoke with enthusiasm of Sidney "him that began to turn it into our tongue" but maintained an invidious silence as to Golding. This Thomas

123

Wilcocks (1549-1608) was a Puritan divine of the sensational type. He was violently opposed to episcopacy and in early life was ready to assume the martyr's rôle according to the milder rule of Elizabeth. In early life he had been in frequent conflict with the ecclesiastical and civil authorities and suffered two terms of imprisonment of one year each for violation of the Act of Uniformity. Even this had not cooled his blood and in later years he was a voluminous writer and correspondent and frequently in trouble on the same general ground. In fact he was quite the opposite of the dignified conservative Golding. Coming from such a person this piece of literary piracy and impudence must have aroused the old man thoroughly. It was bad enough to see one of his most famous works reprinted without remuneration to him but to have it corrected by Wilcocks was adding insult to injury. His vigorous reaction is reflected in his application for a copyright to his own works. Cooper states:

In consequence of a petition addressed by Mr. Golding to the Privy Council of James I., that monarch made order that the Archbishop of Canterbury and the Attorney-General should take into consideration the matters referred to in the petition, and grant to Mr. Golding the sole right of printing such books of his as they might consider meet for the benefit of the church and common-wealth, and that the Attorney-General should draw a book ready for his majesty's signature containing the grant thereof to the petitioner, a blank being left for the number of years, to be filled up according to his majesty's pleasure. This order is dated 25 July. 1605.[1]

This was promising and doubtless comforting to Golding, but nothing seems to have come of it, at least there

[1] Cooper's *Athenae Cantabrigienses*, London, 1861, Vol. II, p. 431.

BELCHAMP ST. PAUL'S PARISH CHURCH

Dedicated to St. Andrew. Paul's Hall is seen in the distance.

is no record that King James signed the "book." Probably the attorney-general and the archbishop took so long to "consider" what books were "meet for the benefit of the church and commonwealth" that Golding died before they made up their minds.

The pirated edition had been dedicated to Henry Frederick, the Prince of Wales, although he was then but ten years of age, so that Wilcocks referred to his "tender years" in the dedication. The young prince was, however, very precocious and showed even then promise of unusual ability. He died in 1612, when only eighteen, distinguished for his scholarly attainments and athletic prowess and much beloved. Whether or not the copyright asked for in 1605 was actually issued and held up Wilcocks' edition, or whether it was stopped by the posthumous copyright of 1606 is not clear, but no further publication seems to have been attempted until 1617 when the seven years of exclusive right granted by the posthumous copyright had expired. Then it was reissued by George Purslowe, without troubling to take out Wilcocks' dedication to Prince Henry Frederick, although the prince had been dead five years and Wilcocks nine.

There are no records of Golding's declining years beyond the borrowings referred to and the application for the copyright in 1605. The end came less than ten months after that application and in the Parish Register of Belchamp St. Paul's, under the heading "Burials" and the date of May 13, 1606, is this entry

"Mr. Arthur Golding, Esquire"

so plainly written that the author had but little trouble

in finding it. Few persons apparently ever really searched this Register. Otherwise the statement that the date of his death is not known, or that it occurred in the years 1570, 1590 or 1605, would not be so general among biographical authorities. The only writer, I have found, who mentions the correct year is W. J. Courthope in his *History of English Poetry.*[2]

His wife, Ursula Reydon, survived him four years, during which she lived at Halstead. She too was buried at Belchamp St. Paul's February 12, 1610.

Golding left no will and died deeply in debt. According to the statement of his son, Henry, some years later, he had borrowed for his father's needs £2,700, part of which he still owed. This was a large sum, in view of the high value of money at the time, which may conservatively be estimated at 10 or 12 to 1 as against present value. Why Golding should have been so heavily in debt is a question to which the author sought the answer through extensive research in the Public Record Office and elsewhere without finding the clue to the mystery. From these sources it was learned, as heretofore related, that he inherited four manors in well-settled fertile portions of Essex and Suffolk counties that had been well developed and prosperous since before the Conquest. These were all in addition to his ancestral home Belchamp Hall, which was entailed upon his eldest son Henry. All of these he sold, three apparently, to save the fourth, Little Birch. Taken together these estates included three thousand two hundred and fifty acres of arable land,

[2] Courthope, W. J., *A History of English Poetry*, London, Vol. 2, p. 140.

meadow, pasture, woodland, heath, and so on. There were sixteen messuages (houses with surrounding grounds), ten tofts (ground suitable for houses), three mills, twenty-five gardens and seven dovecotes. For all this property, according to the records, he received only £1,580. Sixteenth century records were none too explicit and accurate nor were they carefully preserved, so too much reliance is not to be placed in them. However, it is difficult to believe that Golding actually received less than £1,600 for this property, even though it was heavily encumbered with debts to the Queen, especially as his brother had paid £2,200 for less than half of it. On the other hand there is no reason to doubt the accuracy of Henry's statement that his father died heavily in debt.

No ordinary lack of business ability can account for such a condition, especially in a day when the ways in which men lost as well as made fortunes were fewer than at present. The age old vice of reckless personal extravagance through lavish living and domestic display was the most common cause of bankruptcy, but Golding, the Puritan, certainly did not come to poverty from this cause. Political plotting, resulting in sequestrations and fines, was another way, but Golding was no politician and was devotedly loyal to the Queen. There was no stock exchange then where a man might sink his inheritance in vain pursuit of wealth, though the instinct to take long chances for commensurate gains was ministered to by the seamen who were sailing the Seven Seas seeking adventure and profit while incidentally laying the foundation for the world-wide British trade of today. Groups of "Merchant Adventurers" were formed to finance the voyages of the Frobishers, Hawkins's, and Drakes and the large company of their less able and less fortunate imitators. Many a country gentleman subscribed to these undertakings and some profited, but, as is always the case, more lost.

The Earl of Oxford lost £3,000 in the years 1579 to 1581 in backing Frobisher's voyages and Sir Philip Sidney lost £25 in one voyage and £50 in another. Many other famous men of the time were subscribers to these voyages, including Burghley, Walsingham and the Earls of Sussex and Leicester. Dr. Dee was very active in promoting voyages of this sort and in securing subscribers to them.[8] The accounts of many of the ventures of less notable sailors were private and, unless forgotten muniment rooms shall yield up lists of subscribers including Golding's name, we will never know that his financial troubles were brought about in this way, if indeed they were. So we must leave the problem unsolved.

No trace of any monument erected to Golding at the time of his death is to be found at Belchamp St. Paul's; indeed the place of his grave in the churchyard is not known. His day was past. The great Queen and those who had been his contemporaries were gone. A new king sat on the throne who was to achieve the name of "the wisest fool in Christendom" and in some ways to deserve it. The rule of the Stuarts that was to afflict England for three generations had begun. The Elizabethan Era was dead and Golding passed with it. His eldest son was poor and in debt. If he raised a stone to his father, it is

[8] Ward, B. M., *The Seventeenth Earl of Oxford*, London, 1928, pp. 237-239.

gone and, with his sale of the lease some years later, the name ceased to be associated with the Lordship of the Manor of Belchamp St. Paul's. The name, however, is still known in the parish as evidenced by the memorial tablet in the church, dedicated April 17, 1921, to those "men of this parish and congregation who fell in the Great War." There are eighteen names and five of them are those of Goldings, of whom two were named Arthur. Thus the loyal spirit of the Elizabethan scholar lived again, after more than three hundred years, in these gallant defenders of King and Country.

In 1934 a heraldic window was placed in the church as a reminder of the family, and a tablet was raised to Golding's memory. Window and tablet are located in the east bay of the north aisle which is of mid-fifteenth century date. The carved oak roof, with the Tudor rose, different from that of the two western bays which are of later date, but the same as that of the chancel, indicates that this bay was formerly a transept of the present north arch. In this transept, directly opposite what was then the location of the pulpit, the Golding family had their seats.

The tablet which is under the central lancet of the windows bears the following inscription:

Here Worshiped
Arthur Golding, Esq.
Scholar, Translator, Poet.
—1536—1606—
He and his wife are buried in the churchyard.
Erected by his descendant
Louis Thorn Golding.

Window and tablet were dedicated by the Bishop of Chelmsford at a special service held on Whit-tuesday, May 22, 1934. (Appendix No. 15).

Golding left few traces of his personality. He seems to have been singularly lacking in self-consciousness. His portrait was never painted, at least none has been preserved. If he wrote many letters, none are known to have survived. He left no diary, but that is not surprising because the sixteenth century was not a self-conscious age. Men were more concerned in that day with what they did than with what they thought about themselves or what posterity would think about them.

In this Golding was essentially a man of his time. His thoughts were apparently divided between the past and the future; the present was too active to think much about. His interest in the past went back to the classic day; his interest in the future passed out of this life into the life beyond and the only present that he knew was in the preparation for it. When he did deal with the present, it was, as is shown in his two original prose works, to emphasize his puritan attitude towards life. In general he had the purely medieval attitude; this life was but a preparation for the life to come and in it the only light that showed the way was found in the grim and stern puritan philosophy that saw in the Creator a just but patient God whose favor was to be won only by the most rigid and austere practices.

So little of his work was original that it sheds but dim light upon his character. Still it may clearly be seen from his actions that he was a man of courage and frankness. There was nothing of the flatterer or the sycophant in

130

him. When he felt it necessary, he could deal "faithfully" not only with his readers as in the *Discourse on the Earthquake,* but with his brilliant young nephew. His vigorous warning of Edward Vere against popery and his exhortation to a virtuous life were in that day very plain speech to a great noble. This was no sycophant speaking but one "who had never learned to bend the pregnant hinges of the knee where thrift may follow fawning." Golding stood upright on his own feet; there is no evidence that he sought to be or was benefited by the influence of the Earl of Oxford, even when the latter was in high favor with the Queen. It seems clear in fact that as time went on he disapproved of his nephew's wild and spendthrift life, at least he dedicated no more books to him nor is there any record of friendly association.

Even though Queen Elizabeth took Oxford's side in the famous quarrel on the tennis court between the Earl of Oxford and Sir Philip Sidney, there is no evidence that Golding stood by him; indeed indications are that he did not approve of Oxford's actions. Some years later when Sir Philip Sidney was about to go to the wars in the Netherlands, where he lost his life, he desired someone to complete his unfinished work of translating De Mornay's *Trewenesse of the Christian Religion.* He turned naturally to Golding as the acknowledged leader of the translators and did not hesitate on account of his relationship to Oxford to place in his hands this cherished work. Sidney and De Mornay were friends, they had visited at each other's homes and were united by tastes, common interest and similar views of life, and therefore this work was doubly precious to him.

But with all his firm, frank character and his austere, puritan virtue Golding had his human side. He was not a saint. He did not, when smitten, turn the other cheek. We see this side of his nature come out in the long battle of nearly fifteen years to secure possession of the splendid estate of Little Birch. In his contest with the "wild woman," Mary Walgrave-Sanckye-Cryspe, he does not mince words, but thrusts hard at the vulnerable story of her life and does not hesitate to use the means at hand in his effort to win. At the same time, notwithstanding his independent spirit, when he felt he needed Lord Burghley's help he tried to prepare the way for his application to the Exchequer Court by dedicating a book to the statesman in language tipped with a little flattery. This was his translation of *Pomponius Mela,* published in 1585, and he remarks that he expects it to "remain to the behoof of posterity under the security of your Lordship's favor unto which I most humbly commend myself and these my simple doings."

Golding was a hard fighter. He would go to law very readily; but of course that was the common usage, one might almost say the common amusement, of the Elizabethans and when he was in a legal fight, he was not particularly careful of the bystanders' rights or of strict honesty, as was seen when he accepted rentals from his tenants and did not satisfy the Crown's prior claims. One hopes that the unfortunate tenants, who were released by the Court upon their promise to pay the rental a second time, found some way to get their money back from him.

Apparently he was more ready to borrow money than to pay it back and, from the standpoint of worldly wis-

Here worshiped
Arthur Golding Esq.
Scholar, Translator, Poet.
Born 1536 • Died 1606.
He and his wife are buried in the churchyard
Erected by his descendant
Louis Thorn Golding.

THE GOLDING HERALDIC WINDOW AND MEMORIAL TABLET
IN BELCHAMP ST. PAUL'S CHURCH

dom, he showed some skill in being able to hold off his creditor Richard Andrew for a number of years. Again he was shrewd in protecting the title of Little Birch from possible attack by Richard Atkins. But all of this was by no means unusual at that time, even among those most strict in religious observance. The Puritans were bitter fighters whether in the field or at the bar and liked to pay their debts or protect their neighbors no better than did the unregenerate of their day. Their enthusiasm for strict morals was frequently expended in making other people behave according to their own standards.

The apparent lack of confidence in Arthur shown by his brother Henry's will should not be taken too seriously. The will does not necessarily indicate that Henry feared that Arthur would be an oppressor or a despoiler of his widow. It was probably to protect Alice from the puritan in his brother. Henry was a liberal-minded individual and a realist, much under the influence of the soft-headed Alice, as indicated by his handling of the separation of Mary from Walgrave. He knew that the rigorous Arthur was shocked by Mary's conduct and felt that if Alice, who he knew would defend Mary, were to live in peace, he must find a way to keep Arthur quiet.

Golding had that journalistic quality which enabled him to appreciate the current trend of the public's interest and to take advantage of it by producing work suitable to the time and the occasion. In his middle years apparently he was alive to the events in the great world. This was a help when need for money compelled him to produce "pot boilers," especially after he became involved in legal battles. Even before that, however, he had a keen eye

133

to the current and the "newsy." When Bullenger issued his confutation of Pope Pius' bull of excommunication against Elizabeth in 1572 Golding translated it. In 1575, when the English public was watching the development of the Dutch struggle for independence with great interest, and the Dutch patriots headed by the Prince of Orange were eagerly seeking Elizabeth's aid, he published his translation of *The Cleering of the Prince of Orange*. This appeared just at the time that a deputation came from the Netherlands imploring Elizabeth's aid and offering her the sovereignty of Holland and Zealand under certain conditions.

In 1582 he put out his translation from the French of *The Joyfule and Royale Entertainment of the Duke of Brabant in Antwerp*. The policy of a French marriage as a counterpoise to the power of Spain had been trifled with for some time and the Duc d'Anjou had just visited Elizabeth in London in the character of an almost accepted suitor. He went from there to Antwerp to assume the sovereignty of that city, the Dukedom of Brabant, and the leadership of the Netherlands, which the citizens had offered him in the hope of so uniting France to their cause as finally to win the victory over Philip. When Anjou left London, where he had been received with considerable enthusiasm, for there was a party favoring his marriage to Elizabeth, he was accompanied by the Earl of Leicester, Sir Philip Sidney and other great nobles. The presence of these Englishmen in his train had aroused great public interest in the journey. Anjou was received in Antwerp with extraordinary demonstrations of joy and loyalty, which were described in the pamphlet, and, in Golding's translation, eagerly read by the English public, which could not foresee that Anjou's brief reign and the prospects of Elizabeth's French marriage would collapse within a year in his treacherous attack upon Antwerp known as the "French Fury."

Golding not only recognized great world events but he had a sense of the interest of the broad public in local happenings which would have fitted him, in this day, to have edited a sensational newspaper. When, in 1573, a London tailor was murdered by his wife's paramour and his accomplices, and the town was agog with the sensation, he met the curiosity of the public with his *Brief Discourse of the Murther of G. Saunders*, which pleased the popular taste so well that a second edition was issued four years afterward.

In like manner, when the earthquake of April 6, 1580, occurred, he seized the opportunity to impress upon the public's heated imagination his theory that the phenomenon was the work of the Almighty, intended as a warning to the wicked to repent and forsake their evil ways. That he had no sense of humor is indicated by his having argued at length that the earthquake was by direct interposition of the Almighty and then, in his account, relating that the only two persons who were killed were a boy and a girl who were listening to a sermon in a London church, when a stone was shaken down from the roof.

All of this stood outside the main current of his literary labors, either classical or religious. Apparently it represented the necessary bread-and-butter work of a man engaged in making his living. It showed, however, the practical side of a man, who, however, much he might disapprove of the doings of this world, still could and did know how to avail himself of its curiosity and its interest for the satisfaction of his own needs. Golding in maturity was no idealist. He had learned much since his early years, when he had endeavored to present the *Metamor-phoses* in the light of a moral allegory. Life had made him practical.

Chapter XI

THE POSTHUMOUS COPYRIGHT

ONLY two days after Golding had been buried, on May 15, 1606, there was issued to his youngest son Percival and one Thomas Wilson, a copyright granting them the exclusive right to publish seventeen of his most important works, which they duly listed. The haste in procuring this copyright indicates the need to forestall further sales of Wilcocks' pirated edition of De Mornay's *Trewenesse of the Christian Religion.* If the copyright, ordered by the Privy Council ten months before, had really been issued, it was only a grant to Golding personally and would fail at his death. On the other hand, if the Archbishop and the Attorney General were still considering which of his books were "meet for the benefit of the church and commonwealth" the result was the same and Wilcocks and his publisher George Potter were free to market their edition of a book which was still popular.

Speed was evidently of consequence for, as the introduction to the instrument relates, it was within four days of its issuance by the King, delivered to the Lord Chan-. cellor for execution. The full text of the document after the usual formal phraseology of address, is as follows:

Whereas our late Subject Arthure Goldinge of Belchampe St Pawle in the County of Essex Esquire and our loving Subject

137

Thomas Wilson of London Esquire have with great paines travaile and diligence converted or translated out of divers languages into the English tongue many woorkes of great volume and importance as well concerning divinities as alsoe concerning humanities, philosophie, poetrie, historie and other good and laudable matters to the furtherance and benefitt both of the Church and Common wealth of this our Realme, to weet:

The Commentaries of Mr. John Calvin uppon the psalmes;

his sermons uppon Job;

his sermons uppon the Epistle to the Galatheans;

his sermons uppon the Epistle to the Ephesians;

his sermons uppon the booke of deutronomie;

Certaine questions of Mr Bezaes concerning matters of divinity;

Pastills of Hemingius uppon all the Gospelles in the yeare;

The Disposementes of Chitreus uppon all the Epistles in the yeare;

The Trewenesse of Christian religion written in French by Phillippe Mornay;

Marlerattes the exposicion uppon the Apocalipps;

The Testament of the twelve Patriarckes;

The history of Justine;

The Commentaries of Julius Cesar;

Seneca his seaven bookes concerning benefittes;

A Woorke concerning the duties of Magistrates;

The Fifteene bookes of Ovids Metamorphosis in English meeter, and

Leonard Aretayne concerning the warres of the Goths in Italy.

Knowe yee that wee of our gratious favor towardes such good and vertuous actions of our speciall grace meere mocion and certaine knowledg have givin and graunted by theis presentes for us our heires and Successors doe give and graunt full and free libertie licence priviledge and authoritie to the said Thomas Wilson and Percivall Goldinge sonne to the said Arthure Goldinge their and either of theire executors administrators and Assignes That they the said Thomas Wilson and Percivall Goldinge and either of them their and either of their executor administrators and Assignes and every of them during the space of Seaven years next ensueing the date hereof shall and may imprint and cause to be imprinted all and singular the aforesaid bookes mencioned, and the same soe imprinted shall and may from time to time utter, sell and putt to sale within this Realme or any other our dominions and full and free libertie and authority unto the said Percivall Goldinge, that he the said Percivall Goldinge shall and may imprint or cause to be imprinted all such other bookes as he the said Percivall Goldinge shall hereafter translate, collect, gather, compile, make or abridge and all correction, addicions, alteracions and abridgementes of them an every of them, and the same soe imprinted shall and may utter sell and put to sale within the Realme of England or any other our dominions for a terme of seven years and no one else to print the same

Given at Westminster May 15th. 5 Jas. I[1]

The most significant thing about this document is the inclusion of the name of Thomas Wilson and his admission to an equal share with Golding in the honor of having translated the works listed. This Thomas Wilson was an active, self-seeking, and successful officeholder, who had been engaged abroad on diplomatic missions, and who, soon after, became Keeper of the Records in which post he rendered good service. He flourished as a "handy man" for the government and was knighted in 1618. He was born in 1560 and studied at Oxford and afterward toured southern Europe. He translated *Diana* by George de Montemayor from which the story of *Two Gentlemen of Verona* was partly drawn. He apparently had some connection with Golding in former years, for in 1607, the year after this copyright was granted, he asked Sir Thomas Lake, later Secretary of State, the Keeper of the Records whom he succeeded, a very busy and pliant courtier, to

[1] Warrants for the Privy Seal 5 James I, P.R.O.

139

use his influence to secure for him "the privilege of printing certain books (by Sir Phillip Sydney) wherein myself and my late dear friend Mr. Golding have taken paines." The man had undoubted capacity and would be worthy of more attention were it not for the contemptible episode, a few years later, which gave him a bad eminence according even to the very low standards prevailing at the Court of James I. In 1618 Sir Walter Raleigh had been in the Tower some years. James was seeking opportunity and excuse for sending him to the block, as a sop to Spanish anger. More evidence was apparently needed. It could not be had on the outside, so it was sought from the noble victim himself, through the activities of a spy. Wilson who was knighted in July, 1618, may perhaps have accepted this shameful office in payment for that preferment. From September 14th to October 15th of the same year he was shut in the Tower for the purpose of winning his way into the confidence of Raleigh and extracting from him admissions of his guilt. Wilson went at the work wholeheartedly, and, as he afterward admitted, falsely held out the hope of mercy to Raleigh, whom he vigorously denounced as an arch hypocrite.

If Wilson's claim to have worked with Golding upon any of Sidney's works rested upon his unsupported word, it might well be questioned, but, as Percival probably knew the facts, it may be considered. Golding, so far as is known, had nothing to do with Sidney's work except to finish his translation of De Mornay's *Trewenesse of Christianity*. This was done in 1587. Just at this time, Golding was involved in the arbitration, ordered by the Exchequer Court in his suit against Robert Cryspe for possession of Little Birch. With this burden upon him he may well have availed himself of help in the more tedious parts of the work, especially as there is reason to think that his health was then poor. Wilson who was then twenty-seven years of age may well have been employed, as he was probably competent, since he had degrees from St. John's College and Trinity Hall, Cambridge. Golding, however, did not think his aid of sufficient importance for credit on the title page of the book or in any other place of which we have knowledge. The inclusion of Wilson's name as an equal co-worker with Golding was doubtless the price paid for his influence in procuring the copyright and having it enforced so promptly. His efficiency is seen in the speed of the whole performance and the elaborate sufficiency of the document.

That Percival and, possibly Golding himself (for the agreements and arrangements must have been made before the old man's death) should have been forced to make such a bargain, is a measure of the friendlessness of a scholar, who, in his prime, counted among his friends some of the greatest figures of the Elizabethan Age. Lord Burghley, whom he could probably have depended on, had been dead six years and the others had gone before. He stood alone at the end. So we can see some of the reasons why Wilson was credited with work upon Golding's great translations, a perfectly ridiculous statement as Wilson was but five years old when the first four books of the *Metamorphoses* and the *Commentaries of Cæsar* were published.

This copyright is of particular interest, however, on account of the given list of works, which enable us to correct some erroneous attributions which have found respectable support, as will be noted in the list of his works contained in this book. The list as given above is by no means complete and was evidently made up for purely commercial reasons. Wilson and Percival included only Golding's most popular translations which still had a sale. Both his original works were omitted, doubtless because both were merely timely comment upon events, which, however important or sensational at the time, had long been forgotten. The most notable omission was his translation of Theodore Beza's *Abraham's Sacrifice* which he issued in attractive illustrated form in 1577. This does not seem to have been popular, for it was never reissued. Almost all the others however had several editions.

In the list is *A work concerning the duties of magistrates*. Since no author's name is given it might be presumed to have been original, but this is improbable as Golding took no interest in the mechanics of government, nor seems to have possessed any technical knowledge of the law. There is no record of this work ever having been published and it may have been in manuscript without the original author's name. Golding did not always credit his minor works to their authors. The author of *A brief Treatise concerning the Burnynge of Bucer and Fagius,* which he translated and published in 1562, was not given. This was probably the pamphlet published in Latin that year by the Strasburg friends of the reformers after their "restoration" at Cambridge.

The question of the powers and duties of civil magistrates in dealing with forbidden liturgical practices had been a very live one in Golding's early years when the details of the reformation of the English Church were still in controversy. While Bucer was at Cambridge, his opinion on this question was asked by William Bill, a fellow of St. John's College and later Dean of Westminster. Bucer replied at some length in Latin. At the time his views were of much importance, but later, as liturgical forms became fixed by statute and practice, they were merely of academic interest. The correspondence is preserved in the Rawlinson Col. D. 346 Folios 25-36 Bodliean Library. Could this unidentified work have been Golding's translation of Bucer's letter, which he made in an early day, following his interest in the German reformer, but which was never published because no longer timely?

Just what came of the partnership between Wilson and Percival, created by the copyright, is not clear, but in one instance at least there is an indication that the copyright was exercised in a new edition of the *Metamorphoses* in 1612. Apparently the association lasted for several years, for in 1615 one Boyden, a saddler of the Parish of St. Clement Danes, sued Wilson and Percival for the rent of a house in the Strand which he had leased to Wilson and which, in March 1611, Wilson had sublet to Percival "his friend and one with whom he had much dealing" who lived in it with his family for two years.[2] The answers of Wilson and Percival to Boyden's plea do not show them in a very good light, for Wilson disclaimed responsibility on the ground that "he wouldn't pay another man's rent," while Percival said he had paid the rent to Wilson. What became of the poor saddler's claim

[2] Chancery Proceedings James I, B20/80, P.R.O.

does not appear from the record, but his fate was hardly worse than that of Arthur, whose credit as the translator of his famous works the same pair had divided with Wilson.

Percival interpreted very literally the permission granted in the copyright, because, in 1608, he published as his own his father's translation of John Sleydane's *Epitome of Frossard's Chronicles.* The manuscript of this work is in the British Museum in the Harleian MSS., Number 357, Article 5. The book itself was issued by T. Purfoot, whose name also appears on the 1612 edition of the *Metamorphoses.* The manuscript has no mark of identification, but, comparison with the signed manuscript of Percival's history of the Vere family, among the Harleian MSS., and with a photographic reproduction of the only known signed manuscript of Arthur, makes it quite clear that his father wrote it.

After Golding's death we hear of him and Belchamp St. Paul's again in an application by his son, Henry, for a clearing of title to that manor. On the 22nd of April, 1612, Henry filed a bill in Chancery against William Tyffyn of Coln Wake, Co. Essex, Esq., the surviving trustee of Sir Thomas Golding. After reciting the disposal of the property by Sir Thomas as already described and relating how this had come down to his father, Henry goes on to say

holding his fathers said interest & estate for yeres in the premises to be very good & for the sufficiency thereof unquestionable & knowing hymself being the eldest sonne & heire of the said Arthure Golding borne after the said Grant made to the defendant and others deceased, the said Arthur Golding having occasion for the use & imployment of divers great sommes of money, your said Orator at his request was Content to furnish & supply the same, & did accordingly take upp money & ingage himself for the debtes of his said father insomuch that your Orator paid & stood charged at the tyme of his fathers death with the payment of debtes of his to the value of 2,700li or thereaboutes All which your said Orator hath satisfied & is to satisfy & pay accordingly.[a]

Henry had been living at Belchamp St. Paul's since his father's death six years before and probably was in undisputed possession of the premises, but the time had come when he wished to have a lease from Tyffyn, so that he could sell it and provide for his wife and seven children. He secured the lease, and afterward sold it to Mrs. Elizabeth de la Fountaine for £4,000. Thus the property passed out of the hands of the Golding family, after having been in their possession nearly a hundred years.

Henry and Percival are the only two of Arthur Golding's children of whom we have any record. Henry, as we have seen, remained in the country, but Percival went to London. No trace is to be had of the use of his father's works or name, except in the cases above mentioned. Percival, however, has gained a modest place by a performance of his own, which, on its face, is rather creditable. There is in the British Museum Harl. MSS., 4189, a handsome, illuminated manuscript account of the Vere family, written and signed by him. It is entitled *The Arms, Honours, Matches and Issues of the Ancient and Illustrious Family of Veer, and so forth, gathered out of history records and other monuments of antiquity by Persivall Goulding*. This is apparently a somewhat syco-

---

[a] Chancery Proceedings James I, G16/31, P.R.O.

145

phantic attempt to curry favor with a new head of the
Vere family and possible successor to the title. In his
dedication he goes on to say that this is not offered as
"a publike worke to patronize"

but as a testimony of particuler affection; unto which boldnes
my cheife inducements were theis; ffirst, the love and duty wch
not I alone but many of my auncestors, as humble wellwishers
have long borne to the honourable house of Oxenford; whereof
yours being a most eminent branch I presume but rather my
present would not prove ungratefull. Next myne owne earnest
desire by some acceptable meanes to make myself knowne unto
you, being a neare neighbour, and though a stranger to yourself,
yet heretofore well knowne and not a litle beholding to your
worthy brother Mr. John Veer.

The recipient is merely addressed as "Sir." There is no
further identification, but, by examining dates, it is very
clearly indicated that it was addressed to Sir Horace Vere.
With the death of Edward Vere, the seventeenth Earl,
in 1604, the title passed to his son Henry, who died at
the Siege of Breda in the spring of 1625. He had been
wounded and sunstruck in an attempt to relieve the city.
The English army, which took part in this operation, was
then commanded by Sir Horace Vere, one of "The Fighting Veres." With the death of Henry, who left no
children, his distant cousin Robert Vere succeeded to the
title. As he was also childless, Sir Horace became the
heir presumptive to the earldom. Partly for this reason,
but principally because of his great military skill and the
fact that he was the leading English general of his day,
he was created Baron Vere of Tilbury, in July, 1625.
The Mr. John Vere referred to was the elder brother of

Sir Horace Vere, who had spent his life at Kirby, about six miles from Belchamp St. Paul's. He had died in the spring of 1624, and had apparently been a friend and patron of Percival. When John died, Percival was left without any hold upon the Vere family, as Henry, the eighteenth Earl, his second cousin, had been brought up by his mother in London, out of touch with the Veres of Essex, because his father had sold the ancestral Castle Hedingham. He was, at that time, with the English Army in the Netherlands. Therefore when Henry also died without children, and Sir Horace Vere seemed likely to become possessor of the title and head of the family, Percival took this means, as he says, "to make myself knowne unto you, being a neare neighbour." Percival lived in the parish of St. Bartholomew the Great in London, in which parish Sir Horace had a house which he occupied when he was in the city. The fact that Percival uses the simple address "Sir," which was applicable to a knight but not to a baron, shows that this work was written before Sir Horace was created Baron, and probably after the death of Henry, that is between May 15 and July 25, 1625.

These references to Henry and Percival Golding are the only records that have come down to us of Arthur's children. The family seems to have passed from the position of country gentlemen into that of tradesmen. Two of Percival's sons emigrated to the new world, and his grandson, also Percival, was a button seller in London who died in 1690 and was buried in the parish of St. Bartholomew the Great. Of the two emigrant sons, Percival went to the colony of Bermuda about 1637 and was "schoolmaster and reader" for more than forty years; the other, Gideon, had some years before gone to Barbadoes, where he became a wealthy sugar planter, but died leaving no children. Ephraim the son of the Bermuda Percival married Rebecca Gibbs in Barbadoes in 1687. The following year he went to America and settled in the town of Hempstead, Long Island, in the Province of New York. He died in 1707, leaving a numerous family, whose descendants are now scattered throughout the United States and Canada.

TITLE PAGE OF "CALVIN ON JOB" (3RD EDITION, 1584)

This was the most popular of Golding's translations of John Calvin's sermons, passing through three editions, while those on Deuteronomy, Galatians, and Ephesians had but one edition. The volume contains one hundred and fifty-nine sermons.

Chapter XII

HIS PUBLISHED WORKS

O BVIOUSLY the task of compiling a list of Golding's works more than three hundred years after his death is one of considerable difficulty. Contemporaneous records of his books were but fragmentary at best and not distinguished for accuracy.

In the last hundred years several lists have been printed, all incomplete or inaccurate in some respects. An excellent one was included by Dr. M. W. Wallace in his reprint of Golding's *A Tragedy of Abraham's Sacrifice*, by Theodore Beza (Toronto, 1906). This he compiled from Hunter's MSS., Lowndes' *Bibliographer's Manual*, Cooper's *Athenae Cantabrigienses*, Sir Sidney Lee's article in the *Dictionary of National Biography* and the catalogues of the British Museum and Bodleian Libraries—the best sources of information available at the time.

In compiling the list that follows I have used Wallace's list as a basis for elaboration and correction in the light of the discoveries of the last thirty years, particularly, the Posthumous Copyright and my own researches. It is evident, however, that it is impossible to be certain that all the works published by Golding have been traced and recorded. Intimations in some of his works point to others which have not survived or at least are not now known to exist.

Works marked thus ** are listed in the Posthumous Copyright.

A briefe treatise concerning the burnynge of Bucer and Phagius at Cambrydge, in the tyme of Quene Mary, with theyr restitution in the time of our moste gracious souerayne Lady that nowe is. Wherein is expressed the fantasticall & tirannous dealynges of the Romishe Church, togither with the godly, & modest regimet of the true Christian Church, most slaunderouslye diffamed in those dayes of heresye. Translated from the Latin. Thomas Marsh, original member of the Stationers Company, printer. 16 Mo. London, 1562.

**The history of Leonard Aretine, concerning the warres betwene the Imperialles & the Gothes for the possession of Italy: a worke very pleasant & profitable. Translated out of Latin into English by Arthur Goldyng. Dedicated "To Sir William Sicill Knighte principall Secretarie to the Queenes Maiestie, and Maister of her hyghnesse Court of wardes & liueries. Finished at your house in ye Strond the second of Aprill. 1563. Arthur Golding." Rowland Hall, printer. 16 Mo. 360 pages. London, 1563.

**Thabridgemente of the Histories of Trogus Pompeius, gathered & written in the Laten tung, by the famous Historiographer Iustine, and translated into Englishe by Arthur Goldinge: a worke conteyning briefly great plentye of moste delectable Historyes, and notable examples, worthy not only to be Read, but also to bee embraced & followed by al men. Dedicated "To the right Hon.—Edward de Veer, Erle of Oxinforde L.

great Chamberlayne of England, Vicount Bulbeck, &c." Thomas Marsh, printer. Quarto, 400 pages, London, 1564. Reprinted in 1570, 1578.

The Fyrst Fower Bookes of P. Ouidius Nasos Worke, intitled Metamorphosis, translated oute of Latin into English meter. Dedicated to Robert, Earl of Leicester, from Cecil-House, December 23, 1564. Willyam Seres, printer. Quarto. 106 pages. London, 1565.[1]

**The eyght bookes of Caius Iulius Cæsar conteyning his Martiall exploytes in the Realme of Gallia and the Countries bordering vppon the same, translated oute of latin into English by Arthur Goldinge, G. It is dedicated "To the ryghte honorable Syr Willyam Cecill knight, principal Secretorye to the Queenes Maiestie, and maister of her highnes Courtes of wardes and liueries.—At Powles Belchamp the xii. of October. Anno. 1565.—Arthur Golding." Willyam Seres, printer. Octavo. 544 pages. London, 1565. Reprinted by Thomas Este in 1590.

**The XV. Bookes of P. Ouidius Naso, entytuled Metamorphosis, translated oute of Latin into English meeter. Dedicated "To Robert, Earl of Leicester, from Barwicke, the xx. of Aprill, 1567. Willyam Seres, printer. Quarto. 400 pages. London, 1567. Reprinted in 1575 by Seres; 1584 by John Windet and Thomas Judson; 1587 by B. Waldegrave; 1593 by John Danter; 1593 by W. W. (William White); 1603 by W. W.; 1612 by Thomas Purfoot.

---

[1] But four copies of this are known. One each in the British Museum, Bodleian Library, Oxford, Folger Shakespeare Library, Washington, and the Huntington Library, San Marino, California.

John Caluin his Treatise concerning offences, whereby at this day diuers are feared, & many also are quite withdrawen from the pure doctrine of the Gospell: a worke very needful and profitable, transl. out of Latine. Willyam Seres, printer. Octavo. London, 1567.

**A Posthill, or Expositions of the Gospels read in the Churches of God on Sundayes & feast days of Saincts. "Written by Nich. Heminge, and translated into English by Arth. Goldinge." Dedicated "To Sir Walter Myldmay Knight, &c, London, the xij of October, 1569." Then, A warning "Too all the servants of God, and Ministers of Jesu Chryst,—within the famous Realmes of Denmarke and Norwey by Nich. Heminge, Minister of the Gospell in the Vniuersitie of Hafnie.—the xxx. of March, The yere since Chryst was borne, 1561." H. Binneman, printer. Quarto. 690 pages. London, 1569. Reprinted 1574, 1577, 1579.

**A Postil or orderly disposing of certeine Epistles vsually red in the Church of God vppon the Sundayes & Holydayes throughout the whole yeere. Written in Latin by Dauid Chytraeus and translated into English by Arthur Golding. Dedicated "To Sir Walter Myldmay Knight, Chancelour of the— Exchequer, &c.—Finished at Powles Belchamp, the last day of March, 1570. H. Binneman, printer. Quarto. 489 pages. London, 1571. Reprinted 1577.

**The Psalmes of Dauid and others. With M. John Caluins Commentaries. Anno Do. MDLXXI. Dedicated "To Lord Edw. De Vere Erle of Oxinford, by

Arth. Golding, the translator. 20 Octo. 1571. In two parts: the first of 574 pages, the second of 518. Tho. East and H. Middleton, printers. Quarto. London, 1571. Reprinted in 1576.

**A Booke of Christian Question and answers. Wherein are set forth the cheef points of the Christian religion in manner of an abridgement. A worke right necessary and profitable for al such as shal haue to deal with the captious quarelinges and the wrangling aduersaries of Gods truth. Written in Latin by the lerned clarke Theodore Beza Vezelius, and newly translated into Englishe by Arthur Goldinge. Dedicated "To Lorde Henry Earle of Huntingdon, Baron Hastinges, Knight of—the Garter.—London, the 12. of June, 1572." W. How, printer. Octavo. 180 pages. London, 1572. Reprinted in 1574, 1577, 1578.

A Confutation Of the Popes Bull which was published more than two yeres agoe against Elizabeth the most gracious queene of England, Fraunce and Ireland, and against the noble Realme of England: together with a defence of the sayd true Christian Queene, and of the whole Realme of England. By Henry Bullenger the Elder. Translated from the Latin and dedicated to the Earl of Leicester. John Day, printer. Quarto. 172 pages. London, 1572.[2]

ORIGINAL. A Brief Discourse of the Murther of Master George Sanders, a worshipful citizen of Lon-

---

[2] Pope Pius V, who revived the Inquisition and vigorously pressed the battle against heresy and the war against the Turks that culminated in the great naval victory of Lepanto, excommunicated Elizabeth in the Bull (regnans excelsis) dated February 25, 1570 and declared her a usurper. Bullenger was a Swiss reformer whose writings greatly influenced the later phase of the reformation in England.

don. H. Binneman, printer. Octavo. 30 pages. London, 1573-1577.[3]

The benefit that Christians receyue by Iesus Christ crucified. Translated out of French into English, by A. G. It has two epistles prefixed: one, To the English Reader; in which states that the treatise was first written in Italian, and printed at Venice, after that translated into French, and printed at Lions: the other, to all Christians vnder Heaven. Thomas Dawson, printer, for Lucas Harrison and G. Bishop. Octavo. London, 1573. Reprinted by Dawson for Thomas Woodcock and G. Bishop, 1580.

This is ascribed to Golding by the British Museum Catalogue and by Hunter and Cooper. The *Dictionary of National Biography* in the article on Golding says this work was "doubtfully" accredited to him. It is not listed in the posthumous copyright but that can hardly be regarded as conclusive evidence that Golding did not write it, for not all of his books were listed there. It should be noted, however, that it appears to be the only one, that evidenced popularity by more than one edition, which is not mentioned. At the same time none of Anthony Gilby's commentators say that he wrote it, nor is there knowledge of any other contemporary translator who signed his work A. G. On account of the weight of positive evidence and the lack of any to the contrary, it is included in this list.

**Sermons of M. John Caluine vpon the Epistle of Saincts Paule to the Galathians. Dedicated "To Sir William Cecill knight, &c. Written at my lodging in

[3] A copy of each edition is in the British Museum. This book seems not to have been known until of late years, as it is not mentioned by any of Golding's commentators.

the forestreet without Cripplegate the 14. of Nouem-
ber, 1574. Arthur Golding." H. Middleton, printer.
Quarto. 658 pages. London, 1574.

**Sermons by M. John Caluin vpon the Booke of Job.
Translated out of French. Dedicated "the last of
December 1573" to Robert, Earl of Leicester. H.
Binneman, printer. Large folio. 751 pages. London,
1574. Reprinted 1580, 1584.

**A Catholike Exposition vpon the Reuelation of Sainct
John. Collected by M. Augustine Marlorate, out of
diuers notable Writers. Dedicated to Sir Walter
Mildmay. "Finished at my lodging in London the
last day of August 1574." H. Binneman, printer.
Quarto. 636 pages. London, 1574.

**The Testamentes of the twelue Patriarches, the Sonnes
of Jacob: translated out of Greeke into Latine by
Robert Grosthed, sometime bishop of Lincolne, and
out of hys copy into French and Dutch by others:
Now englished by A. G. To the credit whereof an
auncient Greeke copy written in parchment, is kept
in the Vniuersity of Cambridge. John Day, printer.
12 Mo. 154 pages. London, 1575, 1581. Reprinted
in 1589 by Richard Day and in 1590 by the "assigns"
of Richard Day.

This is credited to Anthony Gilby by the British Museum
Catalogue, Cooper's *Cantabrigienses* and the *Dictionary of
National Biography,* the latter saying that it had "often been
wrongfully attributed to Arthur Golding." However, since
it is listed in the posthumous copyright, I have included it
among Golding's work. This was a very popular book for
more than two hundred years. Editions without mention of

the translator were issued in 1660, in 1670; (in the black letter) 1674; 1677, 1684, 1693, 1716 (with new cuts); and in 1813 with new frontispiece.

A Justification or cleering of the Prince of Orendge, agaynst the false Sclaunders wherwith his Illwillers goe about to charge him wrongfully. John Day, printer. Octavo. 188 pages. London, 1575.[4]

The Warfare of Christians: Concerning the conflict against the Fleshe, the World, and the Deuill. Translated out of Latine. Dedicated to Sir William Drewrie. H. Binneman, printer. Octavo. 75 pages. London, 1576.

The Lyfe of the most godly valeant and noble capteine & maintener of the trew Christian Religion in Fraunce, Jasper Colignie Shatilion sometyme greate Admirall of Fraunce. (Written by Jean de Serres). Translated out of Latin. Thomas Vautroullier, printer. Octavo, London, 1576.

An Edict, or Proclamation set forthe by the Frenche Kinge vpon the Pacifying of the Troubles in Fraunce, with the Articles of the same Pacification: Read and published in the presence of the sayd King, sitting in his Parliament, the XIIIJ. day of May, 1576. Translated out of Frenche. Thomas Vautroullier, printer. 16 Mo. 64 pages. London, 1576.

**The Sermons of M. Iohn Caluin vpon the Epistle of S. Paule too the Ephesians. Translated out of French into English by Arth. Golding. Dedicated "To

[4] This was the famous *Justification* addressed to the world by the Prince and issued in 1568. It contained a vivid recital of the crimes and oppressions of the Duke of Alva and was the Prince's defense for openly and finally taking up arms against Phillip II.

First Verses of the translation of "Dr. Haddon's Exhortation" (Harl. MSS. No. 425 leaves 73-74 British Museum) which has been erroneously attributed to Golding.

Edmund—Archbishop of Canterbury, &c.—At Clare in Suffolke, the vii of January, 1576." "To all Christians baptized in the name of the Father, and of the Sonne, and of the holy Ghost, dwelling or abyding in Fraunce. Your brethren in our Lord, the causers of these sermons too bee brought to lyght." H. Middleton, printer. Quarto. 694 pages. London, 1577.

A Tragedie of Abraham's Sacrifice. (Illustrated). Written in french by Theodore Beza. . . . Finished at Pouules Belchamp in Essex, the XI. of August, 1575. Thomas Vautroullier, printer. Octavo. 63 pages. London, 1577.

**The woorke of the excellent Philosopher Lucius Annaeus Seneca concerning Benefyting, that is to say the dooing, receyuing, and requyting of good Turnes. Translated out of Latin by Arthur Golding. Dedicated "To the right honorable Sir Christopher Hatton Knight, Capiteine of the Queenes Maiesties Gard, vice chamberlaine too her highnesse, and one of her—priuie Counsell. Written at my House in the Parish of All Hallowes in the Wall in London the xvii. day of Marche, 1577." John Day, printer. Quarto. 240 pages. London, 1578.

ORIGINAL. A discourse vpon the Earthquake that hapned throughe this realme of England and other places of Christendom, the sixt of Aprill, 1580, between the hours of five and six in the evening. H. Binneman, printer. Octavo. 25 pages. London, 1580.

The Joyful and Royal entertainment of the ryght High and mightie Prince, Francis the Frenche Kings only brother, Duke of Brabande at his entry into his noble citie of Antwerpe. Thomas Woodcock, printer. Octavo. London, 1582.

****The Sermons of M. Iohn Caluin vpon the fifth booke of Moses, called Deuteronomie: Faithfully gathered word for word as he preached them in open Pulpet; together with a preface of the Ministers of the Church of Geneua, and an admonishment made by the Deacons there: Also there are annexed two profitable Tables, one containing the chiefe matters, the other the places of Scripture herein alledged. Translated out of French by Arth. Golding. Dedicated "To Syr Thomas Bromley Knight, Lord Chancelour of England, &c.—21 Dec. 1582. H. Middleton, printer. Folio. 1397 pages of which the sermons occupy 1247. London, 1583.

The Rare and Singuler worke of Pomponius Mela, That excellent and worthy Cosmographer, of the situation of the world . . . with the Longitude and Latitude of euerie Kingdome, Regent, Prouince, Riuers, Mountaines, Citties and Countries. Dedicated to Sir William Cecil, Lord Burghley, on Feb. 6, 1584-5. Thomas Hackett, printer. Quarto. 248 pages. London, 1585. Also in 1590 together with the Julius Solinus. Editions were also published in 1711, 1719, 1739, 1761, and 1775, all Quarto with maps.

The excellent and Pleasant Worke of Iulius Solinus Polyhistor. Contayning the noble actions of humaine creatures, the secretes & prouidence of nature, the description of Countries, the maners of the people: with many maruailous things and strange antiquities, seruing for

158

the benefitt and recreation of all sorts of persons. Translated out of Latin into English, by Arth. Golding, Gent. I. Charlewood, printer. Quarto. London, 1587.

**A woorke concerning the Trewnesse of the Christian Religion, written in French; Against Atheists, Epicures, Paynims, Iewes, Mahumetists, &c. By Philip of Mornay, Lord of Plessie Marlie. Begunne to be translated by Sir Philip Sidney, knight, and at his request finished by Arth. Golding. Dedicated to Robert, Earl of Leicester. George Robinson, printer. Quarto. 552 pages. London, 1587. Reprinted 1592 by Robert Robinson. Revised and corrected by Thomas Wilcocks and dedicated to Henry Frederick Prince of Wales, it was reprinted by George Potter in 1604 and by George Purslowe in 1617.

Politicke, Moral and Martial Discourses. Written in French by M. Iaques Hurault, lord of Vieul & of Marais, and one of the French kings priuie Councell. Dedicated "To William Lord Cobham, L. warden of the Cinque ports, &c. 27, Jan. 1595." Adam Islip, printer. Quarto. 495 pages. London, 1595.

A Godly and Fruteful Prayer, with an Epistle to the right rev. John (Aylmer) bishop of London, from the Latin of Abraham Fleming. T. Purfoot, printer. Octavo. London, not dated.

Epitome of Frossard's Chronicles written in Latin by John Sleydane. T. Purfoot, printer. Quarto. 215 pages. London, 1608, 1611.

On the title page of this work it is stated that the translation is by P. Golding. This is incorrect. The manuscript is in the British Museum (Harl. MS. 357, Art. 5) and is in excellent condition. I have compared it with Percival Golding's manuscript history of the Vere family, also in the British Museum (Harl. MS. 4189) and have compared both with a photographic copy of the only known signed specimen of Arthur Golding's handwriting which is in the Folger Shakespeare Library at Washington. As this comparison makes it perfectly clear that the handwriting is not that of Percival, but that of his father, I have included this among ' Arthur's works.[5]

The fact that both Arthur Golding and Anthony Gilby occasionally signed their work A. G. has led to some confusion. Gilby was a clergyman, a vigorous and leading supporter of the protestant position, a man of learning and a translator of Calvin. With others he was also engaged in the translation of the Geneva Bible. As seen above he was erroneously credited with the translation of *The Testamentes of the Twelve Patriarches.* On the other hand Calvin's *Commentary on Daniel* (London 1570) upon the title page of which appear the initials A. G., has been credited to Golding by the British Museum catalogue, the *Cambridge History of English Literature* and by Cooper's *Cantabrigienses* (Vol. II, p. 432, 1861). However, Cooper had already credited it to Gilby

[5] I am very glad to have the opinion of the eminent authority upon sixteenth century script, Mr. W. W. Greg, of London, to confirm my judgment on this point. At my suggestion Mr. Greg very kindly made the same comparisons and writes me as follows:

"The hand of Harley 357, art. 5., I have no hesitation in identifying with that of the acknowledgment of debt signed by Arthur Golding, which I reproduced in *English Literary Autographs*, Plate XXXV, and which I understand from you to be now in the Folger Library. The hand of Harley 4189 is certainly different and appears to be Percival Golding's autograph.

"22 Oct. 1935."

(Vol. I, p. 518, 1858) with the remark that it had been "erroneously credited to Golding." There is no evidence as to what caused the change in the three years between the publication of the first volume in 1858 and the second in 1861 nor is there any explanation. Of course there is the probability that the conflict is merely the result of oversight, the not unnatural result of uncoördinated work by the two authors, Charles Henry and Thompson Cooper.

Nevertheless why this work should have been credited to Golding is not clear in view of the title page of the copy in the British Museum which reads as follows:

Commentaries of that divine John Calvin, upon the Prophet Daniel, translated into englishe especially for the use of the family of the right honourable Earl of Huntington, to set forth as in a glasse, how one may profitably read the scriptures by considering the text, meditating the sense thereof and by prayer.

This was no ordinary dedication to a noble patron, such as was customary at the time, and indicates the close relation of Gilby to the Earl and his family whose rector he was. Six years before this book was published Huntington had named him to the living of Ashby-de-la-Zouch, the seat of the Hastings family in Leicestershire, where he lived "great as a bishop" until his death in 1585.

An Erroneous Attribution

In the British Museum there is a manuscript translation of Rev. Dr. James Haddon's Latin verses exhorting England to repent at the time of the "Great Sweat" in 1551. (Harl. MS. 425, Leaves 73.74). This has been attributed by Sir Sidney Lee, Dr. Wallace and other commentators to Arthur Golding. The first attribution seems to have been by F. J. Furnivall who wrote in *Notes & Queries,* (4 Series, Vol. VI. Decr. 3rd, 1870) that he would add this translation to the list of Golding's works printed in Warton's *History of English Poetry,* (Edition of 1840) and announced its forthcoming publication in *Ballads from Manuscript* for the Ballad Society which took place in 1871, pp. 325-330.

Examination of the manuscript, however, and comparison of it with the known handwriting of Golding clearly shows that it was the work of another. This will be seen at once by comparing the reproduction (page 156) of the first of the thirty-four verses with the reproduction of Golding's script and signature (page 100).[6]

The writer of the verses was Rev. Dr. James Haddon, an eloquent and vigorous Protestant preacher and controversionalist. The occasion was the last visitation of the epidemic of the sweating sickness in 1551 known as the "Great Sweat." Stow in his *Chronicles* thus describes it:

The sweating sickness began in London on the 9th of July which was so terrible that people being in the best of health were

[6] It was suggested to Mr. W. W. Greg, who had examined the manuscript and compared it with Golding's script, that the difference in the handwriting of this manuscript and that of Golding in his acknowledgment of debt to his sister-in-law reproduced at page 100 was to be accounted for by the possibility that the translation of Dr. Haddon's *Exhortation,* which was written about 1551, was made at the, time when Golding was fifteen years of age, while the acknowledgment of debt was written in 1590, thirty-nine years afterward. In answer to this Mr. Greg writes me as follows:

"I can see no resemblance whatever between the hands of the Haddon MS. and acknowledgment of debt that might lead one to suppose that they were written by the same person at an interval of many years. Nor, though rough, does the Haddon hand look like that of a child. I should say moreover that it appears to be later than 1551.

"19 Nov. 1935."

suddenly taken and died in twelve or twenty-four hours or less. And it is to be noted that this mortality fell chiefly on men of the best age, as between thirty and forty years. Also it followed Englishmen as were within the Realme as in strange countries. The first week died in London eight hundred and six persons.

Dr. Haddon in the years following the outbreak also very earnestly pressed his interpretation of the national visitation in sermons. In Lent, 1553, shortly before Edward VI's death, he preached at Court; and John Knox wrote of him that "he most learnedly opened the causes of the bypast plagues, affirming that worse were to follow unless repentance should shortly be found." He had been tutor to Lady Jane Grey and, having defended the protestant position in joint debate in the early days of Mary's reign, he fled to Strasburg in 1554 and died there in poverty.

When and by whom the statement at the top of the manuscript was made is not known. The hand is so different from that of the translation as to make it seem probable that it was written at a later period and that the attribution was merely an error.

Chapter XIII

HIS ORIGINAL WORK

So FAR as is known Golding left but three original works, two in prose and one in verse. All were short, and, as they afford some insight into his character, they are here reprinted in full, in the chronological order of their publication.

The first is his account of a sensational murder and the punishment of its perpetrators which gives an interesting picture of the manners of the time.

Opposite is the title page (and two pages beyond) the first page of this work reproduced from the copy in the British Museum. Following is the complete text in modern type for easy reading.

The Discourse on the Sanders Murder

Forasmuche as the late murther of M. Saunders, Citizen & Merchant taylor of this Citie, ministreth great occasion of talke among al sorts of men, not only here in the Towne, but also far abrode in the Countrie, & generally through the whole Realme: and the sequeles and accidents ensewing thereupon, breede much diversitie of reports & opinions, while some do justly detest the horriblenesse of the ungratious facte, some lament the grievous losse of their deere frendes, some rejoyce at the comendable execution of upright justice, the godly bewayle the unmeasurable inclination of humayne nature to extreame wickednesse, & therewith magnifie Gods infinite

164

A briefe difcourfe

of the late murther of ma-
fter George Sanders, a worshipful
Citizen of London: and of the ap-
prehenfion, arreignement, and
execution of the principall
and acceffaries of
the fame.

Seene and allowed.

¶ *Imprinted at London by*
Henrie Bynnyman, dwelling in
Knightriders ftreete, at the figne
of the Mermayde.
A N N O. 1577.

TITLE PAGE. DISCOURSE ON THE MURDER
OF G. SANDERS

From the copy in the British Museum.

mercy in revoking of forlone sinners to finall repentance, many delight to heare and tell newes, without respect of the certaintie of the truth, or regarde of dewe humanitie, every man debating of the matter as occasion or affection leades him, & fewe folke turning the advised consideracion of Gods open judgements, to the speedy reformation of their owne secrete faults: It is thought covenient (gentle reader) to giue thee a playne declaration of the whole matter, according as the same is come to light by open triall of Justice, and voluntarie confession of the parties, that thou mayst both know the truth to the satisfying of thy minde, and the avoyding of miscredite, and also use the example to the amendment of thy lyfe. Notwithstanding thou shalte not loke for a full discoverie of every particular by matter appendent to the present case, whiche might serve to feede the fonde humor of such curious apetites as are more inquistive of other folkes offences, than hastie to redresse their owne: for that were neyther expedient nor necessarie. And mens misdoyngs are to be prosecuted no further with open detestation, than till the parties be eyther reclaymed by reasonable and godly perswasion, or punished by orderly and lawfull execution, according to the qualities of theyr offence. When lawe hath once passed upon them, and giuen them the wages of their wicked desertes: the Christian charitie willeth men eyther to burie the faults with the offendours in perpetuall silence, or else so to speak of them, as the vices and not the parties theselves may seeme to be any more touched.

But hereof shall more be spoken (God willing) in the winding up of this matter. Now I will set downe, first

165

the murthering of master Saunders by George Browne, with Brownes apprehension, triall, and execution: then the trial and execution of Anne Saunders, the wife of the sayde George Saunders, of Anne Drewrie, widowe, & of Roger Clement, called among them, Trustie Roger, the servant of ye sayd Anne Drewrie: And lastly, a briefe rehearsall of certaine sayings and dealings of the parties convicted, betweene the time of their apprehensions, and the tyme of theyr execution, whiche are not things proper and peculiar to the very body of the case, but yet incident, and therefore necessarie for the hearer, as whereby will appeare the very originall cause and first grounde of this ungodly deede: And this rehearsall shall be shut up and concluded with a short Admonition how we ought to deale in this and all other such cases.

The Tuisdaye in Easter weeke laste past (which was the xxiiij. day of March) the sayd George Browne receyving secret intelligence by letter from mistresse Drewrie, that master Saunders should lodge the same nyghte at the house of one Mayster Barnes in Woolwich, and from thence go on foote to Saint Marie Craye the nexte mornyng: met him by the way a little from Shooters hill, between seven and eight of the clocke in the forenoone, and there slewe both hym and also one John Beane the servant of the sayd master Barnes.

Assoone as master Saunders felt himselfe to haue his deaths wounde (for hee was striken quite & cleane through at the first blow,) he kneeled downe, and lifting up his handes and eyes unto heaven, sayd, God haue mercy upon mee, and forgiue me my sinnes, & thee too, (speaking to Browne, whome indeede he knew not, what-

166

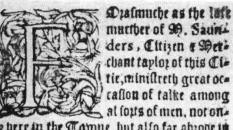

Forasmuche as the late murther of M. Saunders, Citizen & Merchant taylor of this Citie, ministreth great occasion of talke among al sorts of men, not onely here in the Towne, but also far abroue in the Countrie, & generally through the whole Realme: and the sequeles and accidents ensewing therevpon, breede much diuersitie of reportes & opinions, while some do iustly detest the horriblenesse of the vngratious facte, some lament the grieuous losse of their deere frendes, some reioyce at the comendable execution of vpright iustice, the godly bewayle the vnmeasurable inclination of humayne nature to extreame wickednesse, & therewith magnifie Gods infinite mercy in reuoking of forlorne sinners to finall repentance, many delight to heare and tell newes, without respect of the certaintie of the truth, or regarde of dewe humanitie, euery man debating of the matter as occasion or affection leades him, & fewe folke turning the aduised consideration of Gods open iudgements, to the speedy reformation of their owne secrete faultes: It is thought coueni: nt (gentle reader)

A.ij.,

FIRST PAGE. DISCOURSE ON THE MURDER
OF G. SANDERS

From the copy in the British Museum.

soever reporte hath bene made of former acquaintance betwixt them) and with that worde he gaue up the Ghoste. And Browne (as he himself confessed afterward) was thereat striken with suche a terrour & agonie of hart, that he wist not what to do, but was at the poynt to haue faynted even then, and oftentymes else that day, and coulde brooke neyther meate nor drinke that he receyved of al that day after. He was so abashed afterward at the sight of one of master Saunders little yong children, as hee had much ado to forbeare from swounding in the streete: A notable example of the secret working of Gods terrible wrathe in a guiltie and blouddie conscience. But M. Barnes's man hauing ten or eleven deadly woundes, & being left for dead, did by Gods wonderful providence revive agayne, and creepyng a great way on all fours, (for he could neyther go nor stande) was found by an old man and his maiden that went that way to seeke their kine, and conveyed to Woolwich, where he gaue evident tokens and markes of the murtherer: and so continuyng still alive til he had bene apprehended and brought unto him, died the nexte Munday after. Immediatly, upon the deede dooing, Browne sent mistresse Drewrie worde thereof by trustie Roger, he himself repayred forthwith to the Court at Greenewich, and anone after him came thither the reporte of the murther also. Then departed hee thence unto London streyght wayes, and come to the house of Mistresse Drewrie, howbeit hee spake not personally with hyr. But after conference had with him, by hyr servant Roger, she provided him xx. pounds the same day, for the which mistresse Drewrie layde certaine plate of hir owne & of mistresse Saunders to gage.

And upon the nexte day beyng Thursday mornyng (hauing in the meane tyme had intelligence that Browne was soughte for) they sent him sixe poundes more by the sayd Roger, and warned him to shifte for himselfe by flight, whiche thing he forstowed not to doe. Neverthelesse the Lordes of the Queenes Majesties Councel, caused so speedie and narow search to be made for him in all places, that upon the xxviij. of the same moneth he was appreheded in a mans house of his owne name at Rochester, by the Mayor of the towne: and being brought backe againe to the Courte, was examined by the Councell, unto whom he confessed the deede, as you haue hearde, & that he had oftentimes before pretended and sought to do the same, by the instigation of the said widow Drewrie, who (as he sayd) had promised to make a mariage betweene him and mistresse Saunders, (whom he seemed to love excessively,) the desire of which hope hasted him forwarde to dispatche the fact. Neverthelesse he protested, (howbeit untruly) that mistresse Saunders was not privie nor consenting therunto. Upon this confession he was arreygned at the Kings Bench in Westminster Hal on Fryday the xvij. of April, where acknowledging himself giltie, he was condemned as principall of the murther of M. Saunders, according to whiche sentence he was executed in Smithfields on Monday the xx. of the same moneth, at whiche time (though untruly, as she hirself confessed afterward) he laboured by al meanes to cleare mistresse Saunders, of committing evill of hir body with him: and afterwarde was hanged up in chaynes neere unto the place where he had done the fact.

Thus much concerning the very case of the murther it

168

selfe & the punishment of the principall doer thereof. As
for the acknowledgement of the former wickednesse of
his life, & the hartie repentaunce that he pretended for
the same, even to his very death, I deferre them to the
last part of this matter, to whiche place those things do
more peculiarly pertaine. In the meane time mistresse
Drewrie and hir man being examined, and as well by
theyr owne confessions, as by the falling out of the matter
in consequence, & also by Brownes appeachment, thought
culpable, were committed to warde. And anone after
mistresse Saunders being delivered of childe & churched
(for at the tyme of hir husbandes death she looked presently to lie downe) was up on mistresse Drewries mans
confession, and uppon other greate lykelyhoodes and pre-
sumptions, likewise committed to warde, and on wednesday, the sixth of May, arreigned with mistresse Drewrie,
at the Guilde hall, the effect of whole several inditements
is this: That they had by a letter written, bene procurers
of the sayde murther, and so accessaries before the fact:
And knowing the murther done, had by money and
otherwise, relieved and bene ayding to the murtherer, and
so accessaries also after the fact. Wheronto they both of
them pleaded not guiltie. And mistresse Saunders, not-
withstandyng the avouchement of mistresse Drewries man
face to face, and the great probabilities of the evidence
giuen in against hir by M. Geffrey, the Queenes Majesties Sergeant, stoode so stoutly still to the deniall of all
thinges, (in which stoute deniall she continued also a certaine time after hir condemnation) that some were
brought in a blinde beliefe, that eyther shee was not
giltie at all, or else had but brought hir selfe in daunger

of lawe through ignorance, and not through pretenced malice. Howbeit, for asmuch as bare denial is no sufficient barre to discharge manifest matter, & apparant evidence: they were both condemned as accessaries to maister Saunders death, and executed in Smithfielde the thirteenth of May, being the wednesday in the Whitson weeke, at whiche time they both of them confessed themselves guiltie of the fact, for which they were condemned, and with very great repentaunce and meekenesse, receyved the rewarde of their trespasse, in the presence of many personages of Honor and Worship, and of so great a number of people as the lyke hath not bene seene there togither in any mans remembraunce, for almost the whole fields, and all the way from Newgate, was as full of folke as coulde well stande one by another: and besides that, great companies were placed bothe in the chambers neere aboutes (whose windowes and walles were in many places beaten down to looke out at) & also upon the gutters, sides, and toppes of the houses, and upon the batlements and steeple of S. Bartholmewes.

Mistresse Drewries man was arreigned at Newgate on Friday the viij. of May, and beyng there condemned as accessarie, was executed with his mistresse, at the time and place aforesayde.

Thus haue yee hearde the murthering of Maister Saunders, with the apprehension, arreignment, condemnation, and execution of the principall and of the accessaries to the same. Now let us proceede to the incidents that hapned from the times of theyr apprehensions, to the time of their deaths, and so to the admonition, whiche is the conclusion and fruyte of this whole matter.

170

Whereas it was determined that Mistresse Sanders &
mistresse Drewrie should haue suffered upon the next
saterday after theyr condemnation, whiche was Whitson
even: the matter was stayed til the wednesday in Whitson
weeke, upon these occasions ensuing. The booke of M.
Sanders accompts and reckenings, whereupon depended
the knowledge of his whole state, was missing. Certaine
summes of money were sayd to be in the handes of parties
unknowne, the intelligence whereof was desyred and
sought for to the behoofe of M. Saunders children. The
parties convicted were to be reformed to Godwarde, and
to be brought to the willing confessing of the things for
whiche they had bene justly condemned, and whiche as
yet they obstinately concealed.

And besides all this, one Mell, a minister that had
heretofore bene suspended from his Ministerie, accompanying mistresse Saunders, from hir condemnation to
Newgate, & conferring with hir as it had bene to gyue hir
good counsell & comforte, was so blinded with hir solemne
asserverations & protestations of innocencie that notwithstanding he had heard hir inditement, with the exact and
substantiall of hir case: yet neverthelesse, he perswaded
himselfe that she was utterly cleare, & thereupon falling
in love with hir, dealte with mistresse Drewrie to take the
whole guilte upon hir selfe, undertaking to sue for mistresse Saunders pardon. And so, what by his terrifying of
hir, with the horrour of mischarging and casting away of
an innocent, what with his promising of certain money to
the mariage of hir daughter, and with other perswasions:
she was so wholy wonne that way, that as well before
certayne personages of honour, as also before the Deane

of Paules and others, she utterly cleered mistresse Saunders of the facte, or of consent to the same, taking the whole blame thereof to hir selfe, and protesting to stande therein to the death, contrarie to hir former confession at the time of hir arreignement.

Mistresse Saunders also, after the laying of this platte, stoode so stoutely to hir tackling, that when the Deane of Paules gaue hir godly exhortation for the clearing of hir conscience, and for the reconciling of hir selfe unto God, as the time and case moste needefully required (as other had done before) he coulde obtayne nothing at hir hande. By meanes whereof, he was fayne to leave hir that time, whiche was the Friday, not without great griefe and indignation of mind to see hir stubborne unrepentauntnesse. In the meane whyle, the sayd Mell discovering his purpose and whole platforme to an honest Gentleman, whome he unskilfully tooke to haue bene a welwiller to obtaine the pardon of mistresse Saunders, was partely by that meanes, and also by other follies of his own, cut off from his enterprise. For when hee came to sue for hir pardon, whiche thing he did with such outrage of doting affection, that he not onely profered summes of money, but also offered his owne body & life for the safetie of the woman, whom he protested upon his conscience to be unguiltie. The Lordes of the counsell knowing hir to be rightly condemned by good justice, and being privie to the state of the case beforehand, & also finding him out by his owne unwise dealings (wherof among other, one was, that he intended to mary hir) not onely frustrated his desire, but also adjudged him to stande upon the pillorie, with apparant notes & significations to his lewde

172

& foolish demeanour. According to the which appointment he was set upon a Pillorie by the place of execution
at the time of their suffering, with a paper pinned upon
his breast, wherein were written certaine wordes in great
letters conteyning the effect of his fact, to his open shame:
videlicet, For practising to colour the detestable factes of
George Saunders wife. Whiche was a very good lesson to
teach al persons to refrain from any devises or practises
to deface or discredite the honorable procedings of Coun-
sellours, & publike and lawfull forme of trialles & judgements according to Justice, or to hinder the beneficial
course of so good examples.

By this occasion Mistresse Sanders was utterly unpro-
vided to die at that tyme, and therefore as well in respect
of mercie, as for the considerations aforesayde, a further
respyte was gyuen to them unwitting, and a reprivie was
sente by M. Mackwilliams for a tyme if neede were. In
the meane tyme, (that is to wit upon the Saturday morning) the constant report goeth, that as certayne menne
came talking through Newgate, one happened to speake
lowde of the Gallowes that was sette up, and of the
greatnesse and strongnesse of the same, saying it would
holde them bothe and moe, the sounde of whiche wordes
did so pierce into the watchfull eares of mistresse Saunders, who lay nearehand, that being striken to the heart
with the horror of the present death whiche she looked for
that day, she wente immediatly to mistresse Drewrie, and
telling hir that she knew certainly by the wordes whiche
she had hearde, that they should by all likelyhode be
executed that day, asked hir if she would stand to hyr
former promise. But mistresse Drewrie after better con-

sideration of hir selfe, counsayled hir to fell to playne
and simple dealing: telling hir, that for hir owne parte
she was fully determined not to dissemble any longer, nor
to hazarde hir owne soule eternally for the safetie of 'an
other bodies temporall life. Then Mistresse Saunders,
who had determined to acknowledge nothing against hir
selfe, so long as she might be in any hope of life, howbeit
that shee always purposed to utter the truth whensoever
she should come to the instant of death, as she hir self
confessed afterward: being striken both with feare & remorse, did by the advise of M. Cole, (who laboured very
earnestly with hir to bryng hir to repentance, and was
come to hir very early that mornyng, bicause it was
thought they shoulde haue bene executed presently) sendt
for the Deane of Poules agayne, and bewayling hir
former stubburnes, declared unto him and M. Cole, M.
Charke, and M. Yong, that she had giuen hir consent and
procurement to hir husbandes death, through unlawfull
luste and lyking that shee had to Browne, confessing
hir sinfulnesse of lyfe committed with him: and humbly
submitting hir selfe to hir deserved punishment, besought
them of spirituall comforte and councell: which thing
they were glad to perceyve, and thereupon employed
their travel to do them good, and laboured very paine-
fully to instruct them aright: for (God wote) they found
all the three prysoners very rawe & ignorant in all things
perteyning to God and to their soule health, yea and even
in the very principles of the Christen Religion. Neverthelesse, through Gods good workyng with their labour,
they recovered them out of Sathans kingdome unto
Christe, in somuche that besides their voluntary acknowl-

174

edging of their late heynous facte, they also detested the
former sinfulnesse of their lyfe, and willingly yelded to
the death whiche they had shunned, uttering such certayne
tokens of theyr unfayned repentance by all kinde of modestie and meekenesse, as no greater coulde be devised. For
Mistresse Saunders the same daye sente for hir husbandes
brothers and theyr wives, and kinsfolke that were in the
towne, which came unto hyr the day before hir death: in
whose presence shee kneeling mildely on hir knees, with
abundance of sorowfull teares, desired them of forgive-
nesse for bereving them of theyr deere brother & friende:
whereunto M. Saunders the Lawyer in the name of them
al answered, that as they were very sory both for the
losse of theyr friende, and also for hyr heinous fault, so
they hartily forgave hir, and in token thereof kneeled
downe altogither, praying to God with hir and for hir,
that he also would remitte hir sinne.

Besides this pitiful submission, she also bewayled hir
offence towardes hir owne kinred, whome she had stayned
by hir trespasse, and towardes the whole worlde, whome
she had offended by hir crime, but especially hir children,
whome she had not onely berefte both of father and
mother, but also left them a coarsie and shame. Wherefore, after exhortation giuen to suche of them as were of
any capacitie and discretion, that they should feare God,
and learne by hir fall to avoyde sinne: shee gaue eche of
those a booke of M. Bradfordes meditations, wherein she
desired the foresayd three preachers to write some admonition as they thought good: Whiche done, she subscribed
them with these words: Your sorowfull mother Anne
Saunders. And so blessing them in the name of God and

of our Saviour Jesus Christ, shee sent them away out of hir sorowfull sight, & gaue hir selfe wholly to the setting of hyr grieved heart to the quiet receyving of the bitter cup, whiche she dranke of the next day, as hath bene tolde before. Howbeit, without doubt, to hir everlasting comfort.

And mistresse Drewrie no lesse carefull of hir own estate, besides hir humble repentaunce in the pryson, and hir earnest desiryng of the people to pray for hir selfe, and the others with hir as they came towarde execution, did uppon the Carte not onely confesse hir guiltinesse of the facte, as mistresse Sanders had done, but also with great lowlinesse and reverence, firste kneeling downe towardes the Earle of Bedforde and other noble men that were on horsebacke on the East side of the stage, tooke it upon hir death, that whereas it had bene reported of hir that she had poysoned hir late husbande Maister Drewrie, and dealt with witchcraft and sorcerie, and also appeached diverse Merchante mens wives of dissolute and unchast living, shee had done none of all those things, but was utterly cleare both to GOD and the worlde of all suche manner of dealing. And then with lyke obeysaunce, turning hir selfe to the Earle of Darbie, who was in a chamber behinde hir, she protested unto him before God, that whereas shee had bene reported to haue bene the cause of separation betwixte him and my Ladie his wife: She neyther procured nor consented to any suche thing. But otherwise, whereas in the time of hir service in his house, she had offended him, in neglecting or contemning hir duetie, she acknowledged hir faulte, and besought him for Gods sake to forgive hir: who very honourably and even

176

with teares accepted hir submission, and openly protested him selfe to pray hartily to God for hir.

Hir servaunt also, hauing openly acknowledged his offence, kneeled meekely downe, praying severally with a preacher, as eche of them had done at their firste comming to the place. Whiche done, they were all put in a readinesse by the executioner, and at one instant (by drawing away the Carte whereon they stoode) were sent togither out of this worlde unto God.

And Browne also, a good while before, during the time of his imprisonment, comming to a better minde than he had bene of in time past, confessed that he had not heretofore frequented Sermons, nor receyved the holy sacrament, nor used any calling upon God, private or publike, nor giuen himself to reading of holy Scripture, or any bookes of godlinesse: but had altogither followed the appetites and lustes of his sinfull fleshe, even with greedinesse and outragious contempt both of God and man. Neverthelesse God was so good unto him, & schooled him so well in that shorte time of imprisonment, as he closed up his life with a marvellous apparance of heartie repentance, constant trust in Gods mercy through Jesus Christe, and willingnesse to forsake this miserable worlde.

Nowe remayneth to shewe what is to be gathered of this terrible example, and howe wee ought to applie the same to our owne behoofe. Fyrste I note with S. Paule, that when menne regarde not to knowe God, or not to honour him when they knowe hym: God giueth them over to their owne lustes so as they runne on from sinne to sinne, and from mischiefe to mischiefe, to do suche things as are shameful and odious, even in the sight of the

worlde, to their owne unavoydable perils. And when the
measure of their iniquitie is filled up, there is no way for
them to escape the justice of God, whiche they haue provoked. In somuch, that if they might eschue al bodily
punishment: yet the very hell of their owne conscience
woulde prosecute them, and the sting of theyr minde
would be a continuall pryson, torment, and torture to
them, where soever they wente. Againe on the other side,
wee muste marke the infinite greatnesse of Gods wisedome and mercie, who perceyving the perverse wilfulnesse
of mans froward nature to sinning, suffreth men sometimes to runne so long upon the bridle, till it seeme to
themselves, that they may safely do what they liste, and
to the worlde, that they be past recoverie unto goodnesse:
and yet in the ende catching them in theyr chiefpride, he
rayseth them by their overthrowe, amendeth them by
their wickednesse, and revyveth them by their death, in
suche wise blotting out the stayne of their former filth,
that theyr darkenesse is turned into lighte, and theyr terrour to their comforte. Moreover, when God bringeth
suche matters upon the stage, unto the open face of the
worlde, it is not to the intent that men shoulde gaze and
wonder at the persons, as byrdes doe at an Owle, not that
they shoulde delight themselves and others with the fond
and peradventure sinister reporting of them, not upbrayde
the whole stocke and kinrede with the faulte of the offenders: no surely, God meaneth no such thing. His purpose
is, that the execution of his judgementes, shoulde by the
terrour of the outwarde sight of the example, drive us
to the inwarde consideration of our selves. Behold, we
be all made of the same moulde, printed with the same

178

stampe, & indued with the same nature that the offenders are. Wee be the impes of the olde Adam, and the venim of sinne which he receyved from the old Serpent, is shedde into us all, and worketh effectually in us all. Such as the roots is, such are the braunches, & the twigges of a thorne or bramble can beare no grapes. That we stande, it is the benefite of Gods grace, and not the goodnesse of our nature, nor ye strength of our owne will. That they are falne, it was of frayltie: where from we be no more privileged than they: and that shoulde wee oversoone perceyve by experience, if we were lefte to our selves. Hee that looketh severely into other mens faultes, is lightly blynde in his owne: and hee that eyther upbraydeth the repentaunt that hath receyved punishement, or reprocheth the kinred or ofspryng with the fault of the auncester or alye, howe great soever the same hath bene: sheweth him selfe not to haue any remorse of his owne sinnes, nor to remember that he him selfe also is a man: but (whiche thing he would little thinke) he fully matcheth the crime of the misdoer, if he do not surmount by his presumptuousnesse.

When it was tolde our Saviour Christe that Pylate had myngled the bloud of certayne men with theyr owne Sacrifice, what answeare made he? Did he deteste the offenders? Did he exclame against their doings? Did hee exaggerate the faulte of the one, or the crueltie of the other? No. But framing and applying the example to the reformation of the hearer, suppose ye (sayde he) that those Galileans were greater sinners than all the other Galileans, bycause they suffered suche punishment? I tell you nay: but except ye repent, ye shall all likewise perish. Or thinke ye that those eighten on whom ye towre in Silo fell, and slewe them, were sinners above all that dwelt in Hierusalem? I tell you nay: but except ye repent, ye shall all perishe likewise. Let us applie this to our present purpose. Were those whom we saw justly executed in Smithfielde, greater sinners than all other English people? were they greater sinners than al Londoners? Were they greater sinners than all that looked upon them? No verily: but excepte their example leade us to repentance, we shall all of us come to as sore punishment in this worlde, or else to sorer in the worlde to come. Their faults came into the open Theatre, and therefore seemed the greater to our eyes, & surely they were great in deede: neyther are ours the lesse, bycause they lie hidden in the covert of our heart, God the searcher of al secretes seeth them, and if he list he can also discover them. He hath shewed in some, what all of us deserve, to provoke us also to repentance, that all of us might haue mercie at hys hande, and shewe mercy one to another, and with one mouth and one heart glorifie his goodnesse. It is sayde by the Prophete Samuell, that disobedience is as the sinne of Witchcraft. Let every of us looke into himself (but first let him put on the spectacles of Gods Lawe, and carie the light of Gods worde with him) and he shall see such a gulfe of disobedience in himselfe, as he may well thinke there is none offender but himselfe. I say not this as a cloaker of offences, that white shoulde not be called whyte, and blacke, blacke: or as a patrone of misdoers, that they should not haue their deserved hire: but to represse our hastie judgements and uncharitable speeches, that wee might both detest wickednesse with

180

perfect hatred, and rue the persons with Christen modestie: knowing that with what measure we met unto others,
with the same shall it be moten to us agayne.

Finally, let all folkes both maried and unmaried, learne
hereby to possesse and keepe theyr vessell in honestie and
cleannesse. For if the knot betweene man & wife (which
ought to be inseparable) be once broken, it is seldom or
never knit agayne. And though it be, yet is not the wound
throughly healed, but there appeareth some skarre ever
after. But if the sore ranckle and fester inwardly (as commonly it doth, except the more grace of God be) in the
ende it bursteth forth to the destruction or hurt of bothe
parties, not lightly without great harme to others also
besides themselves, as we see by this example. For when
the body whiche was dedicated to God to be his Temple
and Tabernacle of his holy spirite, is become the sinke of
sinne and cage of uncleannesse, the Devil ceasseth not to
dryve the parties still headlong unto naughtinesse, till
they be falne eyther into open shame and daunger of temporall lawe: or into damnable destruction both of body
and soule, according as Salomon in his Proverbes sayth,
that the steps of a harlotte leade down unto death, and
hir feete pierce even unto Hell. Therefore good reader,
so heare and read this present example, as the same may
turne to the bettering of thy state, and not to occasion of
slaunder, nor the hurte of thine owne conscience, nor to
the offence of thy Christian brethren.

Farewell.

Arthur Golding.

Anne Saunders confession as she spake
it at the place of execution.

Good people I am come hyther to dye the death, whereunto I am adjudged, as worthily and as deservedly as ever dyed any: I had a good husband, by whom I had many children, with whome I lived in wealth, & might haue done still, had not the Devill kindled in my hearte, first the hellish firebrande of unlawfull lust, & afterwarde a murtherous intent to procure my sayde husbande to be bereved of his lyfe, whiche was also by my wicked meanes accomplished, as to the worlde is knowne. And as I woulde if he coulde heare me, if it might be, prostrate upon the grounde, at my husbandes feete, aske mercy with plentifull teares of him, so that whiche I maye and I ought to do, I aske mercy of God, I aske mercie of all men and women of the worlde, whom by my deede & example I haue offended: and especially I bewayle my husbande, & aske mercie of my children whom I haue bereaved of so good a father, I aske mercy of his kindred and friendes whome I haue hurt, and of all my frendes and kindred, of whom I am abashed and ashamed: and beyng of my selfe unworthy of pittie, yet I besech them all, and you all, and all the whole world even for Gods sake, and for our saviour Christes sake to forgiue me. And I thanke God with my whole hart, that hee hath not suffred me to haue the reyne and bridle of sinning giuen me at my will, to the daunger of my eternall damnation, but that he hath found out my sin, and brought me to punishment in this world, by his fatherly correction, to amend, to spare, and save me in the worlde to come: & I beseeche him graunte mee his heavenly grace, that all who do beholde or shall heare of my death, may by the example thereof be frayed from like sinning. And I beseeche you all to pray for me and with me.

The Prayer whiche was
sayd by Anne Saunders at the place
of execution, the copie whereof she delivered unto the right honorable the
Earle of Bedford.

As I doe confesse with great sorrow (O deare father) that I haue grevously, and oftentimes sinned against heaven and against thee, and am unworthy to be called thy daughter, so (O deare Father) I acknowledge thy mercy, thy grace and love towardes mee, moste wretched sinner, offred me in my Lorde and saviour Jesus Christ, in whome thou giuest me an hearte to repent. And by repentaunce hast put away my sinnes, and throwne them into the bottome of the Sea: O deare Father encrease and continue this grace untill the ende, and in the ende. I testifie this day (O Lorde my God) thy love, O Lorde, thy saving health is lyfe everlasting, and joy without ende: and bycause thou hast touched my sinful heart with the displeasure of my sinne, and with a desire of thy king-dome, O deare father, for thy Christes sake, as I hope thou wilt, so I beseeche thee to finishe that good worke in me. Suffer me not, mercifull and loving father, to be troubled with death when it layeth holde on me: nor with the love of lyfe, when it shall be taken away. O Lord, now as thou hast, so still lift up my soule as it were with an Eagles winges unto Heaven, there to beholde thee. Lorde into thy hands I commit my body, that it be not troubled in death, and my soule, that it see not damnation. Come Lorde Jesu, come assist me with thy holy spirite, a weake woman in a strong battell, come Lord Jesu, come quickly, save thy handemayde that put-

183

teth hir trust in thee, behold me in Christ, receyve me in Christe, in whose name I pray saying. Our Father. &c.

Anne Saunders dying to the worlde, and living to God.

After this she sayd also a godly Prayer out of the Service booke whiche is used to be sayd at the houre of death.

His Best Known Original Work

The best known of his original works is his discourse on the earthquake of 1580. This event attracted attention out of all proportion to its destructiveness, as but two persons were killed and the wrecking of buildings was not very great. It was not the first earthquake known in England, but was generally regarded as something supernatural. Golding was not the only one to write about it. Abraham Fleming wrote that "six noted poets (including Golding) had written about it. Golding took the view that it was a direct warning from the Almighty.

Opposite is the title page (and two pages beyond) the first page of this work, reproduced from the copy in the British Museum. Following is the complete text in modern type for easy reading.

The Discourse on the Earthquake

Many and wonderfull wayes (good Christian Reader) hathe God in all ages most mercifullye called all men to the knowledge of themselves, and to the amendemente of their Religion and conversation, before he have layd his heavy hande in wrathfull dyspleasure upon them. And this order of dealing he observeth, not onely towardes his owne deare children, but also even towardes the

184

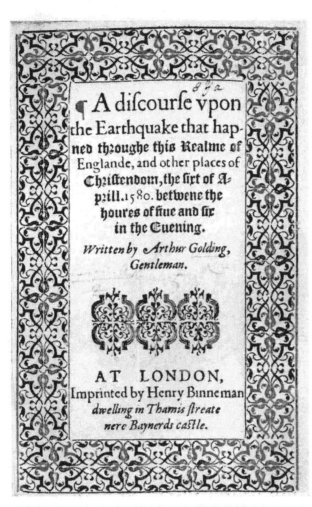

¶ A difcourfe vpon the Earthquake that hapned throughe this Realme of
Englande, and other places of
Chriftendom, the fixt of A-
prill.1580. betwene the
houres of fiue and fix
in the Euening.

*Written by Arthur Golding,
Gentleman.*

AT LONDON,
Imprinted by Henry Binneman
*dwelling in Thamis ftreate
nere Baynerds caftle.*

TITLE PAGE. DISCOURSE ON THE EARTHQUAKE

From the copy in the British Museum.

wicked and castawayes: to the intente, that the one sorte
tourning from their former sinnes, and becomming the
warer al their life after, should glorifie him the more for
his goodnesse in not suffring them to continue in their
sinnes unreformed, to their destruction: and that the other
sorte shoulde be made utterly unexcusable for their wyl-
ful persisting in the stubbornesse of their harde and fro-
warde heartes, against all his friendlie and fatherlie
admontions.

He called Cayne to repentance, before he punished him
for shedding his brothers bloud, and gave him a long time
to have bethought himselfe in.

He warned the olde Worlde a hundred years and more,
before he brought the floud upon the Earth.

He chastized the Children of Israel divers wayes, ere
he destroied them in the wildernesse.

He sent Hornets and wilde Beastes, as foregoers of his
hoste, into the lande of Canaan, before he rooted oute the
inhabiters therof.

He punished not David for his murder and adultery,
untill he had first admonished him by his Prophet.

He removed not the Israelits into captivitie, until all
the warnings of his Prophets, and all the former corrections which he had used in vayne to reforme them, did
shew them to be utterly paste hope of amendment.

Before the last destruction of Jerusalem, there wente
innumerable signes, tokens, and wonders.

Finally, God never poured out his grievous displeasure and wrath uppon any Nation, Realme, Citie, Kingdome, State, or Countrey, but he gave some notable forewarning thereof by some dreadfull wonder.

185

To let passe the examples of forreine Nations, which are many and terrible: what plagues, pestilences, famines, diseases, tempests, overflowing of waters both salte and freshe, and a number of other most prodigeous tokens happened successively long time together, before the displacing of the Britons by the hands of our auncestors, for their neglecting of Gods word preached and planted many hundred yeres among them. Likewise, what great warnings did God give to our forefathers, in divers Princes reignes, before the alteration of the State, both by the Danes, and also by William the Conqueror. Againe, even in these our dayes, how manifestly hath God threatned, and still doth threaten our contempt of his holy Religion, and our securitie and fond sleeping in sinne, shewing us evident tokens of his just displeasure neere at hande, both abroade and at home.

I will not speake of the great civill Warres, nor of the horrible and unnaturall massacres of good men, betrayde under the holyest pretences, which have bin of late yeares in the Countreys bordering upon us: because such dealings being pleasant to suche as seeke bloud, are taken for no wonders. Neyther will I stande uppon the rehearsall of the strange things that befell in the Realme of Naples in the yeare 1566, nor of the Earthquake, whereby a greate part of the Citie Ferrara in Italy was destroyed in the yeare 1570, or of the miraculous sights that were seene in France about Mountpellier, the yeare 1573, or of the like terrible sight that appeared little more than a yeare ago at Prage the chiefe Citie of Boemia: nor of divers other things whiche have hapned in forraine Countreys within the compasse of these fewe yeares: bycause it will per-

Any and wonderfull wayes (good Chꝛistiā Reader) hathe God in all ages most mercifullye called all men to the knowledge of themselues, and to the amendemente of their Religion and conuersation, befoꝛe he haue layd his heauy hande in wꝛathfull dyspleasure vpon them. And this oꝛder of dealing he obserueth, not onely towardes his owne deare childꝛen, but also euen towardes the wicked and castawayes: to the intente, that the one soꝛte tourning from their foꝛmer sinnes, and becomming the warer al their life after, sholo gloꝛifie him the moꝛe foꝛ his goodnesse in not suffring them to continue in their sinnes vnrefoꝛmed, to their destruction; and that the other soꝛte shoulde be

A.ij.   made

FIRST PAGE. DISCOURSE ON THE
EARTHQUAKE

From the copy in the British Museum.

chance bee thought, that those tokens concerne the Countreys where they befell, not us.

Well, I will not say, That whatsoever things haue bin written aforetimes, were written for our learning, that wee might learne to beware by other mens harmes.

We have signes and tokens ynow at home, if we can use them to our benefite.

What shall we say to the sore Famine whiche hapned in the time of oure late soveraigne Lady Queene Mary, whiche was so greate, that men were faine to make bread of Acornes, and foode of Ferne rootes; or to the perticular Earthquake, in the time of oure most gratious soveraigne Lady that now is, which transposed the boundes of mens groundes, and turned a Churche to the cleane contrarie situation: or to the monstrous birthes both of Children and Cattell: or to the unseasonablenesse of the seasons of some yeares, altering (after a sort) Sommer into Winter. and Winter into Sommer; or to the wonderfull new Starre so long time fixed in the heaven; or to the strange appeerings of Comets, the often Eclipses of Sunne and Moone, the great and strange fashioned lights seene in the firmament in the night times, the suddaine falling, and unwonted abiding of unmeasurable abundance of Snow, the excessive and untimely raynes and overflowing of waters, the greatnesse and sharpe continuance of sore frostes, and many other such wonderfull things, one following in anothers necke? Shall we say that none of these also do concerne us? or rather more truly, that bycause they be gone and past (Due to over-great securitie and blindnesse of heart) we haue cleane forgotten them, or at leastwise make no great accompt of them, according to our

187

common proverb, that a wonder lasteth with us but nine dayes.

Therefore, least we should want eyther proofe of the certaintie of Gods irrevocable judgements, or argument of his continuall mercifull dealing towards us, or matter wherewith to convicte us of our excessive unthankefulnesse: beholde, he sendeth us now lastly this Earthquake ye befel ye sixt day of this month, not so hurtful in present operation, as terrible in signification of things to come. For the tryed experience of all ages teacheth us, and the writings of the wise and lerned (specially of holie Scripture) do assuredly witnes unto us, that such tokens are infallible forewarnings of Gods sore displeasure for sinne, & of his just plagues for the same, where amendement of lyfe ensueth not.

And although there bee peradventure some, which (to keepe themselves and others from the due looking back into the time earst misspent, and to foade [1] them still in the vanities of this worlde, least they should see their own wretchednesse, and seeke to shunne Gods vengeance at hande) wil not sticke to deface the apparent working of God, by ascribing this miracle to some ordinarie causes in nature: Yet notwithstanding to the godlie and weldisposed which look advisedly into the matter, pondering the manner of this Earthquake throughly, and considering the manner of our dealings from the late restitution of the Gospell unto this day, and conferring the same wyth the manner of Gods favorable dealing wyth us, and with his ordinary dealing in cases where his truthe hath bin planted & groweth to bee contemned: it must

[1] To beguile with show of kindness (Old English).

188

needes appeare to bee the very finger of God, and as a messenger of the miseries due to such defects.

For, firste of all, whereas naturally Earthquakes are sayde to be engendred by winde gotten into the bowels of the earth, or by vapors bredde and enclosed within the hollowe caves of the earth, where, by their stryving and struggling of themselves to get oute, or being haled outwarde by the heate and operation of the Sun, they shake the earth for want of sufficient vent to issue out at: If this Earthquake has rysen of such causes, it coulde not have bin so universall, bicause there are many places in this Realme, which by reason of their substancial soundnesse and massie firmnesses, are not to bee pierced by any windes fro wythout, nor haue any hollowenesse wherein to conceive and breede any such aboundance of vapors, specially in places farre distant from the Sea, or from Rivers, moores, marishes, fennes, or light & opensoyles.

Neyther coulde it haue bene in so many places universally at one instant both by sea and lande. For the striving therof within the grounde, taking his beginning at some certaine place, and proceeding forwarde to get a vent, would have required same space of time to have attained to so many places so farre off, or else have broken out with great furie in some place that had bin weakest.

Againe, whereas in Earthquakes that proceede of naturall causes, certaine signes and tokens are reported to go before them, as, a tempestuous working and raging of the sea, the wether being fair, temperate, and unwindie, calmenesse of the aire matched with great colde: dimnesse of the Sunne for certaine dayes afore: long and thinne strakes of cloudes appearing after the setting of the Sun, the weather being otherwise cleere: the troublednesse of water even in the deepest welles, yeilding moreover an infected and stinking savour: and lastly, greate and terrible sounds in the earth, like the noise of gronings or thunderings, as wel afore as after the quaking: We finde not that any such foretoken happened against the coming of this Earthquake. And, therefore we may well conclude (though there were none other reason to move us) that this miracle proceeded not of the course of any naturall causes, but of Gods only determinate purpose, who maketh even the verye foundations and pillers of the earthe to shake, the mountaines to melte lyke wax, and the seas to dry up and to becom as a drie field, when he listeth to shewe the greatenesse of his glorious power, in uttering his heavy displeasure against sinne.

But putte the case that some naturall causes or secrete influences had their ordinarie operations in this Earthquake, whereof notwithstanding there is not any sufficient likelyhode: shall we so gaze upon the meane causes, that we, shal forget or let slip the chiefe & principall causes? Knowe we not (after so long hearing and pretelling of the Gospel) that a sparrow lighteth not on the ground without Gods providence? That the neglecting of his loving kindenesse, and the continuing in sin without amendement, provoke his vengeance? And yet that he of his owne fatherlie free goodnesse, doth ever give warning before he stryketh? Surely we can not but know it, yea and see it too, unlesse the God of this worlde have so blynded our eyes, that we will not see it. For it is daylie and almoste hourely tolde us by the Ministers of his

190

word, and the Byble lyes always open for us to reade it ourselves, that as the onely originall cause and welspring of al plagues and punishmentes is sin: to the plagues and punishmentes themselves, and the orderlie disposing, directing, and guiding of all causes to their due endes & effectes, is the onely worke of God, who to make all offendors unexcusable (as I sayde before) doth often cause even the very Elements and senselesse creatures, to foreshow in most terrible maner even by their naturall operations, the approaching of his just vengeance. And truly, as it is sayde in the Psalme, their speaking and talking unto us, is not so softly and whysperingly, as that the voyces of them can not be hearde: but contrarywise, they be so loud in our eares, so manifest to our eyes, and so sensible to oure feeling: that (unlesse we bee stonie and steelie hearted, or given over to a leude minde,) they cannot but bee grievous to our heartes, and terrible to oure consciences.

Nowe then, shall we thinke this rare and unaccustomed miracle, suche as no man lyving nor none of our forefathers hath ever seene or hearde of, to be a thing of no importance, as hapning by chance, or grounded upon some naturall causes: and not rather as a messenger and summoner of us to the dreadful Judgment seate of the almightie & everliving God?

Let us enter into ourselves, and examine our time paste. Since the sharpe tryall which G O D made of us in the raigne of Queene Marie, (at which time we vowed all obedience to G O D, if he woulde voutchsafe to deliver us againe from the bondage of the Romishe Anti-chryst, into the libertie of the Gospell of his sonne Jesus Chryste) he hearkening effectually to our requestes, hath given us a long resting and refreshing-time, blessed with innumerable benefites both of body and soule: For peace, health, and plentie of al things necessarie for the life of man, we have had a golden worlde above all the rest of oure neyghbours rounde aboute us.

The worde of truth hath bin preached unto us earely and late without lette or disturbance. And because our prosperitie hath made us to play the wanton chidren against God, he hath chastized us in the meane season with many fatherlie corrections.

Wee haue bin taught, instructed, exhorted, encouraged, allured, entreated, reprooved, rebuked, upbrayded, warned, threatned, nurtured, and chastized. To be shorte, there is not that means whereby we might be won to the obeying and loving of oure God whether it were by favourable mildnesse or moderate rigor, but he hath ministred the same most mercifully and seasonably unto us. And what are we the better for all this?

Have we so profited in this schole, that of Covetous we bee become Liberall? of Proude and Envious, meek and Lowly? of Leacherous, Chaste? of Gluttons, Measurable feeders? of Drunkards, Sober? of Wrathfull and testie, Milde and patient? of Cruel and hard hearted, Pitifull and gentle? of Oppressors, Relievers? and of Irreligious, Servisable to G O D?

Have we so put off the olde man, & so clothed ourselves with the new, in living sincerely according to ye doctrine we professe, that neyther the enimies of Chrystes Church, nor our owne consciences can reprove us? Then need we not to be afrayde of any signes from the Heaven above,

192

nor of any tokens fro the earth beneath: for wee haue builded our houses wysely upon the rocke, which neither wind, water, nor Earthquake, no nor Sathan himself with al his Fiends can shake downe or empaire.

But alas, it is farre otherwise with us: we haue growen in godliness as the Moone doth in light when she is past the full. For who sees not the emulation that remaynes stil among us for excesse of apparell, fare, and building? Who perceiveth not the disdaine of superiors to their inferiors, the grudge and heartburning of inferiors towardes their superiors, and the want of love in al states one towardes another?

Who complayneth not of corruption in Officers, yea, even in Officers of Justice and ministers of the Lawe? Is it not a common byworde (but I hope not true though comon) that as a man is frended, so the lawe is ended?

In Youth there was never like loocenesse and untimelie libertie, nor in Age like unstayednesse & want of dyscretion, nor the like carelessnesse of duety in eyther towardes other.

The Boye mateth the Man of aged gravity, and is comended for that which he deserveth to be beaten for.

Servants are become maysterlike, & fellowes with Maysters: and Maysters unable to maister their owne affections, are become servants to other folkes servantes, yea and to their owne servantes too.

Men have taken up the garish attire & nice behavior of Women and Women transformed from their own kinde, have gotten up the apparell and stomackes [2] of men: &

[2] A kind of waistcoat worn by men.

193

as for honest and modest shamefullnesse the preferrer of all Vertues, it is so highly misliked, that it is thoughte of some folkes scarce tollerable in children.

Hatred, malice, disdaine, and desire of revenge for the weighte of a feather, are the vertues of our yong Gentlemen in commendation of their manhoods and valiantnesse.

Deepe Dissimulation and Flatterie are counted Courtlie behavior: Mighte overcommeth right: and Truthe is troden under foote.

Idlenesse & Pride bring dayly infinite numbers to that point, that they had rather rob and be shamefully hanged, than labour and live with honesty.

Usurie the consumer of private states, and the confounder of Common weales, is become a common (and in some mens opinions comendable) trade to live by.

Faithfulnesse is fledde into exile, and falshode vaunteth himself in his place, til he have gotten great summes of money into his hands, that hee maye playe the Bankeroute, to the undoing of such as trust him.

The Saboth dayes and holy dayes ordayned for the hearing of Gods word to the reformation of our lives, for the administration & receiving of the Sacramentes to our comfort, for the seeking of all things behovefull for bodye or soule at Gods hande by Prayer, for the mynding of his benefites and to yielde praise and thankes unto him for the same, and finally, for the speciall occupying of ourselves in all spiritual exercizes: is spent full heathenishly, in taverning, tipling, gaming, playing, & beholding of Beare-baytings and Stageplayes, to the utter dishonor of GOD, impeachment of all godlynesse, and unnecessarie

194

consuming of mennes substances which ought to be better employed.

The wante of orderly Discipline and Catechizing, hath eyther sent great numbers both olde and yong backe again into Papistrie, or let them runne loose into godlesse Atheisme.

And wolde God that we which call others to obedience, shewing them the way, and rebuking their vices: mighte not be justly charged to bee as trumpets, which with their sound encourage other men to the battell but fight not themselves. Nay would God that in al degrees, some suche as ought to be Lanternes of light and Ringleaders to Vertue, were not infecters of others by their evill example.

I feare me that if the Prophete were heere alyve, he would tell us hee sometime tolde the Jewes, that from the crowne of our head to the sole of our foot, there is no whole or sounde parte in oure bodie, but that al is ful of sores, blaines, and botches. Thinke we then that such doing shal scape unpunished, or such buildings stande unshaken? Well may we deceive ourselves in to hoping: but God deceiveth not, neyther is deceyved.

It is wrytten, that every plant which our heavenlie Father hath not planted, shal be plucked up by the rootes, and that every tree which beareth not good fruite, shall be cut downe and cast into the fire.

The Axe is layde to the roote of the tree: and the longer that Gods vengeance is in comming, the sorer it smyteth when it is come. Terrible and moste true is this saying of his by the mouth of Salomon: For as much as I have called, and you have refused: and I have stretched oute my handes, and you have not regarded it: but have

195

despised al my counsel, and set my correction at nought: therefore will I also laugh at your destruction, and mock yee when the thing that yee feare commeth upon you: even when the thing that yee be afrayde of breaketh in upon you like a storme, and your miserie like a tempest. When trouble and heaviness come upon you on all sides: then shall ye call upon me, but I wil not answere you, yee shal seeke me early, but yee shall not finde me: even because yee hated knowledge, and didde not chooze the feare of the Lorde. Ye would none of my counsell, but hated my correction: and therfore shal ye eat the fruit of your owne ways, and be filled with your own inventions. Soothly it is a dreadful thing to fall into the handes of the Lorde. For as he is merciful, so is he also just, and in all his determinations he is utterly unchangeable. And (as the Prophet Jeremie sayeth) When sentence is once gone forth of his presence, it shal not retourne without performance.

Wherfore let us not be as horsses and Mules whiche have no understanding: neyther let us tarrie till Judgment be sent forth unto victorie. But let us consider the time of our visitation, and while we have time, let us use it to our benefit.

So long as God calleth unto us, so long as he entreteth us, so long as he techeth, allureth, exhorteth or warneth us, yea so long as he doeth as yet but threaten us: so long the gate is stil open for us, so as he will heare us if we call, and be founde of us if we seeke him. But if he once hold his peace, and begin to smite, then it is too late to call backe his hande, our crying wil not boote us.

Therefore while we have respite, and while it is called

196

today, let us not harden our hartes as in the provocation, and as in the day of Temptation in the wildernesse, but let us hearken to his voyce, & forsaking the lustes and the wicked imaginations and devices of our own harts, let us turne to the Lorde our God wyth harty repentaunce and unfeyned amendment of life, least (beside other meaner plagues both of bodye and minde) our Candlesticke be removed, our light quenched, Christs Gospel taken from us, and we for our unthankefulnesse be caste out with our children into utter darkenesse: and in ye terrible day of Judgement heare this dreadful sentence of the just Judge pronounced against us: Depart from me ye workers of wickednesse, which hardened your harts against me and made your faces as hard as brasse, at such time as my long sufferaunce wayted for you, provoking you by mildenesse and patience to amendement.

FINIS

The reporte of the
said Earthquake, and
howe it beganne.

On Easter Wednesdaye, beeing the sixte of Aprill. 1580. somewhat before six of the clocke in the afternoone, happened thys greate Earthquake whereof this discourse treateth: I meane not greate in respecte of long continuance of time, for (God be thanked) it continued little above a minute of an houre, rather shaking Gods rod at us, than smiting us according to oure desertes: Nor yet in respecte of any greate hurte done by it within thys Realme: For, although it shooke all houses, castles, churches, and buildings, every where as it wente, and put them in danger of ruine: yet within this Realme (praysed be our Savior Jesus Christe for it) it overthrewe fewe or none that I have yet hearde of, saving certaine stones, chimneys, walles, and Pinacles, a highe buildings, bothe in this Cittie and in divers other places: Neyther doe I heare of anye Christen people that received bodily hurte by it, saving two children in London, a boye and a girle, being at Sermon among a great number of people in Christs churche by Newgate market, of whome the boy named Thomas Gray, was slaine out of hand, with the fall of a stone shaken downe from the roofe of the Church: and the girle (whose name was Mabell Everite) beeing sore hurt there at ye same present by like casualtie, dyed within fewe dayes after: But I terme it great in respecte of the universalnesse thereof almoste at one instant, not onelye within this Realme, but also without, where it was muche more violent, and did far more harme: and in respecte of the great terror which it then strake into al mens heartes where it came, and yet still striketh into suche as duely consider howe justely God maye be offended wyth all men for sinne, and speciallye wyth thys Realme of England, which hathe moste abundantly tasted of Gods mercy, and moste unthankfully neglected his goodnesse, whyche yet stil warneth us by thys terrible wonder, what farre more terrible punishmentes are like to lighte uppon us ere long, unlesse we amend our sinful life and conversation betimes.

Only Known Original Verse

These verses, printed as a commendatory introduction to *Barrets Alvearie* (1580), are of interest as indicating

/

1573

his patriotic desire to improve the English language and   ((
his confidence in its capabilities.

ARTHUR GOLDING TO THE READER

The plesant juice that Prime of yeere doth yeeld
In herbe, in flower, in leafe, in plant, or tree,
By natures gift abroad in frith and feeld,
Or mans deuice in gardens not so free
As faire and finelie kept, the busie Bee
    With restlesse trauell gathereth to his Hyue,
    To how great use, they knowe that knowe to thryue.

And Barret here (good Reader) doth present
A Hyue of honie to thy gentle hand,
By tract of time in painefull labor spent:
Well wrought, and brought to such perfection and
Good purpose, as (if truth be rightly scand)
    Thou are to blame, but if thou be his detter
    Of earned thankes, and fare by him the better.

How fit the Tytle of this present Booke
Doth hit the matter written in the same,
Thou shall perceiue the better if thou looke
Throughout the worke, which well doth brooke his name.
For underneath this Hiue yet small in fame,
    Of fower Tungs the flowers hyued bee,
    In one sweete iuice to serue the turne of thee.

Of truth, the skill and labour was not small
To set ech Inglish Phraze in his due place,
And for the match the Latin therewithall,
Of either Language keeping still the grace,
And orderly the Greeke to interlace,
    And last of all to ioyne the French theretoo:
    These things (I saie) requyrde no small adoo.

And furthermore right well thou mayst espie,
There lakt in him no forewardnesse of minde
To haue set downe a sownd Orthographie:
Through want whereof all good inditers find
Our Inglishe tung driuen almost out of kind,
    Dismembred, hacked, maymed, rent, and torne,
    Defaced, patched, mard, and made a skorne.

For who is he that rightly can discerne
The case, the kind, and number of the Nowne?
For my instruction gladly I would lerne,
How men might trie what writer setteth downe
The Article aright, or who doth drowne
    The Pronowne by misplacing it, as now
    Most wryters doe, and yet they marke not how.

I thinke it would a good Gramarian poze
To giue iust rules of Deriuation,
And Composition, as our writing goes.
And yet no tung of other Nation
Hath either greater grace or store of those,
    Than Inglish hath: yee would not thinke ywis
    How rich in Composition Inglishe is.

Moreouer, how shall men directly find
The Conjugation, Number, Person, Tence,
And mode of Verbes togither in their kind?
What man I praie can stand in iust defence
Of due Construction both of wordes and sence?
    And if to Verse men further will proceede,
    Which yeeldes lesse skope and asketh greater heede:

How shall a man assure true quantitie
Of time or tune? Or if he would expresse
The diffrence, and the natiue propertie,

Of brode North speech and Sowthren smoothednesse:
How might he set it downe with cumlinesse,
   Where men in writing doe so fondly dote,
   As nought is done by rule, but all by rote?

But were there once a sound Orthographie
Set out by learning and aduised skill,
(Which certesse might be done full easilie)
And then confirmed by the Souereines will,
(For else would blind and cankred custome still
   His former errors wilfully maintaine
   And bring us to his Chaos backe againe:)

No doubt but men should shortly find there is
As perfect order, as firme certeintie,
As grounded rules to trie out things amisse,
As much sweete grace, as great varietie
Of wordes and phrazes, as good quantitie
   For verse or prose in Inglish euery waie,
   As any comen Language hath this daie.

And were wee giuen as well to like our owne,
And for two clense it from the noisome weede
Of affectation which hath ouergrowne
Ungraciously the good and natiue seede,
As for to borrowe where wee have no neede:
   It would pricke neere the learned tungs in strength,
   Perchaunce and match mee some of them at length.

Wherefore good Reader yeeld they furtherance
To mend the things that yet are out of square,
Thou has a help thy purpose to aduaunce,
And meane to ease they greatest peece of care.
And he that hath done this for thy welfare,
   Upon thy freendely fauor and regard,
   May chaunce to trauell further afterward.
                 Finis.

Chapter XIV

FOUR CENTURIES OF CRITICISM

CRITICISM of Golding's work, which began contemporaneously in the sixteenth century, has continued into the twentieth. Elizabethan England hailed his translations with applause. From the time of his first translation of the first four books of the *Metamorphoses* in 1565 until his death over forty years afterward, his contemporaries expressed their admiration by flattering criticism, by imitation and, in the end, by direct literary piracy. Through the commendation runs the constant note of gratitude to one whose labors had opened the doors to literary treasures hitherto denied save to the learned. This he shared with others who were engaged in similar work, but to none came the remarkable success that attended his translation of *Ovid*, which, in a series of editions, held its preëminence for nearly sixty years.

These commendations began, at least so far as we now have record, in 1566 just after the publication of the first four books of the *Metamorphoses*. In that year T. B. (Thomas Blundeville) in some verses praised the work of his contemporaries, contrasting it, not unfavorably, with the work of Phaer (the translator of *Virgil*) then at the height of its popularity. He mentioned Jasper Heyward, the translator of Seneca's *Thyestes;* Barnaby Googe, translator of Palengenius's *Zodiake of Life,* and especially

Richard Edwards the playwright and Arthur Golding of whom he wrote

> Nor Goldinge can haue lesse renoume,
> Whych Ouid dyd translate;
> And by the thondryng of hys verse
> Hath set in chayre of state.
>
> With him also, as seemeth me,
> Our Edwards may compare;
> Who nothing gyuing place to him
> Doth syt in egall chayre.[1]

Thomas Blundeville (1522-1606) was the translator of Plutarch's *The Fruit of Foes* (1559) and *Three Moral Treatises* (1561) and later of other works from the Italian and Spanish. At the end of the century he published *The Arte of Logike*, a rendition into English of the doctrine of Aristotle.

This was strong praise for a partially completed work, but we may assume that Golding had already made a reputation which backed his admirer's good opinion. Each of the three previous years he had printed a Latin translation. In 1562 the Bucer and Phagius pamphlet, in 1563 Aretine's *History*, and in 1564 Justine's *Abridgement of Trogus Pompeius*. If these received no comment, which has come down to us, they had won him a leading place among the translators of his day, as indicated by Peend's action in abandoning a competitive translation of the *Metamorphoses*.

Comment during the next fifteen years, when he aver-

[1] Verses introductory to *The Eyght Tragedies of Seneca* entitled *Agamemnon* translated by John Studley, printed by Thos. Colwell, London, 1566.

aged more than one new book a year and the same number of re-editions of former ones, has not been preserved. In 1580, however, we find that Abraham Fleming in the preface to his tract on the earthquake of that year, entitled *A Bright Burning Beacon forwarning all wise Virgins to trim their lamps against the comming of the Bridegroome*, lists Golding as one of the "six noted poets" who had written on the same subject.[2]

In 1584 Peele in his *Arraignment of Paris*, complimented him by paraphrasing certain parts of the dedication to Leicester in his complete edition of the *Metamorphoses* in 1567.[3]

In 1586 Webbe in his *Discourse of English Poetry* strikes a high note. He says: "Equally with him (Phaer) may I well adyoine Master Arthur Golding, for hys labour in Englishing Ovids *Metamorphoses* for which gentleman, surely this country hath for many respects greatly to give God thanks: as for him which hath taken infinite paynes without ceasing, traulleth as yet indefatigably, and is addicted without society, by his continual laboure, to profit this nation and speeche in all kind of good learning.[4]

Puttenham in the *Arte of English Poesie* (1589) also couples him with Phaer. He says: "Since him (Phaer) followed Maister Arthure Golding, who with no less commendation turned into English metre the *Metamorphoses of Ovid*," and he praises both "Phaer and Golding for a

[2] Collier, J. Payne, *The Poetical Decameron*, London, 1820, Vol. I, page 117.

[3] *The Works of George Peele.* Edited by A. H. Bullen, London, 1888, Vol. I, page 18, note 4.

[4] Webbe, William, *A Discourse of English Poetry*, ed. E. Arber, London, 1870, page 34.

204

learned and well corrected verse, specially in translation cleare and very faithfully answering their authors intent." [5]

Thomas Nash in Greene's *Menophon*, which appeared in 1589, mentions Golding in the prefatory address. He says: "And in this page of praise I cannot omit aged Arthur Golding for his industrious toile in Englishing *Ouid's Metamorphoses* besides many other exquisite editions of Divinity, turned by him out of the French tongue into our own." [6] This appears to be the only mention of his work on religious subjects, which for many years had occupied most of his time. That is should come from Nash indicates that Golding was orthodox and in tune with the prevailing, or at least controlling, thought of the time.

In 1598 Meres in his *Palladis Tamia* mentions Golding as among those who "for their learned translations are of good note among us" [7] and the century closed with a bracketing of his name with that of the author of *The Faerie Queene*. In 1599 the author of *The First Booke of the Preservation of King Henry VII*, "confesses and acknowledges that we have many excellent and singular good poets in this our age, as Maister Spencer that was, Maister Gowlding, Doctor Phayer, &c." [8]

The comment of later times was more restrained. Warton in his *History of English Poetry* (1774) deals at

[5] *Arte of English Poesie*, ed. Hazelwood, London, 1811, Vol. I, pages 49 and 51.

[6] *The Life and Complete Works in Prose and Verse of Robert Greene*, collected and edited by Rev. Alexander B. Grosart, London and Aylesbury, 1881-1886, Vol. VI, page 20.

[7] *Arte of English Poesie*, ed. Hazelwood, London 1811, Vol. II, page 156.

[8] Quoted by E. Arber in his preface to Richard *Stanyhurst's Aeneis*, Westminster, 1895, pages xx and xxi.

some length with his work quoting quite copiously and sums up his estimate thus: "His style is poetical and spirited and his versification clear: his manner ornamental and diffuse, yet with sufficient observance of the original."

Mr. Sidney Lee in the *Dictionary of National Biography* (1890) says of his style that "it is full of life throughout, and at times reaches a high poetic level."

W. J. Courthope's *History of English Poetry* (1897) says: "The translation itself [*Metamorphoses*] aims simply at telling Ovid's story in a rendering of his own words, but without the slightest effort to reproduce the polish of his style. A fair sample of Golding's manner, which is indeed infinitely superior to Phaer's, will be found in the story of Pyramus and Thisbe (*Metamorphoses*, Book IX.)"

Dr. Wallace in his introduction to the reprint of Golding's translation of Beza's *A Tragedie of Abraham's Sacrifice* (1906) gives it as his opinion that "Golding was endowed with a considerable degree of real literary ability. The 'fourteener' is not a measure calculated to impress favorably a modern ear, but there are many passages in the *Metamorphoses* of which the spirited movement and the author's enthusiastic identification of himself with his subject make the reader forget that the work is not original composition. On the other hand it is inevitable in so long a piece of translation that there should be passages which are suggestive of hack-work; occasionally the metre is halting and awkward, the rhyme forced, and the translation devoid of charm." Referring particularly to the translation of *Abraham's Sacrifice* he says: "On the whole

206

the translation is a piece of excellent idiomatic English, and the noble dignity of the song of Abraham and Sara, which departs entirely from Beza's metre is not unworthy of the Elizabethan age, and may serve as an example of that rare phenomenon—a translator's surpassing his original."

The *Cambridge History of English Literature* (1909) gives him but faint praise, which, however, is shared by Ovid. It says: "The craftsmanship is neither slovenly nor distinguished. The narrative flows through its easy channel without the smallest shock of interruption. In other words, the style is rapid, fluent and monotonous. The author is never a poet and never a shirk. You may read his mellifluous lines with something of the same simple pleasure which the original gives you. Strength and energy were beyond Golding's compass and he wisely chose a poet to translate who made no demands upon qualities he did not possess. He chose a metre too, very apt for continuous narrative—the long line of fourteen syllables, and it is not strange that his contemporaries bestowed upon him their high approval." [9]

Later twentieth century criticism recalls in some degree the enthusiasm of the sixteenth.

Ezra Pound, poet and critic, author of *The ABC of Reading, Selected Poems* and many other books, in *Make It New* (London, 1934), a reconsideration of numerous pithy literary essays, makes some crisp comments on Golding's work. In *Notes on Elizabethan Classicists* he remarks:

[9] *Cambridge History of English Literature*, Cambridge, England, 1909, Vol. IV, Chapter I, page 20.

A great age of literature is perhaps always a great age of translations; or follows it. The Victorians in lesser degree had Fitzgerald, and Swinburne's Villon, and Rossetti. One is at first a little surprised at the importance which historians of Spanish poetry give to Boscan, but our histories give our own translators too little. . . . Golding was no inconsiderable poet, and the Marlowe of the translations has beauties no whit inferior to the Marlowe of original composition.

He quotes from and comments upon Turburville, Marlowe, Drant, Phaer, Surrey and others, but more freely from Golding's *Metamorphoses* and continues:

But Golding's book published before all these others will give us more matter for reverie. One wonders, in reading it, how much more of the Middle Ages was Ovid. We know well enough that they read him and loved him more than the more Tennysonian Virgil. Yet how great was Chaucer's debt to the Doctor Amoris? That we will never know. Was Chaucer's delectable style simply the first Ovid in English? Or is a fine poet ever translated until another his equal invents a new style in a later language? Can we, for our part, know our Ovid until we find him in Golding? Is there one of us so good at his Latin, and so ready in imagination that Golding will not throw upon his mind shades and glamours inherent in the original text which had for all that escaped him? Is any foreign speech ever our own, ever so full of beauty as our lingua materna (whatever lingua materna that may be). Or is not a new beauty created, an old beauty doubled when the overchange is well done? . . . But it is certain that "we" have forgotten our Ovid, "we" being the reading public, the readers of English poetry, have forgotten our Ovid since Golding went out of print.

Contrasting Golding's simple language with Milton's "passion for latinization" he continues:

Golding in the ninth year of Elizabeth can talk of "Charles his wane" in translating Ovid, but Milton's fields are "irriguous,"

(and worse, and much more notably displeasing, his clause structure is a matter of "quem's," "cui's," and "quomodo's."

Another point in defense of Golding: his constant use of "did go," "did say," etc., is not fustian and mannerism; it was contemporary speech, though in a present-day poet it is impotent affectation and definite lack of technique. I am not saying Golding is a greater poet than Milton; (footnote—1929. His Metamorphoses form possibly the most beautiful book in our | language.) these quantitative comparisons are in odium. Milton is the most unpleasant of English poets, and he has certain definite and analyzable defects. His unpleasantness is a matter of personal taste. His faults of language are subject to argument just as are the faults of any other poet's language. His popularity has been largely due to his bigotry, but there is no reason why that popular quality should be for ever a shield against criticism. His real place is nearer to Drummond of Hawthornden than to "Shakespear" and "Dante" whereto the stupidity of our forbears tried to exalt him.

His short poems are his defenders' best stronghold, and it will take some effort to show that they are better than Drummond's Phoebus Arise. In all this I am not insisting on "Charles his wane" as the sole mode of translation. I point out that Golding was endeavouring to convey the sense of the original to his readers. He names the thing of his original author, by the name most germane, familiar, homely, to his hearers. He is intent on conveying a meaning, and not on bemusing them with a rumble. And I hold that the real poet is sufficiently absorbed in his content to care more for the content than the rumble; and also that Chaucer and Golding are more likely to find the mot juste (whether or not they held any theories there-anent) than were for some centuries their successors, saving the author of Hamlet.

He concludes with a lengthy quotation from Gawine Douglas's translation of *Virgil* and remarks:

Gawine Douglas was a great poet, and Golding has never had due praise since his own contemporaries bestowed it upon him.

209

Professor Henry Burrowes Lathrop in his *Translations from the Classics into English* published as No. 35, University of Wisconsin Studies in 1933, deals quite fully, but in a more reserved and judicial style, with Golding's work. The following excerpts are from this book:

Golding's Metamorphoses stands out above all the verse translations of the period. Arthur Golding or Goldyng was a man of letters,—not an amateur giving his vacations to the work of translation,—but a diligent workman, who devoted his main energy to providing English readers with those Latin authors whom he thought it most important for them to know. The Metamorphoses was his largest and most important work, but the bulk of his translations were histories and geographies, and his primary object was to afford knowledge rather than delight.

.   .   .   .   .

Golding's version is less inadequate than Phaer's; he is a better verse-writer, and succeeds in uniting unity of form with variety. His verse, it may be remarked, grows looser as he advances in the work, either from haste or because of increased facility. He dilutes his original, partly for the sake of rhyme and meter, partly like so many authors of the time, to explain allusions. He lacks both elevation and grace. And yet his translation is the best verse translation in English before any original masterpieces existed to set a standard which the versions of the next generation were to attain.

.   .   .   .   .

Golding in his prose is as superior to his contemporaries who translated history as he is in his verse to his contemporaries who translated poetry, and for much the same characteristics. His work, it is true, is not of even quality, being in no small degree dependent on the style of his original, but it all tends definitely toward a certain type. He loosens and breaks up the long periods of his original, with an approach to the analytic type of sentence normal in English idiom. Thus although many intolerably sprawling sentences can be found in his work, they are not typical; he has some sense of the easier flow and clearer outline of the shorter period. His diction is manly and vigorous, presenting an attractive mean between the sheer dryness of Sandford or Stocker, and the slangy and picturesque freedom of Underdowne. It should be said, however, that at best the praise to be given is qualified praise—a norm of good writing for practical purposes had not been attained in his day, but he contributed his part toward developing it.

.   .   .   .   .   .

The Stoic philosophy, indeed, had been largely accepted and embodied in current Christian ethics. Here, too, as in poetry and history, Arthur Golding rendered useful service. His version of Seneca's De Beneficiis shows his usual competence; it is characterized by skillfully idiomatic ease of subordination, without confusion or rigidity, and reproduces Seneca's pointed antitheses without making them too consciously ingenious. Golding's diction is pithily characteristic of the usage of his day on its more vigorous and less artificial side, but is only occasionally very familiar, as for example in satirical passages. His book is therefore important not only in the development of a standard prose English, but in lexicography.

Chapter XV

GOLDING AND SHAKESPEARE

THE influence of Ovid upon Shakespeare was noted while he and Golding were still living. In 1589 Francis Meres wrote: "As the soule of Euphorbus was thought to live in Pythagoras so the witty soule of Ovid lives in mellifluous and honey-tongued Shakespeare."

Although there is internal evidence in the plays that Shakespeare had read Ovid in the original,[1] and it is stated that in his regular school course he had read some of the classics and at least a part of the *Metamorphoses*,[2] there is no reason to doubt that his familiarity with the poet's work was gained from Golding's translation. By the time Shakespeare was nine years old, in 1575, the *Metamorphoses* had become so popular with English readers that a new edition was issued, the first of a long series. Available all his school life, and more and more

[1] "Autolycus, in *A Winter's Tale* is Ovidian, so is Titania (another name for Diana) and Oberon, also called by Shakespeare 'King of Shadows,' and by Ovid 'Umbrarum Rex.' Titania is not the form used by Golding, who calls the lady 'Titan's Daughter,' and it follows, therefore, that 'Shakespeare' could read, and had read, the original Latin!"— Mr. Percy Allen, Shakespearean student and author, in his address at the dedication of the Golding Memorial Window.

[2] "By this time (twelve or thirteen years of age) he would have read in the ordinary course, Valerius Cato, Aesop, Mantuan, a considerable portion of Ovid's Metamorphoses, and something of Cicero, Terence and Virgil." Garnett and Gosse, *English Literature*, Vol. II, page 193.

widely distributed as he grew towards young manhood, the translation was most certainly the source from which the poet gathered his Ovidian allusions. In *English Literature and the Classics* (Oxford 1912, p. 185), S. G. Owen writes: "In one or the other of Shakespeare's plays there are allusions to every one of the fifteen books of the *Metamorphoses*. Similarity of language proves that Shakespeare frequently used Golding's noble and melodious translation."

The most notable example of this use is found in Prospero's invocation in the *Tempest*, which is made very clear from the following comparison taken from *The Plays and Poems of William Shakespeare* (Variorum edition, pages 159-162) edited by Edmond Malone, 1821.

"TEMPEST"

Act. V. Scene I.
(Before the Cell of Prospero)

Pro. Ye elves of hills, brooks, standing lakes, and groves;
    And ye, that on the sands with printless foot
    Do chase the ebbing Neptune, and do fly him,
    When he comes back; you demy-puppets, that
    By moon-shine do the green-sour ringlets make,
    Whereof the ewe not bites; and you, whose pastime
    Is to make midnight mushrooms; that rejoice
    To hear the solemn curfew; by whose aid
    (Weak masters though ye be,) I have be-dimm'd
    The noon-tide sun, call'd forth the mutinous winds
    And 'twixt the green sea and the azur'd vault
    Set roaring war: to the dread rattling thunder
    Have I given fire, and rifted Jove's stout oak
    With his own bolt: the strong-bas'd promontory

Have I made shake: and by the spurs pluck'd up
The pine and cedar: graves, at my command,
Have waked their sleepers; oped, and let them forth
By my so potent art: But this rough magick
I here abjure: and, when I have requir'd
Some heavenly musick, (which even now I do,)
To work mine end upon their senses, that
This airy charm is for, I'll break my staff
Bury it certain fathoms in the earth,
And deeper than did ever plummet sound,
I'll drown my book.

Whoever will take the trouble of comparing this whole passage with Medea's speech, as translated by Golding, will see evidently that Shakespeare copied the translation, and not the original. The particular expressions that seem to have made an impression on his mind, are printed in Italicks:

Ye ayres and windes, ye *elves of hills, of brookes,* of woodes
    alone,
Of *standing lakes,* and of the night, approche ye everych one.
Through help of whom (the crooked bankes much wondering at
    the thing)
I have compelled streames to run clear backward to their spring.
By charms I make the calm sea rough, and make the rough seas
    playne,
And cover all the skie with clouds, and *chase* them thence again.
By charmes I raise and lay the windes, and burst the viper's jaw,
And from the bowels of the earth both stones and trees do draw.
Whole woodes and forrests I remove, I *make the mountains*
    shake,
And even the earth itself to groan and fearfully to quake.
I *call up dead men from their graves,* and thee, O lightsome
    moone,
I darken oft, though beaten brass abate thy peril soone.
Our sorcerie *dimmes* the morning faire, and *darks the sun at*
    noone,

214

The flaming breath of fierie bulles ye quenched for my sake,
And caused their unwieldy neckes the bended yoke to take.
Among the earth-bred brothers you a *mortall warre did set,*
And brought asleep the dragon fell, whose eyes were never shet.

MALONE.

In *Venus and Adonis* Ovid furnished him a description. In Book VIII at line 375 of the *Metamorphoses* [*] is described the boar that Meleager killed.

His eyes did glister blood and fire, right dreadful for to see
His brawned neck, right dredful was his hair that grew so thick
With pricking points, as one of them could well by other stick.
And like a front of Armed pikes set close in battle ray,
The sturdy bristles on his back stood staring up alway.

This in *Venus and Adonis,* stanza 1041, line 619:

> On his bow-back he hath a battle set
> Of bristley pikes that ever threat his foes;
> His eyes like glow worms shine when he doth fret.
> His brawny sides with heavy bristles armed,
> Are better proof than thy spear's point can enter.

And in *Titus Andronicus,* Act IV, Scene I, Shakespeare makes Ovid the necessary peg on which to hang the unravelling of the plot. Thus:

TITUS—"Lucius, what book is that she tosseth so?"
LUCIUS—"Grandsire, 'tis Ovids Metamorphoses. My mother
gave it to me."

In the action of the play the mutilated, ravished, and speechless Lavinia indicates in the book the story of Philomel and Tereus and thus reveals the outrage.

[*] *Shakespeare's Ovid Being Arthur Golding's Translation of the Metamorphoses,* edited by W. H. D. Rouse, London, 1904.

THE END

APPENDICES

Appendix No. 1

WILL OF JOHN GOLDING OF GLEMSFORD
(*Abstract*)

IN THE name of God Amen. 27 June 1495.
John Golding of Glemsforde the elder, clothmaker, in
the Diocese of Norwich, to be buried in the churchyard above
Jesus altar on the south side in the said towne of Glemsforde.

I bequeath the high altar 13/4 and to priests, clerks and poor
folk on my burying 6/8.

I will that a chapell be made over me where I shall ly in the
said churchyard and thereto bequeath £40.

To all the four orders of Freres, i.e. Sudbury, Clare, Babwell
and Cambridge to each of them 10/- to sing Saint Gregory's
Trentall for me and my friends soules.

Item, to Johanne my wife the house I dwell in for life and
£100.

To Dan Thomas my son of Bury £40.

To William my son, house and land which I have in Poslyng-
forth at Bulley Grene and £40 and a meadow called Turpittes
and three acres called Sengeland in Glemsford.

To John my son land in Glemsford except Chambrescroft in
Netherstrete.

To John my son the younger, house in Poslingford.

To Margery Trumbill my daughter £80.

To Kath Wood my daughter £20 and land called Crosses
Land.

To Joan Hill my daughter Chamberscroft and three acres in
Pentlowe and twenty marks.

To all my spinners 12d each.

To Joan Golding daughter to William my son ten marks.

To Joan Pye daughter of William Pye of Melford ten marks.
To each of my children's children 20/-.
To my servants 3/4d each.
To the poor of Melford 6/8d.
Executors: William my son and John Golding my son the elder.
Supervisor: Joan my wife.
Proved 20 May 1497 by the executors named in the will. (P. C. C.)

The chapel for which the £40 was left was duly built. It is twenty-seven feet long by sixteen feet wide, of carved stone, with the customary flint surface filling. A hundred years ago, according to a description written in 1832 and now in the British Museum, there were still remains of the stained glass which once filled its windows. This had probably been destroyed by the Parliamentary soldiers in the Civil War. Today the windows are filled with plain glass, the chapel having been, like the church, no gainer by the repairs and "restorations" of the last century. The outer walls are in generally excellent condition, however, and close up under the eaves is a deeply cut black letter inscription in a single line, the last few words of which have disappeared through the flaking of the stone under the storms of over four hundred winters. Enough is left to make it easy to see that it read:

"John Golding and Joan his wife founded this chapel; on whose souls God have mercy."

VICARS OF BELCHAMP ST. PAUL'S

(*Parish Records*)

		Died or Resigned
Gilbertus, Sacerdos De Belcham	13 Cent. undated	
Baldock, Laurence De	1327	
London, Laurence De	1330	
Corsyn, William	Exchanged with	
Godram, Richard	1381	
Turnom, Henry	Exchanged with	
Bette, John	1408	
Fodringay, William		1423
Harwood, John	1428	March
Smethhurst, John	1428	1434
Kynton, Thomas		1443R.
Hanley, William, M.A.	1443	
Santon, William	1445	
Loker or Lockyer, John, B. D.	1483	1485
Watters or Walter, Thomas		1500D.
Lufkin, Stephen	1545	1558
Poole,		
Stevens, William		
Storer, Richard	1567	
Parminter,	1584	
Nelson, William	1588	1625
Hampton, Barnabas	1625	
Fisher, Robert	1629	
Unwin, Thomas	1667	1701

		Died or Resigned
Pemberton, Francis	1702	1729
Pemberton, Edward	1729	1780
Pemberton, Jeremy	1780	1801
Vandermeulen, John	1812	1863
Pulling, James	1864	1878
Farrer, William	1879	1883
Atkinson, Tindal	1884	1886
Saulez, Robert Travers	1886	1900
Dalton, Edward Neal	1901	1902
Marsh, John Bishop	1902	1910
Flynn, Robert Francis	1910	

Appendix No. 3

FOURTEENTH CENTURY "PRESS GANG"

Thomas Rymer. *Foedera.* London, 1830.

Vol. 3, Part 2, Page 996.   c. 1374

(*Translation*)

"CONCERNING THE SEIZING OF THE MARINERS FOR THE SHIPS AND BARGES OF THE KING."

EDWARD, by the grace of God, King of Anglia and of France, and Lord of Ireland, to his conscript, Thomas Heryng, master of our ship, "La Alice," greeting.

Know that we have committed to you the ordering and the seizing of sixty mariners in the county of Kent, the best, strongest and most skilful mariners, wheresoever it may be possible that they may be found, either serfs or freedmen,

Those mariners excepted whom you have previously ordered or seized for our service,

To be chosen and impressed without delay, and to have them led to London, so that they shall be there at the latest on the first day of March next, at our docks, by the sea, according as you may force this upon them from us,

And that you shall seize all those in this part whom you find contrary, or even rebellious, and sell them as our prisoners, treating malingerers in the same way, until such time as we shall be led to order differently concerning their punishment;

And, therefore, we recommend to you, and enjoin you firmly, that you act with all diligence on these presents, and make and execute them there in the aforesaid manner;

Moreover, we give orders to each and every viscount, mayor, bailliff, officer and to all others faithful to us, both freedmen

223

and serfs, according to the tenor of these presents, that they assist you in making and carrying out these presents all and sundry, that they be your abettors and auxiliaries daily, accordingly as you make known to them, or to anyone of them, this which comes from us.

Witnessed by the king, these our letters are made patent.

Attested by me, myself at Westminster, the 28th day of January, in the year of our reign in England, the 48th, etc.

"In like manner were instructed the subjoined, with reference to the mariners subjoined, in the counties subjoined, to be chosen and seized, in the aforesaid manner, under the same date, to wit:

"Johannes Goldyng, master of the king's ship 'La Mighel' of Hull, with reference to seventy mariners in the counties of Suffolk and Essex," and several other officers.

Appendix No. 4

PEDIGREE OF ELIZABETH WORTHY

(Records College of Arms)

THIS lady had an unusual and ancient pedigree. She was fourteenth in descent from Tihel de Herion, a tenant in chief at the Domesday Survey 1086, who then held the manors of Haverhill and Illegh, Co. Suffolk and Yardley (in Thaxted) Stevington (in Ashdon) and Radwinter, Bumpstead (Steeple and Helion Bumpstead) Sturmer and Tilbury (by Clare.) Under Essex in Domesday he is called Tihel Brittonis (Tihel Breton) deriving from Hellean, a canton of Josselin near Ploermel (Morbihan) in Brittany.

Tihel was one of the "barons" or commissioners appointed by the Conqueror to determine the rights of Ely Abbey in 1080. He was succeeded by William his son, and after him by his grandson, the latter marrying Mabel, daughter of Roger de Helim, had dower in Haverhill in 1185, Robert de Helim her son being the heir. He made a gift of land there and in Bumpstead to Castleacre Priory in Norfolk, and was succeeded by William de Heliun; and he by Andrew who in 1235 was returned to hold ten fees in Essex. His son, another Andrew, was found by inquisition in 1289 to hold the manor of Bumpstead of the Crown in chief, Henry de Helion being his son and heir and then aged seventeen. This Henry died in 1304 and was succeeded by his son Henry, who died 1332 leaving a son John who died 1349 and was succeeded at Bumpstead by his son Henry de Helium who was escheator for the county of Essex, dying 1391. His son John married Alice daughter and heir of Sir Robert Swinborne, Knight, by Joan daughter and heir of John Botetourt of Belchamp, and had a son and heir John Helion, the

225

last male heir of this ancient family. There was also a daughter Elizabeth who married John Warner of Bois Hall in Halstead. This lady had an only daughter and heiress Elizabeth Warner, who married John Worthy of Blamsters in Halstead and also had an only child and heiress Elizabeth Worthy, who married Thomas Golding of Cavendish, as his second wife and became the grandmother of Arthur Golding.

Appendix No. 5

PEDIGREE OF URSULA MARSTON

(Marston Family Records)

THE MARSTONS were an old and distinguished family. Robertus de Marston was lord of the Manor of Marston in Lincolnshire in the time of Edward I and died in 1307 leaving a son only a year and a half old. This child lived to maturity and left a son John, who in his turn also left a son, John, who was still living, very aged, in 1450. This John had four sons, Sir John, Richard, the great grandfather of Ursula, Thomas, who in youth fought at Agincourt and later settled in Shropshire, and Henry Marston, who became a canon of St. Paul's Cathedral. Sir John Marston was a very rich man. He lived at Woodcote Park, adjoining Epsom Downs, now famous for the annual running of the Derby. His estate is now the country club of the Royal Automobile Club. He also had a town house in London, "Leaden Porch," Crooked Lane, E.C. He also held the manors of Horton and Shalford in Surrey. Sir John died in 1461 and his nephew William Marston, Richard's son, was his heir. William died in 1495 and his son, another William, succeeded him. This William Marston married Beatrix, daughter of   .   . Barlow of Havering, Co. Essex, and died in 1511, leaving two daughters, Joan and Ursula, the co-heirs of his large estates. Joan married for her second husband William Saunders, former sheriff of Surrey, and by him became the mother of Nicholas Saunders, the famous Roman Catholic historian of the English Reformation. Ursula married John Golding of Belchamp St. Paul's and became the mother of Arthur Golding.

Appendix No. 6

INQUISITION ON THE WILL OF JOHN GOLDING OF BELCHAMP ST. PAUL'S

(*Court of Wards Inquisition*)
(Public Record Office Vol. 4, No. 70)

INQUISITION made at Walden, co. Essex, 30 June 2 Edw VI (1548) after the death of John Golding, Esq.

The Jurors say that John Golding was seized of a messuage etc. in Belchamp St. Paul, and by his writing dated 23 April 33 Hen VIII (1541) gave same to John Hardy, senr. and Margaret his wife, for the term of their lives, and the said John Golding also conceded a tenement in Belchamp to William Colle, and Margaret his wife one of the daughters and heiresses of Thomas Fox, and also a tenement in Belchamp Otton to John Ashford and Juliana his wife and the said John Golding died seized of these, and before his death made his will and gave the messuages aforesaid to Henry Golding one of his sons forever. John Golding was also seized of land in Belchamp held of the Dean and Chapter of St. Paul, London, land in Hempsted, held of the manor of Blamsters in Halsted, co. Essex, late Rose Bynde, widow, and the said John Golding gave by his will to Ursula his wife the said Tenements in Halsted with remainder to Thomas Golding his son and heir and the said Ursula is in full life. And the Jury finally say that John Golding held tenements called Worthyes place and Holdehall and Peynters in Halsted aforesaid of John, Earl of Oxford in socage, and the said John was seized of the Manor of Boblowe in co. Essex which descends to the said Thomas his son and heir held of the King in chief as one fortieth part of a Knights fee. The said John died 28 November last and the said Thomas Golding is his son and heir and aged 28 years and more.

228

WILL OF THOMAS GOLDING OF CAVENDISH

(*General Clauses*)

IN the name of God Amen The vth day of January in the yeer of Our Lord MVCIIII (1504) and in the xxth yeer of the Reign of Kyng Hery the viith THOMAS GOLD-YNG of CAVENDISSH in the Diocese of NORWICH hooll in mynde and in good and perfite remembrance beying thankid be almighti god make and ordeign this my present testament and last will in maner and forme herafter folwyng.

Furst I bequeath my soule unto the blisfull Tennte our lady, Seint Mary and to al the hooly company of heven My body to be buried in the churcheerd of CAVENDISSH biforsed. Which doon I will that all my detts in the which to any maner persone or persons of right I am bounde be feithfully and hoolly paid into discharge of my soule.

Also I bequeath unto the high aulter of the same chirch into recompense for my tithes or offryngs bi me necligently withdrawen or forgoten xs.

Also I bequeath unto iiii ordiers of Frierys, that is to wete, the frere premonts in SUDBURY, frer Austyns of CLARE, the grey freres at BABWELL, and the white frerys in CAMBRIGGE for iiii trentells of messes bi them ymmediatly after my deceas to be doon for my soule with the soules of AGNEIS my furst wif and all our frends xls.

Also I bequeath unto the Stypendy of an honest pryst to synge bi an hooll yeer in the seid chirch of CAVENDISSH for the soules above-rehersed vi^{li}.

Also I bequeath of my goodes and catells asmoch money as convenyently will serve unto the beyeing of a newe tenor belle to be accordyng in true musyk unto the iiii bellys now hangyng in the steple of CAVENDISSH biforeseid.

Also I bequeath unto the service of an honest pryst that will take upon him the jorney to goo for me my fadir and moder the seid Agneis that was my wif and for all our frends to ROME and to JERUSALEM and to synge for the soules of us at Scale of Cely and Elliswhere in his jorney accordyng unto his duete in such bihalf xx^{li} and more if nede shall require.

Also I bequeath to everych of my godchildren that be now alyve to pray for my soule xiid.

Also I bequeath unto the most nedefull reparacion of the Kyngs highwey to be weell and sufficiantly made and in sesonable tyme betwix CLARE and GLEMSFORD CROSSE xiiiis.

Also I will that ymmediately after my deceas myn executours purchase a pece of land unto the yeerely valu of vi.s or better over and beside al maner of outchargs therof yeerely discharged into which land to be lyeing in CAVENDISSH biforseid or nigh therunto shalbe enfeoffed xxiiii persons dwellers within the same toun to thentent that with the yeerely ferme therof all the payers unto the vi.s of comon fyn atte lete within the same toun may yeerely forever be discharged therof soo that thei of their charite pray for the soules of me and my seid frends.

Appendix No. 8

GOLDING'S SUPPOSITITIOUS EMPLOYMENTS

THE statement that Arthur Golding was in the service of the Lord Protector Somerset, which is made by Sir Sidney Lee in the *Dictionary of Biography*, and by other writers, rests upon the assumption that the letter of the Protector, addressed to   Golding in 1549, was written to him. This letter is as follows:

"We commend us unto you. And for the confidence we have in you, being our servant, we will and require you to solicit and give order for our very good Lord the Earl of Oxford's things, servants, and ordinary power, that he himself and the same also, be in good readiness, whatsoever shall chance to require his service for the King's Majesty; whereof, if any occasion shall chance, we will signify by our letters. Thus we commit the order of the whole unto your good discretion, and will you to use herein convenient secrecy. From Hampton Court the 5th October, 1549.

"Yours loving Lord and Master,

"E. SOMERSET.

"To our loving servant,
  . . . Golding, Esquire."

(Lemon, Robert. *Calendar of State Papers, Domestic*. London, 1856. Vol. I, p. 23, Vol. IX, Domestic, Edward VI, 1549.)

It is incredible that such a letter could have been sent to a boy of thirteen, and Mr. J. Horace Round, the noted genealogical expert, in "Notes on the Great Chamberlain Case" says it went to John Golding, Arthur's father. This cannot, however, be correct because John had died November 28, 1547. It was apparently for Thomas Golding, Arthur's eldest half-brother, then nearly thirty years of age, and, as the evidence shows, close to John de Vere and in all probability an agent of Somerset. He

231

had been appointed one of the commissioners for certifying the Chantry lands in Essex and "knew how to improve his interest to get a large share of them." He had witnessed a will made by John de Vere on February 1, 1548. This will was signed the same day that de Vere agreed to the "fine" which practically stripped his collateral heirs of the great Vere estates in the interest of his eight- or nine-year-old daughter Catherine whom he betrothed to the Protector's son Henry, also a child. This was but a few months before Thomas Golding's sister Margaret was married to John de Vere. Within eighteen months of this marriage and less than a year after the date of the letter Thomas Golding was knighted and, in December 1550, was appointed collector of the subsidy in Essex, both the honor and the lucrative offices coming, of course, from Somerset. These facts indicate that Thomas was the Golding to whom Somerset addressed the letter and whom he called his "servant." They also indicate the extent of his confidence in Thomas, for the letter placed Golding in complete command of the Earl of Oxford and his retainers in case they were called into service. The letter also demonstrates the extent of the control over John de Vere and his affairs which was exercised by the Protector and is quite in line with the interrupted marriage with Mrs. Dorothy, the betrothal of the children, and the "fine" which diverted the de Vere properties to the Somerset family.

The real purpose of the letter is not clear on its face. It seems to have been written under the color of the disturbed conditions in the North, where the Kett rebellion at Norwich had just been suppressed by the Earl of Warwick with a considerable body of troops. As Warwick, however, was head of the party in the government which opposed Somerset in the Privy Council, it is probable that the latter was secretly preparing to defend himself in case of a hostile move. If so, the clash never came and Somerset's brief imprisonment in the Tower nine days later, upon charges which failed at his trial, was accomplished by Warwick before the former could gather his supporters for armed resistance. At any rate it is clear that the letter does not indicate that

232

Arthur Golding was in Somerset's service at that time; there is no evidence that he later was in the employ of the Protector. Somerset fell and was executed in 1551, when Arthur was but fifteen, so there appears to be no reason to think he was ever in his service.

The fact that Sir Philip Sidney later committed to him the task of finishing the translation of De Mornay's "Trewenesse of Christianity" has probably given color to the suggestion that Golding was in the service of the Sidney family. If so, it must have been in his early years, after his return from Cambridge. There appears to be no evidence to that effect. Hunter's "Chorus Vatum" says, "it would seem that the poet was in the service of Sir Henry Sidney (Sir Philip Sidney's father) by the MS. No. 1523, in Heber Library, but this is doubtful." This MS. is a statement prepared by Thomas Nevitt, Keeper of the wardrobe to Robert Sidney the second Earl of Leicester, Sir Philip Sidney's brother, and sets forth for that nobleman's information his expenses, etc., particularly in connection with the marriage of his daughters, Lady Mary and Lady Philip. It begins with the statement that "four years ago your honor was pleased to tell Mr. Golding and myself, etc." In Additional MS. 12066 on the same subject, it is shown that for the expense of Lady Mary's wedding £600 pounds were borrowed of Mr. Golding which was repaid with interest. From this Hunter assumed that this Golding was in Sir Henry Sidney's service although Sir Henry died in 1584. The document is not dated but internal evidence shows that is was written in the reign of Charles I. A letter attached to it is dated October 10, 1626. As the statement to Mr. Golding was made "four years ago" the Mr. Golding to whom it was made and who could lend £600 was clearly not Arthur, who had then been dead sixteen years and who seems never to have been in position to lend any such sum. It is likely that this Golding was the "George Goldinge" who over thirty years before was Provost Marshal for Sir Robert Sidney when he was Governor of Flushing in 1592, as appears from a document in the Hatfield MSS., Vol. 4, p. 292.

Appendix No. 9

GOLDING'S ACCOUNTS AS RECEIVER

(State Papers Domestic Eliz. vol 28 No 57.)

Anno 1563.

MONNEY received by me Arthur Goldyng to thvse of the right Honorable the Erle of Oxinford at thappointment of the right honorable Sir William Cecill knight Master of the Quenes Highnesse Court of Wardes and Lyveries.

Received of the Baylyf of Colbrook in the Countie of Devonshyre the summe of	xvli
Item of the Baylyf of Christen Malford in Comitatu Wylshyre the Summe of	xxli

(State Papers Domestic, Elizabeth 6 vol 28 No 56)

Anno Regni domine Regine Elizabeth quinto.

Manerium de Colbrooke in Comitatu Devon.

Received the xxijth of May in the yere aforesayd of John Dawe Baylyf there for the Collection of the half yerrs Rent of the said Manor due vnto the right honorable the Erle of Oxenford at the feast of Thanunciacion of our Lady last past, the summe of fyvetene powndes	xvli

per me Arthurum Goldyng.

Endorsed in Wm Cecill's hand
Goldyng
Er. Oxford.

Appendix No. 10

SOMERSET'S HOLD ON JOHN DE VERE

JUST what was the nature of Somerset's hold over John de Vere is not clear. It is evident, however, that the Protector could and did control Oxford's actions, whether by fear, as Morant states, or by persuasion, as Sir Clements Markham (*The Fighting Veres*, Boston, 1888, page 19) more moderately indicates. At any rate, Oxford's yielding, in this matter, to either the threats or the blandishments of Somerset, is further evidence of the infirmity of will so clearly shown in his affair with "Mrs. Dorothy." The charge of mental weakness made during a contest for the office of Lord Great Chamberlain a hundred years later, but veiled under the polite words "he was not as wise as his fathers" was founded on these incidents.

Morant's footnote, for which he gives no authority, is found in the second volume of his *History of Essex*, on page 293. It reads as follows:

"The account we have of it is as follows: Edward Seymour, Duke of Somerset, Protector of the Realm, out of his extreme avarice and greedy appetite did under color of justice convent before himself for certain criminal causes John Earl of Oxford and so terrify him that to save his life he was obliged to alienate to the said Duke by deed all his estates, lordships, castles, manors, &c."

A possible hint as to the nature of the accusation is found in J. Horace Round's article on the Lord Great Chamberlain case in the *Monthly Review*, June, 1902. Mr. Round says that "the Sixteenth Earl of Oxford was sharply rebuked in 1647 by the Privy Council for his pretended claim to the office of Lord Great Chamberlain, 'whereunto he could show nothing of good grounds to have the right to the same.'"

235

This office had been held by Somerset under grant from Henry VIII and he transferred it to Warwick, after whose death it was granted to John de Vere, who had always insisted that it was hereditary in his family. His heirs maintained this claim in many contests for the office.

ADDRESS TO THE READER—FIRST FOUR
BOOKS OF THE METAMORPHOSES

I WOULD not wish the simple sort offended for too bee,
 When in this booke the heathen names of feynèd Godds they
 see.
The trewe and everliving God the Paynims did not knowe:
Which causèd them the name of Godds on creatures too bestowe.
For nature beeing once corrupt and knowledge blynded quyght
By Adams fall, those little seedes and sparkes of heavenly lyght
That did as yit remayne in man, endevering foorth too burst
And wanting grace and powre too growe too that they were at
 furst,
Too superstition did decline: and drave the fearefull mynd,
Straunge woorshippes of the living God in creatures for too fynd.
The which by custome taking roote, and growing so too strength,
Through Sathans help possest the hartes of all the world at
 length.
Some woorshipt al the hoste of heaven: some deadmens ghostes
 & bones:
Sum wicked feends: sum woormes & fowles, herbes, fishes, trees
 & stones.
The fyre, the ayre, the sea, the land, and every ronning brooke,
Eche queachie grove, eche cragged cliffe the name of Godhead
 tooke.
The nyght and day, the fleeting howres, the seasons of the yeere,
And every straunge and monstruous thing, for Godds mistaken
 weere.
There was no vertue, no nor vice: there was no gift of mynd
Or bodye, but some God thertoo or Goddesse was assignde.

237

Of health and sicknesse, lyfe and death, of needinesse and
wealth
Of peace and warre, of love and hate, of murder, craft and
stealth,
Of bread and wyne, of slouthfull sleepe, and of theyr solemne
games,
And every other tryfling toy theyr Goddes did beare the names.
And looke how every man was bent too goodnesse or too ill,
He did surmyse his foolish Goddes enclyning too his will.
For God perceyving mannes pervers and wicked will too sinne
Did give him over too his lust too sinke or swim therin.
By meanes wherof it came too passe (as in this booke yee see)
That all theyr Goddes with whoordome, theft, or murder blotted
bee,
Which argues them too bee no Goddes, but woorser in effect
Then they whoose open poonishment theyr dooings dooth detect.
Whoo seeing Jove (whom heathen folke doo arme with triple
fyre)
In shape of Eagle, bull or swan too winne his foule desyre?
Or grysly Mars theyr God of warre intangled in a net
By Venus husband purposely too trappe him warely set?
Whoo seeing Saturne eating up the children he begate?
Or Venus dalying wantonly with every lustie mate?
Whoo seeing Juno play the scold? or Phoebus moorne and rew
For losse of hir whom in his rage through jealous moode he slew?
Or else the suttle Mercurie that beares the charmed rod
Conveying neate and hyding them would take him for a God?
For if theis faultes in mortall men doo justly merit blame,
What greater madnesse can there bee than too impute the same
Too Goddes, whoose natures ought too bee most perfect, pure
and bright,
Most vertuous, holly, chaast, and wyse, most full of grace and
lyght?
But as there is no Christen man that can surmyse in mynd
That theis or other such are Goddes which are no Goddes by
kynd:

238

So would too God there were not now of christen men profest,
That worshipt in theyr deedes theis Godds whose names they doo
    detest.
Whoose lawes wee keepe his thralles wee bee, and he our God
    indeede.
So long is Christ our God as wee in christen lyfe proceede.
But if wee yeeld too fleshlye lust, too lucre, or too wrath,
Or if that Envy, Gluttony, or Pryde the maystry hath,
Or any other kynd of sinne the thing the which wee serve
Too bee accounted for our God most justly dooth deserve.
Then must wee thinke the learned men that did theis names fre-
    quent,
Some further things and purposes by those devises ment.
By Jove and Juno understand all states of princely port:
By Ops and Saturne auncient folke that are of elder sort:
By Phoebus yoong and lusty brutes of hand and courage stout:
By Mars the valeant men of warre that love too feight it out.
By Pallas and the famous troupe of all the Muses nyne,
Such folke as in the sciences and vertuous artes doo shyne.
By Mercurie the suttle sort that use too filch and lye,
With theeves, and Merchants whoo too gayne theyr travell do
    applye.
By Bacchus all the meaner trades and handycraftes are ment:
By Venus such as of the fleshe too filthie lust are bent,
By Neptune such as keepe the sea: by Phebe maydens chast,
And Pilgrims such as wandringly theyr tyme in travell waste.
By Pluto such as delve in mynes, and Ghostes of persones dead:
By Vulcane smythes and such as woorke in yron, tynne or
    lead.
By Hecat witches, Conjurers, and Necromancers reede,
With all such vayne and devlish artes as superstition breede.
By Satyres, Sylvanes, Nymphes and Faunes with other such
    besyde,
The playne and simple country folke that every where abyde.
I know theis names too other thinges oft may and must agree:
In declaration of the which I will not tedious bee,

But leave them too the Readers will too take in sundry wyse,
As matter rysing giveth cause constructions too devyse.
Now when thou readst of God or man, in stone, in beast, or tree
It is a myrrour for thy self thyne owneestate too see.
For under feyned names of Goddes it was the Poets guyse,
The vice and faultes of all estates too taunt in covert wyse.
And likewise too extoll with prayse such things as doo deserve.
Observing alwayes comlynesse from which they doo not swarve.
And as the persone greater is of birth, renowne or fame,
The greater ever is his laud, or fouler is his shame.
For if the States that on the earth the roome of God supply,
Declyne from vertue untoo vice and live disorderly,
Too Eagles, Tygres, Bulles, and Beares, and other figures
    straunge,
Bothe too theyr people and themselves most hurtfull doo they
    chaunge,
And when the people give themselves too filthie life and sinne,
What other kinde of shape thereby than filthie can they winne?
So was Licaon made a Woolfe: and Jove became a Bull:
The tone for using crueltie, the toother for his trull.
So was Elpenor and his mates transformed intoo swyne,
For following of theyr filthie lust in women and in wyne.
Not that they lost theyr manly shape as too the outward showe:
But for that in their brutish brestes most beastly lustes did growe.
For why this lumpe of flesh and bones, this bodie is not wee;
Wee are a thing which earthly eyes denyed are too see.
Our soule is wee, endewed by God with reason from above:
Our bodie is but as our house, in which wee woorke and move.
Tone part is common too us all, with God of heaven himself;
The toother common with the beastes, a vyle and stinking pelf.
The tone bedect with heavenly giftes and endlesse; toother
    grosse,
Fraylie, filthie, weake, and borne too dye as made of earthly
    drosse.
Now looke how long this clod of clay too reason dooth obey,
So long for men by just desert account our selves wee may.

240

But if wee suffer fleshly lustes as lawlesse Lordes too reigne,
Than are we beastes, wee are no men, wee have our name in
    vaine.
And if wee be so drownd in vice that feeling once bee gone,
Then may it well of us bee sayd, wee are a block or stone.
This surely did the Poets meene when in such sundry wyse,
The pleasant tales of turned shapes they studyed too devyse.
There purpose was too profite men, and also too delyght
And so too handle every thing as best might like the sight.
For as the Image portrayd out in simple whight and blacke
(Though well proportiond, trew and faire) if comly colours
    lacke,
Delyghteth not the eye so much, nor yet contentes the mynde
So much as that that shadowed is with colours in his kynde:
Even so a playne and naked tale or storie simply told
(Although the matter bee in deede of valewe more than gold)
Makes not the hearer so attent too print it in his hart,
As when the thing is well declarde, with pleasant termes and
    art.
All which the Poets knew right well: and for the greater grace.
As Persian kings did never go abrode with open face,
But with some lawne or silken skarf, for reverence of theyr
    state:
Even so they folowing in their woorkes the selfsame trade and
    rate,
Did under covert names and termes theyr doctrines so emplye,
As that it is ryght darke and hard theyr meening too espye.
But beeing found it is more sweetee and makes the mynd more
    glad,
Than if a man of tryed gold a treasure gayned had.
For as the body hath his joy in pleasant smelles and syghts:
Even so in knowledge and in artes the mynd as much delights.
Wherof aboundant hoordes and heapes in Poets packed beene
So hid that (saving untoo fewe) they are not too bee seene.
And therfore whooso dooth attempt the Poet woorkes too reede,
Must bring with him a stayd head and judgement too proceede.

For as there bee most wholsome hestes and precepts too bee
    found,
So are theyr rockes and shallowe shelves too ronne the ship
    a ground.
Some naughtie persone seeing vyce shewd lyvely in his hew,
Dooth take occasion by and by like vices too ensew.
Another beeing more severe than wisdome dooth requyre,
Beeholding vice (too outward shewe) exalted in desyre,
Condemneth by and by the booke and him that did it make,
And willes it too be burned with fyre for lewd evample sake.
These persons overshoote themselves, and other folkes deceyve:
Not able of the authors mynd the meening too conceyve.
The Authors purpose is too paint and set before our eyes
The lyvely Image of the thoughts that in our stomackes ryse.
Eche vice and vertue seemes too speake and argue too our face,
With such perswasions as they have theyr dooinges too embrace.
And if a wicked persone seeme his vices too exalt,
Esteeme not him that wrate the woorke in such defaultes too halt,
But rather with an upryght eye consyder well thy thought:
See if corrupted nature have the like within thee wrought:
Marke what affection dooth perswade in every kynd of matter:
Judge if that even in heynous crymes thy fancy doo not flatter.
And were it not for dread of lawe or dread of God above,
Most men (I feare) would doo the things that fond affections
    move.
Then take theis woorkes as fragrant flowers most full of pleasant
    juce
The which the Bee conveying home may put too wholsome use:
And which the spyder sucking on too poyson may convert,
Through venym spred in all her limbes and native in hir hart.
For too the pure and Godly mynd, are all things pure and cleene,
And untoo such as are corrupt the best corrupted beene:
Lyke as the fynest meates and drinkes that can be made by art,
In sickly folkes too nourishment of sicknesse doo convert.
And therefore not regarding such whose dyet is so fyne
That nothing can digest with them onlesse it bee devine,

Nor such as too theyr proper harme doo wrest and wring awrye
The thinges that too a good intent are written pleasantly:
I purpose now (if God permit) as here I have begonne
So through al Ovid's turnèd shapes with restless race to ronne
Until such time as bringing him acquainted with our toong,
He may a lyke in English verse as in his own bee soong.
Wherein although for pleasant style, I cannot make account,
Too match myne author who in that all other dooth surmount:
Yit (gentle Reader) I doo trust my travell in this cace
May purchace favour in thy sight my dooings too embrace:
Considring what a sea of goodes and Jewelles thou shalt
    fynd,
Not more delyghtfull too the eare than frutefull too the mynd.
For this doo lerned persons deeme, of Ovids present woorke:
That in no one of all his bookes the which he wrate, doo lurke
Mo darke and secret misteries, mo counselles wyse and sage,
Mo good ensamples, mo reprooves of vyce in youth and age,
Mo fyne inventions too delight, mo matters clerkly knit,
No nor more straunge varietie too shew a lerned wit.
The high, the lowe: the riche, the poore: the mayster, and the
    slave:
The mayd, the wife: the man, the chyld: the simple and the
    brave:
The yoong, the old: the good, the bad: the warriour strong and
The wyse, the foole: the countrie cloyne: the lerned and the lout:
And every other living wight shall in this mirrour see
His whole estate, thoughtes, woordes and deedes expresly shewd
    too bee.
Moreover thou mayst fynd herein descriptions of the tymes:
With constellacions of the starres and planettes in theyr clymes:
The Sites of Countries, Cities, hilles, seas, forestes, playnes and
    floods:
The nature both of fowles, beastes, wormes, herbes, mettals,
    stones and woods,
And finally what ever thing is straunge and delectable,
The same conveyed shall you fynd most featly in some fable.

And even as in a cheyne, eche linke within another wynds,
And both with that that went before and that that followes
    binds:
So every tale within this booke dooth seeme to take his ground
Of that that was reherst before, and enters in the bound
Of that that folowes after it, and every one gives light
Too other: so that whoo so meenes to understand them ryght,
Must have a care as well to know the thing that went before,
As that the which he personally desyres too see so sore.
Now to thinent that none have cause heereafter too compleine
Of mee as setter out of things that are but lyght and vaine:
If any stomacke be so weake as that it cannot brooke,
The lively setting forth of things described in this booke,
I give him counsell to absteine untill he bee more strong,
And for to use Ulysses feat ageinst the Meremayds song.
Or if he needes will heere and see and wilfully agree
(Through cause misconstrued) untoo vice allured for too bee:
Then let him also marke the peine that dooth therof ensue,
And hold himself content with that that too his fault is due.

FINIS

LETTER DEDICATORY, THE FIFTEEN BOOKS
OF THE METAMORPHOSES

TO THE RYGHT HONORABLE AND HIS SINGULAR
GOOD LORD, ROBERT ERLE OF LEYCESTER

Baron of Denbygh, Knyght of the Most Noble
Order of The Garter, &c. Arthur Golding
Gent. Wisheth Continuance of
Health, with Prosperous
Estate and Felicitie.

THE EPISTLE

At length my chariot wheele about the mark hath found the way,
And at their weery races end, my breathlesse horses stay.
The woork is brought too end by which the author did account
(And rightly) with eternall fame above the starres too mount,
For whatsoever hath bene writ of auncient tyme in greeke
By sundry men dispersedly, and in the latin eeke,
Of this same dark Philosophie of turned shapes, the same
Hath Ovid into one whole masse in this booke brought in frame.
Fowre kynd of things in this his worke the Poet dooth conteyne.
That nothing under heaven dooth ay in stedfast state remayne.
And next that nothing perisheth: but that eche substance takes
Another shape than that it had. Of theis twoo points he makes
The proof by shewing through his woorke the wonderfull ex-
    chaunge
Of Goddes, men, beasts, and elements, too sundry shapes right
    straunge,
Beginning with creation of the world, and man of slyme,
And so proceeding with the turnes that happened till his tyme.

245

Then sheweth he the soule of man from dying to be free,
By samples of the noblemen, who for their vertues bee
Accounted and canonizèd for Goddes by heathen men,
And by the peynes of Lymbo lake, and blysfull state agen
Of spirits in th' Elysian feelds. And through that of theis
    three
He make discourse dispersedly: yit specially they bee
Discussed in the latter booke in that oration where
He bringeth in Pythagoras disswading men from feare
Of death, and preaching abstinence from flesh of living things.
But as for that opinion which Pythagoras there brings
Of soules removing out of beasts too men, and out of men
Too birdes and beasts both wyld and tame, both too and fro agen:
It is not too be understand of that same soule whereby
Wee are endewd with reason and discretion from on hie:
But of that soule or lyfe the which brute beasts as well as wee
Enjoy. Three sortes of lyfe or soule (for so they termèd bee)
Are found in things. The first gives powre too thryve, encrease
    and grow,
And this in senselesse herbes and trees and shrubs itself dooth
    show.
The second giveth powre too move and use of senses fyve,
And this remaynes in brutish beasts, and keepeth them alyve.
Both theis are mortall, as the which receyvèd of the aire
By force of Phebus, after death, doo thither eft repayre.
The third gives understanding, wit and reason: and the same
Is it alonly which with us of soule dooth beare the name.
And as the second dooth conteine the first: even so the third
Conteyneth both the other twaine. And neyther beast, nore
    bird,
Nor fish, nor herb, nor tree, nor shrub, nor any earthly wyght
(Save only man) can of the same partake the heavenly myght.
I graunt that when our breath dooth from our bodies go away,
It dooth eftsoones returne too ayre: And of that ayre there may
Both bird and beast participate, and wee of theirs likewyse.
For whyle wee lyve, (the things itself appeereth to our eyes)

Bothe they and wee draw all one breath. But for too deeme or
    say
Our noble soule (which is divine and permanent for ay)
Is common too us with the beasts, I think it nothing lesse
Than for too be a poynt of him that wisdome dooth professe.
Of this I am ryght well assurde there is no Christen wyght
That can by fondnesse be so farre seducèd from the ryght
And finally hee dooth procede in shewing that not all
That beare the name of men (how strong, feerce, stout, bold,
    hardy, tall,
How wyse, fayre, rych, or hyghly borne, how much renownd by
    fame,
So ere they bee, although on earth of Goddes they beare the
    name)
Are for too be accounted men: but such as under awe
Of reasons rule continually doo live in vertues law:
And that the rest doo differ nought from beasts, but rather bee
Much woorse than beasts, bicause they doo abace theyr owne
    degree.
To naturall philosophye the formest three perteyne,
The fowrth too morall: and in all are pitthye, apt and pleyne
Instructions which import the prayse of vertues, and the shame
Of vices, with the due rewardes of eyther of the same.

Out of the first booke.

As for example, in the tale of Daphnee turnd to Bay
A myrror of virginitie appeere untoo us may,
Which yeelding neyther untoo feare, nor force, nor flatterye,
Doth purchace everlasting fame and immortalitye.

Out of the second.

In Phaetons fable untoo syght the Poet dooth expresse
The natures of ambition blynd, and youthfull wilfulnesse.
The end whereof is miserie, and bringeth at the last
Repentance when it is to late that all redresse is past.

And how the weaknesse and the want of wit in magistrate
Confoundeth both his common weale and eeke his owne estate.
This fable also dooth advyse all parents and all such
As bring up youth, too take good heede of cockering them too
    much.
It further dooth commende the meane: and willeth too beware
Of rash and hasty promises which most pernicious are,
And not too bee performèd: and in fine it playnly showes
What sorrow too the parents and too all the kinred growes
By disobedience of the chyld: and in the chyld is ment
The disobedient subject that ageinst his prince is bent.
The transformations of the Crow and Raven doo declare
That Clawbacks and Colcariers ought wysely too beware
Of whom, too whom, and what they speake. For sore against his
    will
Can any freendly hart abyde too heare reported ill
The partie whome he favoureth. This tale dooth eeke bewray
The rage of wrath and jelozie too have no kynd of stay:
And that lyght credit too reports in no wyse should be given,
For feare that men too late too just repentance should bee driven.
The fable of Ocyroee by all such folk is told
As are in serching things too come too curious and too bold.
A very good example is describde in Battus tale
For covetous people which for gayne doo set theyr toongs too sale.

Out of the iij

All such as doo in flattring freaks, and hawkes, and hownds
    delyght
And dyce, and cards, and for too spend the tyme both day and
    nyght
In foule excesse of chamberworke, or too much meate and drink:
Uppon the piteous storie of Acteon ought too think.
For theis and theyr adherents usde excessive are in deede
The dogs that dayly doo devour theyr followers on with speede.
Tyresias willes inferior folk in any wyse too shun
Too judge betweene their betters least in perill they doo run.

248

Narcissus is of scornfulnesse and pryde a myrror cleere,
Where beawties fading vanitie most playnly may appeere.
And Echo in the selfsame tale dooth kyndly represent
The lewd behaviour of a bawd, and his due punishment.

Out of the iiij

The piteous tale of Pyramus and Thisbee doth conteine
The headie force of frentick love whose end is wo and payne.
The snares of Mars and Venus shew that tyme will bring too
    lyght
The secret sinnes that folk commit in corners or by nyght.
Hermaphrodite and Salmacis declare that idlenesse
Is cheefest nurce and cherisher of all volupteousnesse,
And that voluptuous lyfe breedes sin: which linking all toogither
Make men too bee effeminate, unweeldy, weake and lither.

Out of the v.

Rich Piers daughters turnd too Pyes doo openly declare,
That none so bold too vaunt themselves as blindest bayardes are.
The Muses playnly doo declare ageine a toother syde,
That whereas cheefest wisdom is, most meeldnesse dooth abyde.

Out of the vj.

Arachnee may example bee that folk should not contend
Ageinst their betters, nor persist in error too the end.
So dooth the tale of Niobee and of hir children: and
The transformation of the Carles that dwelt in Lycie land,
Toogither with the fleaing of of piper Marsies skin.
The first doo also show that long it is ere God begin
Too pay us for our faults, and that he warnes us oft before
Too leave our folly: but at length his vengeance striketh sore.
And therefore that no wyght should strive with God in word nor
    thought
Nor deede. But pryde and fond desyre of prayse have ever
    wrought

Confusion too the parties which accompt of them doo make.
For some of such a nature bee that if they once doo take
Opinion (be it ryght or wrong) they rather will agree
To dye, than seeme to take a foyle: so obstinate they bee.
The tale of Tereus, Philomele, and Prognee dooth conteyne
That folks are blynd in thyngs that too their proper weale per-
     teyne,
And that the man in whom the fyre of furious lust dooth reigne
Dooth run too mischeefe like a horse that getteth loose the
     reyne.
It also shews the cruell wreake of women in their wrath
And that no hainous mischiefe long delay of vengeance hath.
And lastly that distresse doth drive a man too looke about
And seeke all corners of his wits, what way too wind him out.

Out of the vij.

   The good successe of Jason in the land of Colchose, and
The dooings of Meda since, doo give too understand
That nothing is so hard but peyne and travell doo it win,
For fortune ever favoreth such as boldly doo begin:
That women both in helping and in hurting have no match
When they too eyther bend their wits: and how that for too catch
An honest meener under fayre pretence of freendship, is
An easie matter. Also there is warning given of this,
That men should never hastely give eare too fugitives,
Nor into handes of sorcerers commit their state or lyves.
It shewes in fine of stepmoothers the deadly hate in part.
And vengeaunce most unnaturall that was in moothers hart.
The deeds of Theseus are a spurre too prowesse, and a glasse
How princes sonnes and noblemen their youthfull yeeres should
     passe.
King Minos shewes that kings in hand no wrongful wars should
     take
And what provision for the same they should before hand make.
King Aeacus gives also there example how that kings
Should keepe their promise and their leages above all other things.

250

His grave description of the plage and end thereof, expresse
The wrath of God on man for sin: and how that nerethelesse
He dooth us spare and multiply ageine for goodmens sakes.
The whole discourse of Cephalus and Procris mention makes
That maried folke should warely shunne the vice of jealozie
And of suspicion should avoyd all causes utterly.
Reproving by the way all such as causelesse do misdeeme
The chaste and giltlesse for the deedes of those that faultie
  seeme.

Out of the viij.

The storie of the daughter of King Nisus setteth out
What wicked lust drives folk untoo too bring their wills about.
And of a rightuous judge is given example in the same,
Who for no meede nor frendship will consent too any blame.
Wee may perceyve in Dedalus how every man by kynd
Desyres to bee at libertie, and with an earnest mynd
Dooth seeke too see his native soyle, and how that streight dis-
  tresse
Dooth make men wyse, and sharpes their wits to fynd their owne
  redresse.
Wee also lerne by Icarus how good it is too bee
In meane estate and not too clymb too hygh, but too agree
Too wholsome counsell: for the hyre of disobedience is
Repentance when it is too late for thinking things amisse
And Partrich telles that excellence in any thing procures
Men envie, even among those frendes whom nature most
  assures.
Philemon and his feere are rules of godly pacient lyfe,
Of sparing thrift, and mutuall love betweene the man and wyfe,
Of due obedience, of the feare of God, and of reward
For good or evill usage shewd too wandring straungers ward.
In Erisicthon dooth appeere a lyvely image both
Of wickednesse and crueltie which any wyght may lothe,
And of the hyre that longs theretoo. He sheweth also playne
That whereas prodigalitie and gluttony dooth reigne,

A world of riches and of goods are ever with the least
Too satisfye the appetite and eye of such a beast.

Out of the ix.

   In Hercules and Acheloyes encounters is set out
The nature and behaviour of twoo wooers that be stout.
Wherein the Poet covertly taunts such as beeing bace
Doo seeke by forgèd pedegrees to seeme of noble race.
Who when they doo perceyve no truth uppon their syde too stand,
In stead of reason and of ryght use force and myght of hand.
This fable also signifies that valiantnesse of hart
Consisteth not in woords, but deedes: and that all slyght and Art
Give place too prowesse. Furthermore in Nessus wee may see
What breach of promise commeth too, and how that such as bee
Unable for too wreake theyr harmes by force, doo oft devyse
Too wreake themselves by pollicie in farre more cruell wyse.
And Deyanira dooth declare the force of jealozie
Deceyved through too lyght beleef and fond simplicitie.
The processe following peinteth out true manlynesse of hart
Which yeeldeth neyther untoo death, too sorrow, greef, nor
   smart.
And finally it shewes that such as live in true renowne
Of vertue heere, have after death an everlasting crowne
Of glorie. Cawne and Byblis are examples contrarie:
The Mayd of most outrageous lust, the man of chastitie.

Out of the x.

   The tenth booke cheefly dooth containe one kynd of argument,
Reproving most prodigious lusts of such as have bene bent
Too incest most unnaturall. And in the latter end
It shewed in Hippomenes how greatly folk offend,
That are ingrate for benefits which God or man bestow
Uppon them in the tyme of neede. Moreover it dooth show
That beawty (will they nill they) aye dooth men in daunger
   throw:

252

And that it is a foolyshnesse too stryve ageinst the thing
Which God before determineth too passe in tyme too bring.
And last of all Adonis death dooth shew that manhod stryves
Against forewarning though men see the perill of theyr lyves.

Out of the xi.

The death of Orphey sheweth Gods just vengeaunce on the
  vyle
And wicked sort which horribly with incest them defyle.
In Midas of a covetous wretch the image wee may see
Whose riches justly too himself a hellish torment bee,
And of a foole whom neyther proof nor warning can amend,
Untill he feele the shame and smart that folly doth him send.
His Barbour represents all blabs which seeme with chyld too bee
Untill that they have blaazd abrode the things they heare or see,
In Ceyx and Alcyone appeeres most constant love,
Such as betweene the man and wyfe too bee it dooth behove.
This Ceyx also is a lyght of princely courtesie
And bountie·toward such whom neede compelleth for too flye.
His viage also dooth declare how vainly men are led
Too utter perill through fond toyes and fansies in their head.
For Idols doubtfull oracles and soothsayres prophecies
Do nothing else but make fooles fayne and blynd their bleared
  eyes.
Dedalions daughter warnes too use the toong with modestee
And not too vaunt with such as are their betters in degree.

Out of the xij.

The seege of Troy, the death of men, the razing of the citie,
And slaughter of king Priams stock without remors of pitie,
Which in the xii. and xiii. bookes bee written, doo declare
How heynous wilfull perjurie and filthie whoredome are
In syght of God. The frentick fray betweene the Lapithes and
The Centaures is a note wherby is given too understand
The beastly rage of drunkennesse.

Out of the xiij.

Ulysses dooth expresse
The image of discretion, wit, and great advisèdnesse.
And Ajax on the other syde doth represent a man
Stout, headie, irefull, hault of mynd, and such a one as can
Abyde too suffer no repulse. And both of them declare
How covetouse of glorie and reward mens nature are.
And finally it sheweth playne that wisdome dooth prevayle
In all attempts and purposes when strength of hand dooth fayle.
The death of fayre Polyxena dooth shew a princely mynd
And firme regard of honor rare engraft in woman kynd.
And Polymnestor king of Thrace dooth shew himself to bee
A glasse for wretched covetous folke wherein themselves to
    see.
This storie further witnesseth that murther cryeth ay
For vengeance, and itself one tyme or other dooth bewray.
The tale of Gyant Polypheme doth evidently prove
That nothing is so feerce and wyld, which yeeldeth not to love.
And in the person of the selfsame Gyant is set out
The rude and homely wooing of a country cloyne and lout.

Out of the xiiij.

The tale of Apes reproves the vyce of wilfull perjurie,
And willeth people too beware they use not for too lye.
Aeneas going downe too hell dooth shew that vertue may
In saufty trauvell where it will, and nothing can it stay.
The length of lyfe in Sybill dooth declare it is but vayne
Too wish long lyfe, syth length of lyfe is also length of payne.
The grecian Achemenides dooth lerne us how we ought
Bee thankfull for the benefits that any man hath wrought.
And in this Achemenides the Poet dooth expresse
The image of exceeding feare in daunger and distresse.
What else are Circes witchcrafts and enchauntments than the
    vyle
And filthy pleasures of the flesh which doo our soules defyle?

And what is else herbe Moly than the gift of stayednesse
And temperance which dooth all fowle concupisence expresse?
The tale of Anaxaretee willes dames of hygh degree
To use their lovers courteously how meane so ere they bee.
And Iphis lernes inferior folkes too fondly not too set
Their love on such as are too hygh for their estate too get.

Out of the xv.

Alemons sonne declares that men should willingly obay
What God commaundes, and not uppon exceptions seeme to stay.
For he will find the meanes too bring the purpose well about,
And in their most necessitie dispatch them saufly out
Of daunger. The oration of Pithagoras implyes
A sum of all the former woorke. What person can devyse
A notabler example of true love and godlynesse
Too ones owne natyve countryward than Cippus dooth expresse?
The turning to a blazing starre of Julius Cesar showes,
That fame and immortalitie of vertuous doing growes.
And lastly by examples of Augustus and a few
Of other noble princes sonnes the author there dooth shew
That noblemen and gentlemen shoulde stryve to passe the fame
And vertues of their auncesters, or else too match the same.
Theis fables out of every booke I have interpreted,
Too shew how they and all the rest may stand a man in
sted.
Not adding over curiously the meening of them all,
For that were labor infinite, and tediousnesse not small
Bothe untoo your good Lordship and the rest that should them
reede
Who well myght thinke I did the bounds of modestie exceede,
If I this one epistle should with matters overcharge
Which scarce a booke of many quyres can well conteyne at large.
And whereas in interpreting theis few I attribute
The things too one, which heathen men to many Gods impute,
Concerning mercy, wrath for sin, and other giftes of grace,
Describèd for examples sake in proper time and place:

Let no man marvell at the same. For though that they as blynd
Through unbeleefe, and led astray through error even of kynd,
Knew not the true eternall God, or if they did him know,
Yit did they not acknowledge him, but vaynly did bestow
The honor of the maker on the creature: yit it dooth
Behove all us (who ryghtly are instructed in the sooth)
Too think and say that God alone is he that rules all things
And worketh all in all as lord of lords and king of kings,
With whom there are none other Gods that any sway may beare,
No fatall law too bynd him by, no fortune for too feare.
For Gods, and fate, and fortune are the termes of heathennesse,
If men usurp them in the sense that Paynims doo expresse.
But if wee will reduce their sence too ryght of Christian law,
Too signifie three other things theis termes wee well may draw.
By Gods wee understand all such as God hath plaast in cheef
Estate to punish sin, and for the godly folkes releef.
By fate the order which is set and stablishèd in things
By Gods eternall will and word, which in due season brings
All matters too their falling out, which falling out or end
(Bicause our curious reason is too weake too comprehend
The cause and order of the same, and dooth behold it fall
Unwares too us) by name of chaunce or fortune wee it call.
If any man will say theis things may better lernèd bee
Out of divine philosophie or scripture, I agree
That nothing may in worthinesse with holy writ compare.
Howbeit so farre foorth as things in whit impeachment are
Too vertue and too godlynesse but furtherers of the same,
I trust we may them saufly use without desert of blame.
And yet there are (and those not of the rude and vulgar sort.
But such as have of godlynesse and lerning good report)
That thinke the Poets tooke their first occasion of theis things
From holy writ as from the well from whence all wisdome
    springs.
What man is he but would suppose the author of this booke
The first foundation of his woorke from Moyses wryghtings
    tooke?

256

Not only in effect he dooth with Genesis agree,
But also in the order of creation, save that hee
Makes no distinction of the dayes. For what is else at all
That shapelesse, rude, and pestred heape which Chaos he dooth
    call,
Than even that universall masse of things which God did make
In one whole lump before that ech their proper place did take.
Of which the Byble saith that in the first beginning God
Made heaven and earth: the earth was waste, and darknesse yit
    abod
Uppon the deepe: which holy wordes declare unto us playne
That fyre, ayre, water, and the earth did undistinct remayne
"In one grosse bodie at the first:
  "For God the father that
"Made all things, framing out the world according too the plat,
"Conceyved everlastingly in mynd, made first of all
"Both heaven and earth uncorporall and such as could not fall
"As objects under sense of sight: and also aire lykewyse,
"And emptynesse: and for theis twaine apt termes he did devyse.
"He called ayer darknesse: for the ayre by kynd is darke.
"And emptynesse by name of depth full aptly he did marke:
"For emptynesse is deepe and waste by nature. Overmore
"He formed also bodylesse (as other things before)
"The natures both of water and of spirit. And in fyne
"The lyght: which beeing made too bee a patterne most divine
"Whereby too forme the fixed starres and wandring planets
    seven,
"With all the lyghts that afterward should beawtifie the heaven,
"Was made by God both bodylesse and of so pure a kynd,
"As that it could alonly bee perceyvèd by the mynd."
To thys effect are Philos words. And certainly this same
Is it that Poets in their worke confused Chaos name.
Not that Gods woorkes at any tyme were pact confusedly
Toogither: but bicause no place nor outward shape whereby
To shew them too the feeble sense of mans deceytfull syght
Was yit appointed untoo things, untill that by his myght

257

And wondrous wisdome God in tyme set open too the eye
The things that he before all tyme had everlastingly
Decreed by his providence. But let us further see
How Ovids scantlings with the whole true patterne doo agree.
The first day by his mighty word (sayth Moyses) God made
    lyght,
The second day the firmament, which heaven or welkin hyght.
The third day he did part the earth from the sea and made it
    drie,
Commaunding it too beare all kynd of fruits abundantly.
The fowrth day he did make the lyghts of heaven to shyne from
    hye,
And stablishèd a law in them too rule their courses by.
The fifth day he did make the whales and fishes of the deepe,
With all the birds and fethered fowles that in the aire doo
    keepe.
The sixth day God made every beast, both wyld and tame, and
    woormes.
That creepe on ground according too their severall kynds and
    formes,
And in the image of himself he formed man of clay
Too bee the Lord of all his woorkes the very selfsame day.
This is the sum of Moyses woords. And Ovid (whether it were
By following of the text aright, or that his mynd did beare
Him witnesse that there are no Gods but one) dooth playne
    uphold
That God (although he knew it not) was he that did unfold
The former Chaos, putting it in forme and facion new,
As may appeere by theis his words which underneath ensew.
"This stryfe did God and nature breake and set in order dew
"The earth from heaven the sea from earth he parted orderly,
"And from the thicke and foggie aire he tooke the lyghtsome
    skye."
In theis few lynes he comprehends the whole effect of that
Which God did woork the first three dayes about this noble
    plat.

258

And then by distributions he entreateth by and by
More largely of the selfsame things, and paynts them out too
    eye
With all their bounds and furniture: And whereas wee doo
    fynd
The terme of nature joynd with God: (according to the mynd
Of lerned men) by joyning so, is ment none other thing,
But God the Lord of nature who did all in order bring.
The distributions being doone right lernedly anon,
Too shew the other three dayes workes he thus proceedeth on.
"The heavenly soyle too Goddes and starres and planets first he
    gave
"The waters next both fresh and salt he let the fishes have,
"The suttle ayre to flickring fowles and birds he hath assignd,
"The earth too beasts both wylde and tame of sundry sorts and
    kynd,"
Thus partly in the outward phrase, but more in verie deede,
He seemes according too the sense of scripture too proceede.
And when he commes to speake of man, he dooth not vainely
    say
(As sum have written) That he was before all tyme for ay,
He mencioneth mo Gods than one in making him. But thus
He both in sentence and in sense his meening dooth discusse.
"Howbeeit yit of all this whyle the creature wanting was
"Farre more divine, of nobler mynd, which shoulde the resdew
    passe
"In depth of knowledge, reason, wide and hygh capacitee,
"And which of all the resdew should the Lord and ruler bee.
"Then eyther he that made the world and things in order set,
"Of heavenly seede engendred man: or else the earth as yet
"Yoong, lustie, fresh, and in her flowre, and parted from the
    skye
"But late before, the seedes therof as yit hild inwardly.
"The which Prometheus tempring streyght with water of the
    spring,
"Did make in likenesse to the Goddes that governe every thing."

What other thing meenes Ovid heere by terme of heavenly
    seede,
Than mans immortall sowle, which is divine, and commes in
    deede
From heaven, and was inspyrde by God, as Moyses sheweth
    playne?
And whereas of Prometheus he seems too adde a vayne
Devyce, as though he ment that he had formed man of clay,
Although it bee a tale put in for pleasure by the way:
Yit by thinterpretation of the name we well may gather,
He did include a misterie and secret meening rather.
This woord Prometheus signifies a person sage and wyse,
Of great foresyght, who headily will nothing enterpryse.
It was the name of one that first did images invent:
Of whom the Poets doo report that he too heaven up went,
And there stole fyre, through which he made his images
    alyve:
And therefore that he formèd men the Paynims did contryve.
Now when the Poet red perchaunce that God almyghty by
His providence and by his woord (which everlastingly
Is ay his wisdome) made the world, and also man to beare
His image, and too bee the lord of all the things that were
Erst made, and that he shapèd him of earth or slymy clay:
Hee tooke occasion in the way of fabling for too say
That wyse Prometheus tempring earth with water of the spring,
Did forme it lyke the Gods above that governe every thing.
Thus may Prometheus seeme too bee theternall woord of God,
His wisdom, and his providence which formèd man of clod.
"And when all other things behold the ground with goveling
    eye:
"He gave too man a stately looke replete with majesty:
"And willd him too behold the heaven with countnance cast on
    hye,
"Too mark and understand what things are in the starrie skye."
In theis same woordes, both parts of man the Poet dooth expresse
As in a glasse, and giveth in instruction too addresse

260

Our selves too know our owne estate: as that wee bee not borne
Too followe lust, or serve the paunch lyke brutish beasts for-
    lorne,
But for too lyft our eyes as well of body as of mynd
Too heaven as too our native soyle from whence wee have by
    kynd
Our better part: and by the sight thereof too lerne too know
And knowledge him that dwelleth there: and wholly too bestow
Our case and travell too the prayse and glorie of his name
Who for the sake of mortall men created first the same.
Moreover by the golden age what other thing is ment,
Than Adams tyme in Paradyse, who beeing innocent
Did lead a blist and happy lyfe untill that thurrough sin
He fell from God? From which tyme foorth all sorrow did
    begin.
The earth accursèd for his sake, did never after more
Yeeld foode without great toyle. Both heate and cold did vexe
    him sore.
Disease of body, care of mynd, with hunger, thirst and neede,
Feare, hope, joy, greefe, and trouble, fell on him and on his
    seede.
And this is termd the silver age. Next which there did succeede
The brazen age when malice first in peoples harts did breede,
Which never ceasèd growing till it did so farre outrage,
That nothing but destruction could the heate thereof asswage
For why mens stomackes wexing hard as steele ageinst their God,
Provoked him from day too day too strike them with his rod.
Prowd Gyants also did aryse that with presumptuous wills
Heapt wrong on wrong, and sin on sin lyke howge and lofty
    hilles
Whereby they strove too clymb too heaven and God from thence
    too draw,
In scorning of his holy woord and breaking natures law.
For which anon ensewd the flood which overflowèd all
The whole round earth and drowned quyght of creatures great
    and smal,

Excepting feaw that God did save as seede whereof should grow
Another offspring: All these things the Poet heere dooth show
In colour, altring both the names of persons, tyme and place.
For where according too the truth of scripture in this cace,
The universall flood did fall but sixteene hundred yeeres
And sixandfifty after the creation (as appeeres
By reckening of the ages of the fathers) under Noy,
With whom seven other persons mo like saufgard did enjoy
Within the arke, which at the end of one whole yeere did stay,
Uppon the hilles of Armenie: The Poet following ay
The fables of the glorying Greekes (who shamelessely did take
The prayse of all things too themselves) in fablying wyse dooth
    make
It happen in Deucalions tyme, who reignd in Thessaly
Eyght hundred winters since Noyes flood or thereupon well
    nye,
Bicause that in the reigne of him a myghty flood did fall,
That drownde the greater part of Greece, townes, cattell, folk,
    and all,
Save feaw that by the help of boats atteyned untoo him,
And too the highest of the forkt Parnasos top did swim.
And forbycause that hee and his were driven a whyle to dwell
Among the stonny hilles and rocks until the water fell,
The Poets hereupon did take occasion for too feyne,
That he and Pyrrha did repayre mankynd of stones ageyne.
So in the sixth booke afterward Amphious harp is sayd
The first foundation of the walles of Thebee to have layd,
Bycause that by his eloquence and justice (which are ment
By true accord of harmonie and musicall consent)
He gathered intoo Thebee towne, and in due order knit
The people that disperst and rude in hilles and rocks did sit.
So Orphey in the tenth booke is reported too delight
The savage beasts, and for too hold the fleeting birds from flyght,
Too move the senseless stones, and stay swift rivers, and too
    make
The trees too follow after him and for his musick sake

Too yeeld him shadowe where he went. By which is signifyde
That in his doctrine such a force and sweetenesse was implyde,
That such as were most wyld, stowre, feerece, hard, witlesse,
    rude and bent
Ageinst good order, were by him perswaded too relent,
And for too bee conformable too live in reverent awe
Like neybours in a common weale by justyce under law.
Considring then of things before reherst the whole effect,
I trust there is alreadie shewd sufficient too detect
That Poets tooke the ground of all their cheefest fables out
Of scripture: which they shadowing with their gloses went about
Too turne the truth too toyes and lyes. And of the selfsame rate
Are also theis: Their Phelgeton, their Styx, their blisfull state
Of spirits in th' Elysian feelds. Of which the former twayne
Seeme counterfetted of the place where damned soules remayne,
Which wee call hell. The third dooth seeme too fetch his
    pedegree
From Paradyse which scripture shewes a place of blisse too bee.
If Poets then with leesings and with fables shadowed so
The certeine truth, what letteth us too plucke those visers fro
Their doings, and too bring ageine the darkened truth too lyght,
That all men may behold thereof the cleerenesse shining bryght?
The readers therefore earnestly admonisht are too bee
Too seeke a further meaning than the letter gives too see.
The travell tane in that behalf although it have sum payne
Yit makes it double recompence with pleasure and with payne.
With pleasure, for varietie and straungenesse and the things,
With gaine, for good instruction which the understanding brings.
And if they happening for to meete with any wanton woord
Or matter lewd, according as the person dooth avoord
In whom the evill is describde, doo feele their myndes therby
Provokte too vyce and wantonnesse, (as nature commonly
Is prone to evill) let them thus imagin in their mynd.
Behold, by sent of reason and by perfect sight I fynd
A Panther heere, whose peinted cote with yellow spots like gold
And pleasant smell allure myne eyes and senses too behold.

But well I know his face is grim and feerce, which he dooth hyde
To this intent, that whyle I thus stand gazing on his hyde,
He may devour mee unbewares. No let them more offend
At vices in this present woork in lyvely colours pend,
Then if that in a chrystall glasse fowle images they found,
Resembling folkes fowle visages that stand about it round.
For sure theis fables are not put in wryghting to thenent
Too further or allure too vyce: but rather this is ment,
That men beholding what they bee when vyce dooth reigne in
    stead
Of vertue, should not let their lewd affections have the head,
For as there is no creature more divine than man as long
As reason hath the sovereintie and standeth firme and strong:
So is there none more beastly, vyle, and develish, than is hee,
If reason giving over, by affection mated bee.
The use of this same booke therefore is this: that every man
(Endevoring for too know himself as neerly as he can
As though he is a chariot sat well ordered) should direct
His mynd by reason in the way of vertue, and correct
His feerce affections with the bit of temprance, least perchaunce
They taking bridle in the teeth lyke wilful jades doo praunce
Away, and headlong carie him to every filthy pit
Of vyce, and drinking of the same defyle his soule with it:
Or else all headlong harrie him uppon the rockes of sin,
And overthrowing forcibly the chariot he sits in
Doo teare him woorse than ever was Hippolitus the sonne
Or Theseus when he went about his fathers wrath too shun.
This worthie worke in which of good examples are so many,
This Ortyard of Alcinous in which there wants not any
Herb, tree, or frute that may mans use for health or pleasure
    serve,
This plenteous horne of Achelory which justly dooth deserve
Too beare the name of treasorie of knowledge, I present
Too your good Lordship once ageine not as a member rent
Or parted from the resdew of the body any more:
But fully now accomplishèd, desiring you therefore

264

Too let your noble courtesie and favor countervayle
My faults where Art or eloquence on my behalf dooth fayle.
For sure the marke whereat I shoote is neyther wreathes of bay,
Nor name of Poet, no nor mede: but cheefly that it may
Bee lykèd well of you and all the wise and lerned sort,
And next that every wyght that shall have pleasure for to sport
Him in this gardeine, may as well beare wholsome frute away
As only on the pleasant flowres his rechlesse senses stay.
But why seeme I theis doubts too cast, as if that he who tooke
With favor and with gentlenesse a parcell of the booke
Would not likewyse accept the whole? or even as if that they
Who doo excell in wisdome and in lerning, would not wey
A wyse and lerned woorke aryght? or else as if that I
Ought ay too have a speciall care how all men doo apply
My dooings too their owne behoof? as of the former twayne
I have great hope and confidence: so would I also fayne
The other should according too good meening find successe:
If othervyse, the fault is theyrs not myne they must confesse,
And therefore breefly too conclude, I turne ageine too thee
O noble Erle of Leysecter, whose lyfe God graunt may bee
As long in honor, helth and welth as auncient Nestors was,
Or rather as Tithonussis: that all such students as
Doo travell too enrich our toong with knowledge heretofore
Not common too our vulgar speech, may dayly more and more
Proceede through thy good furtherance and favor in the same,
Too all mens profit and delyght, and thy eternall fame.
And that (which is a greater thing) our natyve country may
Long tyme enjoy thy counsell and thy travell too her stay.

At Barwicke the xx of Aprill, 1567.

Your good L. most humbly too commaund

ARTHUR GOLDING.

RECORD OF GOLDING'S ADMISSION TO THE INNER TEMPLE

(Calendar of the Inner Temple Records)

Vol I, p 273.
Parliament held on 25 January 16 Elizabeth, A.D. 1573-4, before Robert Kellawaye, George Bromley, Francis Gawdye, Robert Withe, Thomas Marryott and others.

Admission of Arthur Golding, without payment, and he is to have the benefit of a special admission.

ARCHBISHOP PARKER'S ANTIQUARIAN SOCIETY

In *Notes and Queries* April 7, 1852 appeared the following:

Antiquaries of the Time of Queen Elizabeth

I have a copy of Weever's *Ancient Funerall Monuments*, which once belonged to William Burton, the historian of Leicestershire; on a flyleaf at the end of the volume is the following list in the autograph of that celebrated antiquary, which, perhaps, may not be without its interest to the readers of "N. & Q." I have appended some notes of identification, which I have no doubt some of your correspondents could easily render more complete.

"Antiquarii temp. Eliz. Reg.

1. Recorder Fletewode, Wm.
2. Mr. Atey.
3. Mr. Lombard, Willm.
4. Mr. Cope.
5. Mr. Broughton ye Lawyer.
6. Mr. Leigh.
7. Mr. Bourgchier.
8. Mr. Broughton ye Preacher.
9. Mr. Holland, Joseph.
10. Mr. Cartier.
11. Mr. Cotton, Robt.
12. Mr. Thinne, Francis.
13. Jo. Stowe.
14. ———— Coombes.
15. ———— Lloyd.
16. ———— Strangman.
17. Hen. Spelman.
18. Arthur Gregory.
19. Anth. Cliffe.
20. Tho. Talbot.
21. Arthur Goulding.
22. Arthur Agard.
23. Willm Camden.
24. Merc. Patten.
25. Samson Erdeswike.
26. ———— Josseline.
27. Hen. Sacheverell.
28. Wm. Nettleton de Knocesborough.
29. John Ferne.
30. Robt. Bele.
31. John Savile de Templo.
32. Daniell Rogers.
33. Tho. Saville.
34. Henry Saville.
35. Rog. Keymis.
36. John Guillim.
37. ———— Dee.
38. ———— Heneage.
39. Rich. Scarlet.
40. ———— Wodhall.
41. Dent de Baco Regis.
42. ———— Bowyer.
43. Robt. Hare.
44. ———— Harrison, schoolem[r].
45. ———— Harrison, minist[r]."

John Weever's (1576-1632) *Ancient Funerall Monuments,* was published in 1631. William Burton (1575-1645) who made the list above given must therefore have made it between 1631 and 1645, which indicates the probability that it is fairly accurate.

The *Notes and Queries* writer identified a number of the names, most of which are not now familiar but the following may be noted:

1. William Fleetwood, Recorder of London, "a learned man and good antiquary," ob. 1593. (Wood, ed. Bliss, i. 598.)

2. Mr. Atey. Was this Arthur Atey, Principal of St. Alban Hall, and Orator of the University of Oxford, who was secretary to the Earl of Leicester, knighted by King James, and who died in 1604?

5. Mr. Broughton the Lawyer, i.e. Richard Broughton, Justice of North Wales, called by Sir John Wynne, in the History of the Gwedir Family, "the chief antiquary of England."

8. Mr. Broughton the Preacher. Could this be the learned divine Hugh Broughton, author of *The Consent of Scriptures,* born in 1549, ob. 1612?

11. Sir Robert Cotton, the founder of the Cottonian Library, died in 1631.

3. John Stow, author of *The Chronicles of England* and *The Survey of London;* died in 1605.

21. Arthur Golding; the same, I suppose who finished the translation of a work concerning *The Trueness of Christian Religion against Atheists,* &c., began by Sir Philip Sidney, and also published other translations. (Wood and Gough.)

25. —— Josseline, secretary to Archbishop Parker, was the author of a short account of Corpus Christi or Ben'et College, Cambridge, to the year 1569. (Gough.)

30. Robert Bele, secretary to the embassy of Sir Francis

Walsingham at Paris in 1571, Clerk of the Privy Council, &c.; ob. 1601.

37. Dr. John Dee, the celebrated philosopher of Mortlake, died in 1608.

Appendix No. 15

DEDICATION OF THE GOLDING
MEMORIAL WINDOW

THE Golding Memorial Window in the parish church of
Belchamp St. Paul's was dedicated by the bishop of the
diocese (Chelmsford) the Rt. Rev. Dr. Henry Albert
Wilson, at a special service on Whit Tuesday, May 22nd, 1934.
The church was well filled with residents of the neighborhood
and a considerable number of persons from London and elsewhere including a group from the Shakespeare Fellowship, who
were interested in the occasion not only because of the influence
of Golding's translations upon Shakespeare but on account of
their belief that Edward de Vere, the seventeenth Earl of
Oxford, Golding's nephew, was the author of some of the works
attributed to Shakespeare.

The short service was conducted by the Vicar, the Rev. R. F.
Flynn, Mr. Louis Thorn Golding reading the lesson and, with
Mrs. Golding, unveiling the window. After the church service
addresses were made in the schoolhouse. Col. M. W. Douglas,
President of the Shakespeare Fellowship presided. Sir Charles
Marston, the archaeologist and author of *New Light on the Old
Testament* and other books, who is a collateral descendant of
Ursula Marston, Arthur Golding's mother, spoke of the Golding
and Marston families and traced them from ancient times.
Mr. Arthur Gray, Master of Jesus College, Cambridge, and his-
torian of the University, spoke of Golding at that college.

Mr. Percy Allen, Vice President of the Shakespeare Fellowship, Shakespearean student, critic, lecturer and author of *Shakespeare and Chapman as Topical Dramatists* and other books made
an address upon Golding's work, dealing principally with his
influence upon Shakespeare.

270

Appendix No. 16

ELIZABETH'S VISIT TO CASTLE HEDINGHAM

QUEEN ELIZABETH'S progresses were reported, in the sparse account, in Latin, of Thomas Weldon, cofferer of her household, whose duty evidently was to take note of the expenditures for the entertainment of the royal party, for he goes into detail as to the amounts spent for this purpose wherever the Queen stayed. In his report of the progress in Essex and Suffolk in 1561 he names "Hemingham" as the place of her stay August 14th-18th.

H. Ranger, in *Castle Hedingham, Its History and Associations, Halstead, 1887,* points out on page seven that this spelling was one of the dozen or more variations of the name by which the home of the Earls of Oxford had been known up to that time and on page twenty-eight quotes "The Genealogist" as stating that the place referred to was Castle Hedingham.

"Hemingham" was doubtless the form then in use, for Cecil, who as principal secretary was in attendance on the Queen, wrote a letter from there on August 17th dating it thus. Thirty years later, on a plan of the Castle made by order of Cecil, the name was spelled Hedingham. Nichols did not identify "Hemingham" with Hedingham, confusing it with Helmingham a place in Suffolk, overlooking the fact that the night before going to "Hemingham" the Queen was at Smallbridge only ten miles away but over twenty-five from Helmingham. Also that after a five days' stay she moved on to Gosfield five miles distant but nearly thirty-five from Helmingham. Such a long stay, the longest on this progress, and a cost of £556 1s. 11d., the highest for her entertainment, point not only to ample space to care for a large party, such as Castle Hedingham afforded, but wealthy and hospitable hosts, as John de Vere, the Lord Great Chamberlain, and his wife, a lady-in-waiting to the Queen, are well known to have been.

ARTHUR GOLDING'S ARMS—The quarterings are those of his mother (Marston) and his grandmother (Worthy). Drawn from the brass escutcheon on the tomb of his brother, William Golding, in Belchamp St. Paul's Church.

INDEX

273